NATIVE AMERICAN FLAGS

NATIVE
AMERICAN
FLAGS

Donald T. Healy
Peter J. Orenski

FOREWORD BY
Carl Waldman

UNIVERSITY OF OKLAHOMA PRESS • NORMAN

Native American Flags
is a revised edition of *Flags of the Native Peoples of the United States,*
by Donald T. Healy, *Raven: A Journal of Vexillology,* vols. 3–4, Trenton, N.J.:
North American Vexillological Association, 1996–1997.

Library of Congress Cataloging-in-Publication Data

Healy, Donald T.
  Native American flags/ Donald T. Healy, Peter J. Orenski; foreword by Carl Waldman.
    p. cm.
  Revision of an article, Flags of the native peoples of the United States, by Donald T.
Healy, published in Raven : a journal of vexillogy, v. 3/4 (1996–1997).
  Includes bibliographical references and index.
  ISBN 0–8061–3556–5 (pbk. : alk. paper)
    1. Indians of North America—Material culture. 2. Flags—United States. 3. Ban-
ners—United States. I. Orenski, Peter J., 1949–II. Title.

E98.M34H43 2003
929.9'2'08997—dc21

                                                            2003047397

Contents

— *Intertribal Organizations* —

— *Tribes without Federal Recognition* —

Foreword

CARL WALDMAN

Flags are a loaded concept. For millennia, they have conveyed information about the identity of peoples—information that is at once political, historical, cultural, and aesthetic. But for Native Americans the tribal flag is a relatively new concept. Few were created during the nineteenth century and much of the twentieth century. Only in recent decades have they been widely adopted, to the point that most tribal entities in the United States now have flags. Many groups in Canada and Latin America also have adopted flags. Yet, for native peoples, using images to express identity is an ancient tradition. It can therefore be said that the flag for Native Americans, at the start of the twenty-first century, is a new and powerful tradition that has drawn on earlier traditions. In that regard, this important book, the first on the subject matter, is a celebration of the Native American past, present, and future.

Flags are works of art, and such works play a part in the traditional Native American worldview. Since in Native American languages there is no equivalent word for "art"—that is, objects created for the sake of pure aesthetics—some scholars have maintained that for Native Americans, until modern times, art was never separate from other aspects of daily life: practical, social, and spiritual. Yet, like other peoples who do define art as a discrete concept, Native Americans traditionally took visual pleasure in well-conceived and well-constructed objects. They valued elements that make up the generally held notion of art—mastery of materials, use of stylistic conventions, and individual powers of invention and conceptualization. Some early works by indigenous peoples certainly indicate a sense of beauty for the sake of beauty. And there is of course no way to know what was in the mind of individuals when they shaped artful pieces. In any case, it can be said that flags, like most traditional Native American works of art, are functional.

One function of Native American artwork has been to communicate meaning through symbols, as flags and their images do. A pictograph is a picture or sign representing a word or idea as opposed to representing a sound. Native American pictographs appear as etchings in stone, bone, horn, antler, shell, wood, bark, pottery, and hide; as woven patterns on basketry and textiles; as paintings on hide and other materials; and as paintings and tattoos on the human body. Some pictographs are abstract designs, often in geometric perfection. The circle, for instance, stands for that which is connected, never-ending, and all-embracing—a meaning that now appears in tribal flags.

Pictographs on dwellings (in particular, hide tipis of the Plains Indians) and on weapons (in particular, hide shields) proclaim identity, as flags do. And consider pictographs drawn in place on rocks, known by the general term of rock art (or petroglyphs when carved, pecked, or abraded). Perhaps the purpose of these ancient rock images, specific to a place and permanent enough in many cases to survive for modern eyes, was similar to the purpose of a flag, proclaiming a people's territory.

Colors in images, like both representational and abstract designs, often had symbolic content for native peoples. The Navajos, for example, in their sand paintings—temporary altars for the purpose of healing made with trickled sand—used five sacred colors: white, black, blue, red, and yellow. The colors chosen for tribal flags likewise have special significance, specific to the various tribal entities.

The myriad symbols in Native American flags offer a window into traditional indigenous culture. Nature (the sun, eagles, wolves, turtles, and trees, as revealed in this book) is integral to Native American philosophy. Traditional arts (the making of dwellings, boats, clothing, arrows, pipes, etc.) are also represented in the new art of flag-making. Another point revealing a meeting of old behavior and new is that storytelling is often a central part of Native American gatherings, and the contents of the flags tell a public story. Some of the flags even show human images—images of culture heroes that have special meaning to a people.

Beliefs surrounding the totem also relate to the modern use of flags by Native Americans. A totem can be an animal, plant, legendary being, or natural phenomenon. It serves as a symbol and guardian spirit of an individual or of a group—a tribe, clan, family, or secret society. The best-known representations of totems are found on the totem poles of Northwest Coast Indians. Standing tall over villages and homes, these poles seem like a kind of flag. Northwest Coast Indians also make use of crests, sometimes called "clan emblems," in their artwork. The totemic designs woven by the Tlingits into the ceremonial Chilkat blankets are an example.

The concept of the totem is intrinsic to the concept of the palladium, a Greek-derived word referring to an object considered sacred to a people that helps safeguard them. The Lakotas have the Buffalo Calf Pipe; the Cheyennes have the Medicine Arrows and the Sacred Buffalo Hat; the Omahas have the Sacred Pole, representing Venerable Man; and so on. These objects possess "medicine" or "magic," the mysterious power inherent in the universe, and are kept by chiefs or shamans in "medicine bundles." That is to say, these inanimate objects possess animating spirits. And so it is with a flag. The flags themselves become powerful and valued objects and instruments of magic to protect the people and assure unity among them. Tribes' flags thus are sacred objects. And when they blow in the wind—becoming, in the view of certain tribes, one with the Wind People—they seem to manifest this special power.

The existence of Native American flags also tells us something about the historical process of acculturation: how, despite the tragedy of much interaction between Native Americans and nonindigenous peoples—including disease, warfare, displacement from homelands, and dispossession of culture—separate traditions can come together in an inspiring way. The political content is at the heart of the meaning of a flag, and tribal flags are a powerful and inspiring statement of sovereignty, survival, and self-determination. We stand for nations, flags proclaim. We stand for a united people who have endured within the pressures of another nation.

The flag of the United States shows how design and color give meaning, and such an object becomes powerful in a people's consciousness. The stars represent the states; the stripes, the original thirteen colonies; and, as described by the Continental Congress, "White signifies purity and innocence; red, hardiness and valor; and blue, vigilance, perseverance and justice." The American flag tells the story of the founding of a nation. For many people, the flag is a sacred object, not to be desecrated. The various nicknames reveal this phenomenon: "Stars and Stripes" and "Star-Spangled Banner" refer to symbols; "Red, White, and Blue," to colors; and

"Old Glory," to historical significance. Interestingly, there is a tradition of the Native American use of the U.S. flag (and no doubt colonial flags and banners as well) as an article of clothing or as an ornamental feature on other objects, especially horse trappings. Different uses evolved with time—as a trophy taken in warfare, displayed in one form or another for its captured power or magic; as a parade item with a unifying message between formerly opposing cultures (and, perhaps, a pure appreciation of aesthetics); and as a prestige item valued by people who fought in the world wars, such as the Navajo code talkers of World War II. The making of modern-day flags is once again tied to a historical practice.

The designs and colors of tribal flags are now as powerful in their content as those of the flags of nations around the world. And the flags themselves have become sacred objects.

Each section of this beautiful and informative book, presenting a tribe's flag in a detailed context, stands on its own. Yet all the sections together offer us a broad view. The compendium becomes a chronicle. Through their lifelong dedication to the subject of Native American flags, Donald Healy and Peter Orenski have gifted us—another Native American tradition, as in the Northwest Coast Indian *patshatl* (potlatch) or the Lakota Otu'han. They have gifted the rest of us with entrance to Native America.

Acknowledgments

This book originated as a paper written to be presented at a North American Vexillological Association (NAVA) meeting. It subsequently grew into a book-length feature in NAVA's scholarly periodical, *Raven*. Many members of NAVA contributed information, photos, stories, and leads to allow the volume of information to grow ever larger.

Much credit for the original *Raven* article (and this book, its successor) must be given to the Executive Board of NAVA, particularly its president, Charles A. Spain, Jr. Edward B. Kaye of the *Raven* staff served as a dedicated editor, fine-tuning the original document, and his touch can still be felt throughout this version. Several members of NAVA and its boards and commissions helped hone the document into something both the author and NAVA could regard with pride. In numerous ways this was an effort by many, many people.

Thanks must be given to the hundreds of people in tribal headquarters across the country as well as in tribal libraries and schools who helped document their flags and acted as conduits to other tribes and sources. Thanks to chiefs, shamans, and council members who graciously supplied copies of ordinances, creation stories, and actual flags and in several instances passed special ordinances to allow us to obtain copies of their flags.

Most of all, thanks—and an apology—to my artist *par excellence* and co-author, Dr. Peter Orenski, who spent countless hours on the phone talking to various tribal leaders as well as members of the national and regional organizations and is the actual author of over two dozen tribal stories contained herein. He has developed a close relationship with many tribes and has an ability to elicit tales of tribal myth, lore, and explanations of symbols to a remarkable degree. The reader will see his fine touch with these tribal leaders in the stories about the Ottawas, the Tainos, the Oneidas, the Mohegans, the Micmacs, and others.

The apology is for having infected Peter, in the seven-odd years we have been teamed on this project, with the same fascination, the same vision, the same need to present the first-ever compendium of tribal flags. On many an occasion when I tired of the struggle, it was Peter's enthusiastic drive that kept this venture going. The work's coming to fruition owes as much to him as to any effort on my part. I am deeply grateful for his friendship.

Authors' note: The flags of the Confederated Tribes of the Grand Ronde Community of Oregon and of the Penobscot Tribe of Maine are rendered entirely in black and white; therefore they do not appear in the color section.

Introduction

INDIANS AND NORTH AMERICA

Native Americans or Indians have inhabited the Americas for anywhere between 12,500 and 33,000 years, depending upon the anthropological study consulted. They are not limited, as too many people presume, solely to the United States and Canada but occupy every corner of the Western Hemisphere, from South America to the islands at the extreme north of Canada. Their origins lie in the eastern reaches of Asia.

Once on the American continents, the people diverged and adapted to the myriad of ecological environments that they encountered. The cultures of the Peruvian Incas, the Arizona Navajos, the Florida Seminoles, and the Alaskan Haidas are in many ways more diverse than alike. Today that diversity is being recognized.

The mass media (especially the motion picture industry) have created a stereotypical image for Native Americans that has had the effect of quashing an awareness of the diversity of cultures found across the continent. This is especially true in the eastern part of the United States and Canada. Here, all too frequently, in order to be recognized as Indians in public events, photo ops, and ethnic celebrations, eastern tribes adopt the clothing, artifacts, and image of the Plains Indians—the warriors seen attacking Fort Apache or chasing down that wagon train in a 1950s western. A tipi at a Native American festival in New York, New Jersey, or Florida is as culturally bizarre as an igloo in the Bahamas!

SOVEREIGNTY AND/OR
FEDERAL AND STATE RECOGNITION

Legally, the various tribes and bands that range from Maine to California have a unique status. They are considered sovereign domestic nations within the borders of the United States—if they have received federal recognition.

Federal recognition involves many different issues, most of which do not pertain to this book; but a few points are relevant. To receive federal recognition, a tribe or band must reside either in its traditional homeland (e.g., the Navajos in Arizona) or in a location designated by the federal government in the past (e.g., the Seminoles in Oklahoma). A tribe must have a continuity of cultural traditions and cannot have become too "Americanized." This is especially problematic for many tribes of the lower Great Lakes, since the policies of the United States government once encouraged assimilation. A tribe must have the typical structures of a government—executive, legislative, and judicial branches and a constitution. As of 2002, nearly 600 tribes, bands, pueblos, and rancherías have been awarded this status.

A less desirable but still important status is state recognition. This does not have all the benefits associated with federal acceptance, but it does mean that a tribe's current home state has legally accepted it as a representative group of a particular nation. This is usually one step below federal recognition. Nearly 200 tribal units have this status.

Finally, some entities lack either state or federal recognition. Many of these fall into one of two major categories: they are alien to their geographic locale or they have become too integrated into the surrounding society.

ECONOMIC CHANGES
AMONG NATIVE PEOPLES

Two major pieces of legislation in the last thirty years have had an impact on the Native American population of the United States. The 1975 U.S. Indian Self-Determination and Education Assistance Act established the current level of independence of federally recognized Indian nations. This spurred tribes to find ways to employ their resources, tap their work force, and offer incentives for businesses looking for alternatives to state red tape. Since the federally recognized tribes do not fall under legislative control of the state governments within whose territory they reside, they can create islands of opportunity for many businesses.

The 1988 U.S. Indian Gaming Regulatory Act led to a rapid creation of job- and revenue-producing casinos on Native American reservations. According to the U.S. General Accounting Office, in 1996 there were 184 tribes running 281 gaming facilities with US$4.5 billion in annual revenues. Almost a third of the members of the Coeur d'Alene Tribe in Idaho, for example, are employed in the gaming industry.

These two acts helped give tribes the right to determine their own development and a means to acquire capital to do so.

A SHORT HISTORY OF NATIVE AMERICANS' USE OF FLAGS

The use of flags is not a traditional Native American custom. The flag is basically an object created in the "Old World." The earliest known flags are some 3,000-year-old vexilloids from what is now Iran. The spread of flags was the result of noblemen's desire to identify themselves on battlefields and later, with the appearance of the nation-state, the need to identify borders, ships, government buildings, and similar trappings of nationhood.

The earliest known use of flags by Indians within the United States actually occurred in the Confederacy during the Civil War. The Confederate States of America designed and gave flags to the "Five Civilized Tribes" in the Indian Territory—the Cherokees, Chickasaws, Choctaws, Creeks, and Seminoles. These five nations were offered independence if they allied themselves with the Confederacy and fought under the supplied banners. Between the end of the Civil War and the beginning of the twentieth century, Indians rarely used flags. These were almost exclusively flags given to friendly chiefs by the United States military. The only known flag created by a Native American was that of Smohalla, a Warapam shaman associated with the Dreamer religion of the 1800s, centered in the Pacific Northwest.

During World War II, a few tribes (most notably the Arapahoes of the Wind River Reservation in Wyoming) wanted to give flags to their soldiers fighting overseas. The Arapahoes even designed a flag for that purpose, but it was not until the 1950s that actual flags were created.

The 1960s saw the addition of a few more tribal flags. In his 1970 work *The Flag Book of the United States,* Dr. Whitney Smith described five tribal flags known to exist—those of the Oglala Sioux, the Crows, the Northern Cheyennes, the Seminoles of Florida, and the Miccosukees. In a footnote,

Dr. Smith allowed for the possibility that there might be others. As an aside, that very footnote was the inspiration for this work.

With the advancement of tribal government and tribal sovereignty in the 1970s and 1980s, symbols of that sovereignty became increasingly important. In surveying tribes for this book, the opening of gaming resorts was a seemingly unusual but very common reason given for adopting a flag. The idea appeared to be that "if people are coming to our casino, we had better let them know they are on our lands, not lands of the state of X." Now, at the beginning of the twenty-first century, most tribes have flags.

WHAT FLAGS TELL US ABOUT NATIVE AMERICANS

Looking at the native peoples of the United States through their symbols serves many purposes. All too often books dealing with indigenous people treat them solely or almost entirely in a historic context. Too frequently contemporary issues are minimized. Flags offer a means to analyze much of what is important to Native Americans from their history.

Flags also offer tribes a way to affirm their distinct identity. As someone who has researched this topic for some twenty years, I am frequently asked about a Sioux flag as opposed to a Standing Rock Sioux flag. The use of flags identifies the political entities that exist today—rarely a generic population. There are over a dozen Sioux tribes in the United States and still more in Canada. Each band of the Chippewas (or Ojibwes) has a distinctive flag, yet no flag exists that could truly be called a Chippewa flag.

In amassing information about the flags of the tribes, I gained an appreciation of the importance of design and symbolism among native peoples and in their other types of artifacts: styles in clothing, canoes, dwellings, the paint schemes for decorating horses, pipes, weapons, and so on.

Flags also indicate the similarities between widely scattered peoples who represent only a small percentage of the 300 million greater population. As the reader looks at the various flags and reads their descriptions, recurring themes will become evident on two levels—the greater tribal level and a "universal" Native American level.

Examples of tribal themes can be seen in the use of Hiawatha's Belt in the flags of the component tribes that form the Iroquois League of Six Nations and the floral motifs and wild rice found in many Chippewa (Ojbwe) flags. Universal themes that occur over and over are the four sacred colors—red, white, yellow, and black; the number four; the appearance of structures; and maps. These help build a sense of unity between people scattered from one end of the continent to the other.

A SHORT INTRODUCTION
TO VEXILLOLOGY

Vexillology is the study of flags, their history, and their symbolism. As an embodiment of a group's self-image, flags can help give a sense of the people they represent. Such study has gone on for several hundred years; but vexillology dates back only to the 1960s, when the term was coined by noted flag researcher and author Dr. Whitney Smith. The practice has since become more codified. Thousands of people around the world study and research various aspects of flags. Many organizations have been founded to further vexillology, including the North American Vexillological Association (NAVA), the largest such group in the United States and Canada. The topic of Native American flags was first presented to a NAVA audience and at an international congress of vexillology in Warsaw, Poland.

Guide to References Cited

This work is primarily concerned with the flags of the various Native American tribes found in the United States. To gain a full understanding of the symbols employed by the tribes, it is necessary to know at least a little about the people themselves. To this end, these books became a constant resource in providing the thumbnail sketches of very complex histories, beliefs, and achievements. Readers who are interested in furthering their understanding of the cultures embodied by Native Americans are urged to consult these resources and others for more detailed information.

Appleton, LeRoy H. *American Indian Design & Decoration.* New York: Dover Publications, Inc., 1971. Code: *AIDD.*

Arizona Commission of Indian Affairs. *1989 Tribal Directory of Arizona Indian Tribes.* Phoenix: Arizona Commission of Indian Affairs, 1989. Code: *TDAI.*

Hirschfelder, Arlene, and Martha Kreipe de Montano. *The Native American Almanac.* New York: Prentice-Hall General Reference, 1993. Code: *NAA.*

Klein, Barry T. *Reference Encyclopedia of the American Indian.* 6th ed. West Nyack, N.Y.: Todd Publications, 1993. Code: *REAI.*

Marquis, Arnold. *A Guide to America's Indians.* Norman: University of Oklahoma Press, 1974. Code: *GAI.*

Smith, Whitney. *The Flag Book of the United States.* Revised ed. New York: William Morrow & Co., 1975. Code: *FBUS.*

Stoutenburgh, John, Jr. *Dictionary of the American Indian.* New York: Bonanza Books, 1960. Code: *DAI.*

Terrell, John Upton. *American Indian Almanac.* New York: Barnes & Noble Books, 1970. Code: *AIA.*

Waldman, Carl. *Atlas of the North American Indian.* New York: Facts on File, Inc., 1985. Code: *ANAI.*

―――. *Encyclopedia of Native American Tribes.* New York: Facts on File, Inc., 1988. Code: *ENAT.*

— *Tribes* —
with Federal Recognition

Absentee-Shawnee Tribe of Indians of Oklahoma

Located in central Oklahoma is the Historic Trust Area of the Absentee Shawnees, the westernmost outpost of their people. The term "Absentee" is applied to the Native Americans who accepted U.S. citizenship under the Citizenship Act of 1924 and gave up claims to reservation lands. "Shawnees" meant "southerners" in the language of the Algonquins, their original northern neighbors.

The Shawnees originated in the Midwest in areas now in Ohio, Indiana, West Virginia, Kentucky, and Tennessee; the modern Shawnees still live in their traditional homelands. In Ohio they do not enjoy federal recognition as an official nation, while in Oklahoma there are three federally recognized bands of the Shawnee Nation: the Eastern Shawnee Tribe in the northeast corner of the state; the Loyal Shawnees, who have reemerged from the Cherokees; and the larger Absentee-Shawnee Tribe just outside Oklahoma City.

In 1974 the Absentee Shawnees adopted a flag (Janet Hubbard-Brown, *The Shawnee* [New York: Chelsea House Press, 1995], 104). The flag, designed by tribal member Leroy White, honors the great Shawnee leader Tecumseh (see Eastern Shawnee Tribe of Oklahoma). The central white oval of the red flag bears a stylized profile of Tecumseh in red and black, facing left. Behind Tecumseh two large crossed eagle feathers extend beyond the oval. Surrounding the oval is the tribe's name in Shawnee and in English in white: "LI-SI-WI-NWI" on top and "ABSENTEE SHAWNEE" below. Two white stars separate the Shawnee and English names on each side of the oval.

Ak-Chin Indian Community (Tohono O'odham and Pima)— Arizona

The Tohono O'odhams ("Desert People") and the Pimas ("River People") share a 22,000-acre reservation in southern Arizona located between the two main reservations of those tribes. The main Tohono O'odham lands are on the Tohono O'odham Reservation to the south. The main concentration of the Pimas is to the north on the lands of the Gila River Indian Community. These two small tribes, totaling 405 people in 1990, function as a single entity within the Ak-Chin Community. In 1962 they adopted a tribal seal designed by Wilbert "Buddy" Carlyle and drawn by Sylvester Smith.

The seal's symbols speak of the ideals on which the Ak-Chin Community is based. An arrow in the center symbolizes the Ak-Chin people as a community of Native Americans. Scales balanced on the arrow represent equality and justice. A red rising sun tells of their belief in a brighter tomorrow, while crossed lightning bolts show their inspiration and energy in upholding the ideals of their community. These elements appear on a white circular background, along with the tribal motto "EQUALITY FOR ALL" above the symbols and "FOR A BRIGHTER TOMORROW" below in black. A wide black band surrounds the circle, with the official tribal name "AK-CHIN INDIAN COMMUNITY" across the top in white and "ARIZONA" on the bottom, separated by two white stars representing the two nations.

All elements are black and white on both the seal and flag except for the rising sun, which is red on the flag and black on the seal. When used as part of the flag, the seal is set on a plain white background. The flag was adopted in 1987 on the twenty-fifth anniversary of the adoption of the tribal seal.

Alabama-Quassarte Tribal Town (Creek)— Oklahoma

The Alabama people originated in the southeastern part of the United States in the state that today bears their name. As French allies in the French and Indian War, the Alabamas moved west after the British victory into lands now part of Louisiana and Texas. Those who remained in their original lands became close allies of the Creek (Muscogee) Indians. When the Creeks were removed to the Indian Territory in 1830, their Alabama allies left with them (*ENAT*, 6).

Today the only recognized distinctive Alabama Tribe is located in Texas, where it has united with the Coushatta Nation. The Alabamas, whose name means "Weed Gatherers," also live on as part of the Creek Nation in Oklahoma. There they share the town of Eufaula with the Quassartes (their spelling of the name of the people called the Coushattas in Texas).

The Quassartes (Coushattas) also originated in what is now Alabama and shared much of the same recent history as their Alabama cousins. Those who merged with the Creeks in the early nineteenth century were sent to Oklahoma with the Creeks. The remnants of these two nations in Oklahoma are now considered to be Creeks rather than members of their ancient tribes.

The flag of the Alabama-Quassartes consists of a central white square between two red panels that are half the width of the white panel (this form is known as a "Canadian Pale," since the flag of Canada was the first national flag to employ three vertical stripes—in heraldry a pale—in these

4

proportions). Centered on the white area is a representation of a Red Tailed Hawk. The hawk's outspread wings nearly reach the edges of the white square. It has a black face, brown body and upper part of the wings, yellow central wings and tail feathers, and red wing-tips. All feathers are outlined in black. In its talons the hawk holds a white scroll bearing the legend "ETVLWVOMVLKV YRVKKV" in black (presumably the tribal name).

Above the hawk, in two lines, is the official name in black: "Alabama Quassarte Tribal Town"; below is "Est. 1939," the date of its founding.

Apache Tribe of Oklahoma

With fewer than 600 enrolled members, the Apache Tribe of Oklahoma is one of the smallest of the nearly forty different tribes based in modern Oklahoma. Its membership includes not only Apaches but also those of Kiowa ancestry. The tribe was once known as the Kiowa-Apaches.

The Apache Tribe is composed mainly of descendants of the Plains Apaches, an offshoot of the Apaches of New Mexico, Arizona, and Mexico. They had very close ties with the Kiowa Tribe of the Plains and had a similar lifestyle, which was as different from the lifestyle of their fellow Apaches as the grasslands of Kansas and Oklahoma are from the deserts of Arizona.

In celebrating the unique cultural ancestry of the Apache Tribe of Oklahoma, the number two occurs in several ways in the flag of the Apache and Kiowa people who make up this modern nation.

Their flag is divided in two: the left half is red, the right blue. The colors combine with white elements to incorporate the colors of the United States; but red and blue also recall the colors of the blankets used by Plains Indians (see Comanche Indian Tribe). Centered on the flag is a white or light-buff map of Oklahoma.

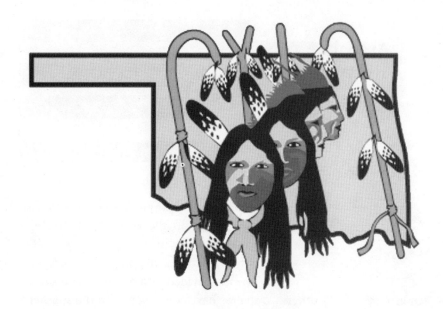

Superimposed on the map are four heads of Indian warriors: two (facing forward) in the attire of the Apaches, two (facing right) wearing Kiowa headdresses (combs plus feathers). Each warrior is adorned with "war paint" in red, white, and blue but also has natural skin tones. The four warriors are bracketed by two coup sticks, and behind them are two lances. Each coup stick bears two pairs of two feathers. The warrior in the front wears a yellow kerchief tied around his neck, and each of the two Apaches wears a single feather in his hair.

The words "APACHE TRIBE" appear in white lettering across the top of the flag and "OKLAHOMA" across the base of it.

This is a flag of twos: sets of warriors, coup sticks, colored sections, and pairs of feathers, all reflecting the dual nature of the Apaches of Oklahoma, a tribe of two worlds, the Great Plains and the Great Southwest.

Arapahoe Tribe of the Wind River Reservation— Wyoming

The Arapahos are believed to have migrated from the headwaters of the Mississippi River in the early 1700s (*ENAT*, 17–19). During the 1800s, the Arapaho people divided into northern and southern groups. The Southern Arapahos have combined with the southern Cheyennes in Oklahoma to form the current Cheyenne and Arapaho Nation. The Northern Arapahoes (spelled with an *e*) remain a distinct tribal entity, although they share the Wind River Reservation in northwestern Wyoming with the Shoshones.

The origin of the name "Arapaho" is uncertain. It may have derived from the Shawnee *tirapihu* ("trader") or from the Kiowa term for the Arapahos, "Ahyato." The Arapahos called themselves "Inuna-ina" ("Our People").

The Arapahoes of the Wind River Reservation may be one of the first tribes to adopt a flag ("History of the Arapaho Flag" [1997], www.uwlax. edu/ls/history/students/springer/docs3.html). The flag dates from the 1940s, when the Arapahoes saw their young men going off to war in Europe and the Pacific. After the death of the first Arapahoe soldier in World War II, John L. Brown, the tribal elders decided that there should be a distinct symbol of the Arapahoes since their sons were now dying not only for the United States but also for the Arapahoe Nation.

The elders designed a flag with seven stripes representing seven ceremonial and sacred elements. At the top of the flag (at that time flown vertically) a white triangle contained a circular device of red, white, and black—red because they are human beings and Arapahoes; white because they want a long life; and black because they seek happiness.

After the war's end, the concept of a flag for the Arapahoe Nation faded until the Korean War, when the people asked their tribal elders to adopt a flag to identify the Arapahoes. On 15 June 1956 the current flag of the Arapahoe Nation was adopted by the general council of the Arapahoes. That flag consists of seven stripes (the central stripe being one-half the width of the other six). The two outermost stripes are red, the second and sixth stripes are white, the third and fifth stripes are black, and the narrow central stripe is white. At the left is a white triangle edged in black containing a red semicircle over a black semicircle, separated by a narrow white band.

Aroostook Band of Micmac Indians of Maine

 The Micmacs of the Aroostook Band, federally recognized since 26 November 1991, trace their ancestry to some twenty-eight Micmac communities in the Maritime Provinces of Canada (New Brunswick, Newfoundland, Nova Scotia, Prince Edward Island, and Québec). Traditionally the Micmacs have been a highly mobile society, and the Canadian communities mirror the far-flung Micmac settlements throughout New England states. The Boston, Massachusetts, area alone, for instance, is home to some 4,000 people of Micmac origin. The headquarters for the approximately 800 members of the band living in the United States is on seventeen acres of trust land on Presque Isle, within Aroostook County in northern Maine, a scant ten minutes' drive from the Canadian border. The Aroostook Band, which also owns parcels of land throughout the county, represents all Micmacs in the United States.

Given the dispersed locations and traditional mobility of the Micmacs, it is not surprising that the two circular designs of the Aroostook Band flag stress the unity-in-diversity theme that also dominates the Micmac flag (see Micmac Nation). In fact, this flag differs in only two important features: the addition of the logo of the Micmac Council in the upper portion of the central red panel and the flag's three- by six-foot dimensions (the same 1:2 ratio of width to length as in the Canadian Maple Leaf flag).

The richly symbolic logo of the Elders' Council has a black circular outline, signifying the unity of the Micmac people. The upper part of the circle is divided in half by a black vertical band punctuated by four yellow disks, which honor the four women of the band (or tribe), all Micmac mothers, who promoted the advancement of the Micmacs. The upper left

quarter shows two black bear claws on a white background, symbolizing strength and the readiness to provide assistance. A black deer looking toward the right stands in the upper-right quarter on a white background. It represents the gratitude the Micmacs feel toward this animal, which provides vital assistance to the community with both clothing and food.

Separating the upper from the lower portions of the circle, a center band celebrates the original members of the Aroostook Council. There were five women though only four are visible here (white inverted wigwams) and four men (black upright tipis with yellow outlines), each with his or her own household; council members still oversee tribal business and work together for the welfare of the band community.

The black triangle in the lower half of the circle stands for the wigwam of the council's lodge. A small white triangle marks the entrance to the wigwam, and three white disks honor the three original women sachems (council members). This triangle, topped by the middle black tipi in the central band, forms the Arrow of Peace—symbol of the arrows used by hunters to provide food and by warriors to defend the band against enemies. Framing the lower half of the circular logo are seven eagle feathers, which represent seven future Micmac generations and the seven districts of the Micmac Nation.

The wings and lower body of the Invisible Thunderbird—representing strength and wisdom—are suggested by the central band and the lower black and white triangles, although its head remains invisible.

Thanks to Bernard Jerome, cultural director and member of the Elders of the Micmac Tribe, who provided information to Peter Orenski. The flag is courtesy of TME Co., Inc., from a commercial production run in 2001, based on specifications from Mr. Jerome.

Assiniboine and Sioux Tribes of the Fort Peck Indian Reservation— Montana

In northeastern Montana, sprawling across five counties, lies the 905,000-acre Fort Peck Reservation, home to the Assiniboine and Sioux Tribes. It was established in 1871 to serve both groups (*Tribal History of the Fort Peck Reservation, Fort Peck Tribes,* undated pamphlet). Today the reservation is home to several bands from each tribe. The Assiniboines include the Canoe Paddler Band and the Red Bottom Band. The Sioux include parts of the Sisseton, Wahpeton, Yanktonai, and Hunkpapa Teton Bands (the great Chief Sitting Bull was a Hunkpapa).

According to Ray K. Eder, vice-chairman of the Fort Peck Tribes:

> . . . the flag was designed and sketched by the renowned Indian artist Roscoe White Eagle. . . . The colorful flag of the Fort Peck Tribes is contrastingly depicted on a field of blue sky. The two chiefs displaying the robe of the prairie buffalo is befitting of the fact that two Tribes, Assiniboine and Sioux, reside together in harmony on the same 40 × 85-mile reservation. The sacred robe of the buffalo symbolizes the tight and lasting bond of friendship and understanding between the two Tribes. Native Americans find this to be very gratifying during these trying years of our Indian self-determination era. (Ray K. Eder, letter dated 25 January 1995)

Upon the sky-blue field is a goldenrod-yellow hide bearing the words "FORT PECK TRIBES" in red. The tribes' names appear in white on red above the trailing feathers of the two chiefs' headdresses. The chiefs and their costumes are shown in full natural colors (Carol Lenz, interim business manager, Fort Peck Community College, letter dated 25 January 1995).

Bay Mills Indian Community of the Sault Ste. Marie Band of Chippewa (Ojibwe) Indians— Michigan

One of the two easternmost homes of the Ojibwe (or Chippewa) people in the United States is the Bay Mills Indian Community on the northeastern tip of the Upper Peninsula of Michigan (the other is the Sault Ste. Marie Band located nearby). Flying over this eastern outpost of the third-largest Native American nation in the United States (after the Navajos and Cherokees) is a flag designed by tribal member Richard LeBlanc.

The flag is divided diagonally by a central yellow stripe running from the lower-left corner to the upper-right corner, leaving a medium- to dark-blue triangle in the upper left and a red triangle in the lower right. Centered upon this is the seal of the Bay Mills Indian Community.

A narrow green ring surrounds the seal, bearing the legend "BAY MILLS INDIAN COMMUNITY" across the top and the Ojibwe word "GNOOZ-HEKAANING" ("place of the pike" [fish]) across the bottom in white. The center is divided diagonally into four equal sections, recalling the sacred number four and using the four primary Native American colors: white at the top and (clockwise) yellow, red, and black. These colors reflect the human races, the four primary directions, the four stages of human life, the four seasons, and many other recurring elements of Native American and human existence. Separating the four colored quadrants are four stylized white feathers with brown tips and brown spines. The flag was adopted sometime after 1994.

Thanks to Angie Carrick, of the Bay Mills Tribal Headquarters.

Big Pine Band of Owens Valley Paiute Shoshone Indians— California

In east-central California, south of Yosemite National Park, are several small reservations or rancherías (*GAI*, 42). A band of Paiutes shares the Big Pine Ranchería with a band of Shoshones.

The flag of this branch of the widespread Paiute Nation, officially known as the Paiute Tribe of the Owens Valley, is the tribal seal on a white background. The circular seal shows the back of a seated Indian man facing into a golden sunrise, alluding to the location of the ranchería in the eastern part of California. Glimpses of a brilliant blue sky separate the sun's rays. The landscape is white, and the horizon forms a jagged edge against the rising sun. The man has black hair, tan skin, red pants, and a yellow breechcloth. From his uplifted arms flow two light-blue streams with black detailing. This image probably refers to the clear springs in the mountains that nourish the lands of the Big Pine Ranchería and the entire Owens Valley. The seal on the flag is unusually large.

A black ring surrounds the seal. Across the top of the ring in red are the words "THE GREAT SEAL OF THE BIG PINE" and around the bottom "PAIUTE TRIBE OF THE OWENS VALLEY."

Thanks to NAVA member Jim Ferrigan for providing data on this flag.

Blackfeet Tribe— Montana

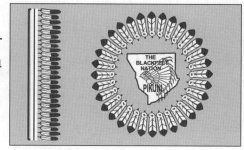

The Piegans, or Pikuni branch of the Blackfoot Confederacy, are the southern-most group of Blackfeet Indians, located in western Montana (other branches are in Canada). The Pikunis (which means "Poorly Dressed") occupy a reservation established in 1855, straddling the border with Canada. The term "Blackfeet" comes from their reputation for dyeing their moccasins black.

The Blackfeet people were known for their beautiful craftwork—their tipis, clothing, weapons, and riding equipment were of exceptional design. Their war-bonnets, one of which appears on the flag, were unique: the feathers stood straight up. Examples of Blackfeet art can be found in the Museum of the Plains Indian, located in the Blackfeet capital of Browning, Montana.

On the left side of the flag's medium-blue field is a ceremonial lance or coup stick with twenty-eight white-and-black eagle feathers (sample flag provided by Elmer's Flag & Banner, Portland, Oregon). To the right of center is a ring of thirty-eight white-and-black eagle feathers surrounding a map of the reservation in white. On this map are a war-bonnet and the tribal names "THE BLACKFEET NATION" and "PIKUNI" in black.

Bois Forte Band (Nett Lake) of Chippewas (Ojibwes)— Minnesota

Minnesota, the "Land of Ten Thousand Lakes," is home to many of this band of Chippewas, also called Ojibwes or in their own language Anishinabes. Six of the reservations within Minnesota have banded together to form the Minnesota Chippewa Tribe. One of these six is the Bois Forte Band, which is based on the Nett Lake Reservation in northernmost Minnesota. The other five members are the Fond du Lac, Grand Portage, Leech Lake, Mille Lacs, and White Earth Chippewas.

On the Nett Lake Reservation, some 1,300 members reside on about 42,000 acres of land. The band's population size places it at the median for the six Minnesota Chippewa tribal members.

The top half of the flag of the Bois Forte Band is white and the bottom half light blue, with the tribal seal in the center. The seal, which occupies almost three-quarters of the height of the flag, has many elements in common with the seal of the Mille Lacs Chippewas.

The seal is circular, ringed by a white band bearing the name "BOIS FORTE BAND" above and "OF CHIPPEWA" below in black letters. The inside of the seal is divided in half horizontally, and the bottom half is

further subdivided into two parts. The top half of the seal is light blue and represents the clear skies of northern Minnesota. Rising into the sky is an orange sun, with white birds flying on each side. The bottom part is divided into brown and light-blue segments, representing the earth and the waters of Nett Lake. Wild grasses shown in green grow skyward from the land, and green reeds rise above the surface of the lake. Superimposed on the entire backdrop is a green representation of the most important plant in the daily life of the ancient Anishinabes, the wild rice plant, which grows in the lakes of the upper Midwest.

Both the Bois Forte Band and the Mille Lacs Chippewas recall the sun, water, plant life, and wild rice on their seals (see Mille Lacs Band of Chippewas [Ojibwes]). The repetition of these symbols on flags of differing Chippewa bands shows the importance of these elements in the life and history of the Chippewas of northern Minnesota.

Cabazon Band of Cahuilla Mission Indians—California

The members of the Cabazon Band of Cahuilla Mission Indians are the descendants of Chief Cabazon, head of the Desert Cahuilla Indians during the middle decades of the nineteenth century. Although the Cabazon Cahuillas were never under the control of the Spanish mission system, the European-American settlers who arrived in what was then the Alta California state of Mexico in the 1840s referred to most of the Native Americans as Mission Indians. The name stuck. The Cabazons have lived in the Coachella Valley (Riverside County) for more than 2,500 years!

The Cahuillas (pronounced Kah-we-ahs, which means "masters" or "powerful ones" in the Cahuillan/Kawiyan language) learned to survive in harsh desert conditions by digging wells and harvesting available foods such as acorns, mesquite, and piñon pine nuts. Their homes (individually known as a *kish*) were made from reeds, branches, and brush. There are two main branches of the Cahuillas: the Wildcat and Coyote groups. These two major groups were further subdivided into about a dozen clans, each with its own name, territory, and common ancestry.

Cahuilla populations started shrinking in the 1850s as the Southern Pacific Railroad laid claim to local water rights. This deprived the Cahuillas of the most precious resource in the desert and resulted in poor crop yields. The loss of water forced the Cahuilla people to move frequently.

Chief Cabazon's people were living near Indio, California, when President Ulysses S. Grant issued an executive order on 15 May 1876, creating the Cabazon Reservation for the 600 tribal members then surviving.

Today there are fewer than 50 members of the Cabazon Tribe. Their reservation covers 1,450 acres in various small parcels spread over 16 miles. The largest section contains the tribal offices, police and fire departments, their gaming operation, and a family bowling center.

The Cabazon Cahuillas employ a white flag bearing their tribal seal in the center, with an intricate pattern in red along the top and bottom edges of the flag. These two stripes, which are mirror images of each other, almost reach the hoist and outer edges of the flag. Each stripe consists of an extended rectangle with a relatively thick outer border, containing a series of contiguous triangles. Within each triangle are two smaller triangles, which share the same baseline. These triangles point toward the center of the flag. The design between the outer triangles is evocative of saguaro cacti or stick figures like the "Man in the Maze" seen on flags of the Salt River Pima and Maricopa Tribes of Arizona (see Salt River Pima-Maricopa Indian Community).

The seal of the Cabazon Cahuillas is round, with a red-triangle edging. A white ring edged in black bears the tribal name "CABAZON BAND OF MISSION INDIANS" above and its location, "Indio, CA," below in black lettering. This encloses an artistic representation of the lands of the Cabazon Cahuillas: on a tan landscape of desert sand a large saguaro cactus in green casts a dark shadow to its left. In front, to the right of the cactus, sits a curled white rattlesnake. Behind the saguaro are the purple mountains that surround the desert, capped by white snow—the source of much of the water that served the Cahuillas for centuries. A red sun appears on the right above the mountains in a cloud-filled light-blue sky, recalling the harsh conditions facing the desert-dwelling Cahuilla people.

Thanks to Janice Kleinschmidt, public information officer of the Cabazon Band of Cahuilla Mission Indians, for providing information about the flag and seal.

Caddo Indian Tribe
of Oklahoma

The modern Caddo people are the descendants of many different tribes that once inhabited the present states of Louisiana, southern Arkansas, and coastal Texas as far west as the Brazos River (*ENAT*, 33–34). These included the tribes of the Kadohadacho Confederacy (which gives the modern Caddos their name), the Hasinai Confederacy, and the Natchitoches Confederacy.

Today the more than 1,200 Caddos share joint control of small parcels of tribal lands in Oklahoma with the Delaware and Wichita Nations around the areas of Fort Cobb and Fort El Reno.

Over their lands flies the orange banner bearing their tribal seal. On the flag the seal is separated from the orange field by a medium-blue ring bearing the name "CADDO NATION" in black at the top. This blue ring recalls the spirit's journey through life and beyond.

The seal of the Caddo Nation features three women in nineteenth-century Caddo dress performing the traditional Turkey Dance, an old dance that is still performed today (Caddo Nation, *Flag of the Caddo Nation,* 1997). The women and children of the tribe dance and also sing. The background of the seal shows (in outline) five Caddo men singing and playing the drums. The Turkey Dance fosters a sense of confidence and well-being. It provides the Caddos with an outlet for mental stress and promotes physical endurance, since the dance can last from one hour to all day! The three dancing women wear dresses of green (on the left), red-orange and white (in the center), and lavender with a white apron (on the right).

At the base of the seal is a small round design (in yellow, red, green, and white), symbolizing the door to the world beyond; it also recalls the four stages of life and the four primary directions of the compass.

This flag was designed by a member of the Caddo Tribe, Mrs. Billie Hoff, and has been manufactured commercially by the Homer Miller Co. of Oklahoma City. The flag had a buff-colored background when originally conceived and executed, and the name read "Caddo Indian Nation in Oklahoma."

Thanks to LaRue Parker of the Caddo National Council for supplying information on the flag.

Catawba Indian Nation— South Carolina

The Catawbas ("People of the River") are an ancient people who have lived in the border regions between the Carolinas for centuries. The federal government revoked their recognition in 1962 and restored it in the mid-1990s.

The Catawbas are known for their beautiful pottery, which serves as the principal device on the tribal seal and flag. The seal of the Catawba Nation dates from 1974–75, when the executive director of the Catawbas needed official stationery. Wanda George Warren, a high school student, designed an appropriate seal for the tribe in her commercial art class. She contacted leaders and tribal elders for ideas on symbolism and offered several designs, one of which was selected. That seal (with slight artistic modifications in 1994) has been in use ever since (survey response, Dewey L. Adams, Catawba Indian Nation).

A pale orange pot centered on the circular seal represents Catawba pottery. On it is an image of Chief Haigler, first chief of the Catawba Nation, in burnt orange. Behind the pot are the Catawba River in blue and the lands of the Catawbas in green. Ringing the central device is an orange band with "GREAT SEAL OF THE CATAWBA INDIAN NATION" in black. Outside this is a yellow serrated "sunburst" ring, backed by a burnt-orange field. The entire seal is ringed by a narrow black band. When used as a flag, the seal is on a burnt-orange field, recalling terra-cotta pottery. The Catawba people thus bring pottery—the symbol of their past—into the flag—the newest symbol of their sovereignty.

A historic flag associated with the Catawbas is the banner of the Catawba Rangers, who fought for the Confederacy during the Civil War. This flag of blue silk with a light-blue silk fringe had two scrolls—the upper one bore the words "OUR BATTLE CRY" and the lower one the motto "LIBERTY OR DEATH," both in gold lettering. Between the scrolls were an old-style gun, two crossed swords, and a red star in the center flanked by a gold "S" on one side and "C" on the other. Below this was a wreath held by a hand pointing up to the star. On the reverse, the top scroll bore the words "CATAWBA RANGERS" and the center depicted a palmetto palm, symbol of South Carolina, with a snake stretched ready to strike from the grass beneath. A ring of red stars and gold "beads" circled the central emblem (*Confederate Veteran*, 170, undated excerpt).

Cherokee Nation— Oklahoma

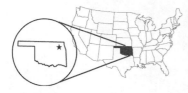

The modern Cherokee Nation is one of the largest nations in the United States in the number of enrolled members. The name "Cherokee" was probably given to them by their neighbors, the Creeks, who called them "Tciloki," meaning "People of a Different Speech." They called themselves "Ani Yun Wiya" or "Real People" (*ENAT*, 43–48).

The Cherokee people are now located in two distinct regions, reflecting their history under the United States. Most are in Oklahoma, while the small Eastern Band of Cherokees (see Eastern Band of Cherokee Indians of North Carolina) remains in North Carolina and Tennessee, their traditional homeland.

In 1830, when President Andrew Jackson signed the Indian Removal Act that displaced all Indians in the Southeast to what is now Oklahoma, the Cherokees were a nation that lived in towns and cities, with a written constitution and newspapers in their own language. The great Cherokee chief Sequoyah had invented the script, which became the first Indian language in written form. While some truly feared that the Cherokees would take steps to become an independent nation on the western boundaries of the United States, the primary motivation for their removal was to obtain Cherokee lands in Georgia, the Carolinas, Tennessee, and Alabama.

The eviction of the Cherokee people and their relocation to Indian Territory (Oklahoma) has become known as the "Trail of Tears." The federal government's treatment of the Cherokees and other tribes in the 1830s bore bitter fruit thirty years later when all five of the "Civilized Tribes" (the Cherokees, Chickasaws, Choctaws, Muscogees or Creeks, and Seminoles) allied with the Confederate States of America and fought in the Civil War against the Union.

The Western Cherokees, based in Oklahoma, use an orange flag (sample flag provided by the Cherokee Nation of Oklahoma, Tahlequah, Oklahoma) bearing the tribal seal (sample seal provided by Annin & Co., Roseland, N.J.). In the seal's center is a single seven-pointed star, with each point half-yellow, half-orange. This star recalls the seven original clans of the Cherokee people. Around it is an oak wreath in orange and green; the oak symbolizes the sacred eternal fire kindled from its wood. The star and wreath lie on a gray circle. Ringing this central emblem is an orange band bearing the legend "SEAL OF THE CHEROKEE NATION" in both English and Cherokee script. In Cherokee, it is pronounced *Tsa la gi yi a ye hli,* meaning "The Cherokee Nation" (from a postcard, "Seal of the Cherokee Nation"). At the base of the orange ring is "Sept. 6, 1839," the date of the constitution of the Cherokee Nation in Oklahoma. The seal is edged in green.

Around the seal is a ring of seven yellow seven-pointed stars, for the seven original clans. These stars also recall the seven holidays in the Cherokee life cycle and the seven sacred rites of the traditional Cherokee religion. One point of each star is aimed toward the central seal. The entire flag has a border of green and black diagonal stripes, similar to the rope-like border frequently found around a seal. The flag was designed by Stanley John (*Cherokee Advocate,* August 1978), a full-blood Navajo and husband of a member of the Cherokee Nation. It was approved by the

Tribal Council on 9 October 1978 and officially raised over tribal headquarters on 30 September 1979 (*Cherokee Advocate*, September 1979).

A resolution of the Cherokee Council on 9 September 1989 added a single black seven-pointed star to the upper right corner (Cherokee Council Resolution #73-89). This star is a constant reminder of the Cherokees who lost their lives during the terrible ordeal of the Trail of Tears, recalled each year in Tahlequah.

The earliest documented Cherokee flag is that of the Cherokee Brigade. This flag was presented to Principal Chief John Ross on 7 October 1861 by the Confederate Indian commissioner, Albert Pike. A similar flag has been attributed to the First Cherokee Mounted Rifles, possibly pointing to the base design as a de facto national flag for the Cherokee Nation (Devereaux D. Cannon Jr., *The Flags of the Confederacy: An Illustrated History* [Memphis, Tenn.: St. Luke's Press & Broadfoot Publishing, 1988], 64). The

 Cherokee Brigade flag was based on the first Confederate national flag, with three horizontal stripes (red, white, red) and a blue canton (rectangle in the upper left) bearing a ring of eleven white stars. The Cherokees added a large red star in the center of the ring and surrounded it with four smaller red stars. The five additional stars stood for the "Five Civilized Tribes," while the large one represented the Cherokees. On the white stripe "CHEROKEE BRAVES" appears in red letters.

The Cherokees are also reported to have a flag bearing seven red seven-pointed stars (*FBUS*, 254–55). This flag, called a "peace flag," was used in ceremonies marking the Cherokee national holiday on 7 September 1968. The Cherokee peace flag is symbolic in both color and design. The red stars stand for victory and success, while the white background represents peace and happiness. The seven points of each star recall the seven clans of the Cherokee people. The stars are arranged in the pattern of the constellation Yonegwa (Ursa Major, the Big Dipper). According to Cherokee history, the peace flag was carried by the Cherokees along the Trail of Tears. Before that journey began, the Cherokee war flag was buried with a hatchet. The "war flag" was the exact opposite—a red flag bearing the seven stars in white.

Special thanks to NAVA member Devereaux Cannon for detailed information on the changes in the Cherokee flag.

Cheyenne and Arapaho Tribes of Oklahoma

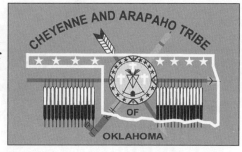

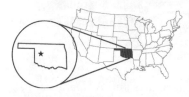

The Cheyennes and Arapahos of Oklahoma unite two of the most famous tribes in the American West. Both nations are actually the southern branches of their respective tribes (see Arapahoe Tribe of the Wind River Reservation and Northern Cheyenne Tribe). The Southern Cheyennes, now officially just the Cheyennes, are survivors of the Sand Creek Massacre (*ENAT*, 48–53). Today the Arapahos and Cheyennes share tribal trust lands in western Oklahoma, where they earn income by farming and leasing mineral rights.

The flag of the Cheyennes and Arapahos is a slightly modified version of the old flag of the Southern Cheyennes and Arapahos. A white outline of the state of Oklahoma fills the center of a light-blue field. Across this outline is a lance bearing two sets of fourteen white-and-black eagle feathers, standing for the fourteen members of the old tribal council. In the center is the seal of the two tribes, depicting a tipi with three crosses in white above and beside it (the cross is often used as a star in Indian symbolism). Ringing this is a band with fourteen stars, again for the tribal council members. At the four prime directions of the ring are triangles pointing inward, each containing a small black cross. Except for the white crosses, all items appear in black against a background of peach, apricot, or light beige, probably recalling the color of the rawhide used on Cheyenne and Arapaho shields.

Behind the shield and the map are traditional emblems of war and peace used by many Native Americans. The arrow, traditionally a symbol

of war, points downward, meaning the Cheyennes and Arapahos are at peace. The sacred pipe, not only a symbol of peace, is also very important in the ceremonies of many tribes. These symbols cross, forming an "X."

Arching over the entire device in black capital letters is "CHEYENNE AND ARAPAHO TRIBE" and below the seal "OF OKLAHOMA." The flag was altered to reflect both the name change of the Cheyennes and the makeup of the Tribal Council. The word "SOUTHERN" was removed, and a row of eight white stars was added across the top of the map of Oklahoma to show the new council's structure.

A variant of the flag was created for the Flag Plaza in Oklahoma City (made by Homer Miller Co., Oklahoma City). The background is white, not blue. The official seal has two arrows for the two tribes rather than one; the feathers are gold and white rather than black and white.

Cheyenne River Sioux Tribe— South Dakota

The Sioux Nation is divided into four major groups: the Tetons, Santees, Yanktons, and Yanktonais. The Cheyenne River Sioux are part of the Teton branch, which includes the Oglala, Brulé, Hunkpapa, Miniconjou, Oohenonpa, Sans Arc or Itapzico, and Sihasapa Bands (*ENAT*, 222–28). All seven of these bands refer to themselves as Lakotas ("Allies").

The Lakotas of the Cheyenne River Sioux fly a white flag bearing a large tribal seal that stretches across nearly the entire length of the flag. The central element is a rainbow in red over yellow over blue, representing the Cheyenne River Sioux people themselves. Atop the rainbow curve six blue thunderclouds, for the region above the world where the thunderbirds, who control the four winds, live.

The two white-and-black eagle feathers hanging from the ends of the rainbow represent the spotted eagle, the protector of all Lakotas. Two fused sacred pipes symbolize unity: one for the Lakotas, the other for all other Indian nations. Two yellow hoops represent the Sacred Hoop that shall not be broken. In many Native American cultures, the Sacred Hoop symbolizes life on earth, and breaking the Sacred Hoop dooms the planet. The Sacred Calf Pipe Bundle in red stands for Wakan Tanka, the Great Mystery (Arlene Thompson, letter dated 27 November 1994). The flag contains the six colors sacred to the Lakotas: red, white, yellow, and black for the human races, blue for the heavens, and green for Mother Earth.

The Cheyenne River Sioux are known as the "Keepers of the Most Sacred Calf Pipe," a gift to all the Lakotas from the White Buffalo Calf Maiden. The white buffalo is a sacred omen to the Sioux, portending great times for Native Americans. A white buffalo calf born in Minnesota in 1994 brought joy and excitement to many Indians of the upper Plains.

Thanks to Arlene Thompson and to the Cheyenne River Sioux Tribal Headquarters for the sample flag.

Chickasaw Nation— Oklahoma

The Chickasaw Nation, one of the "Five Civilized Tribes" of Oklahoma, was constituted on 4 March 1856, after its forced removal from the banks of the Mississippi (*ENAT*, 53–54). Its constitution was adopted on 16 August 1867, and its tribal seal was designed in 1907 (*FBUS*, 255–56). The original capital, Tishomingo, was named for the last great war chief of the Chickasaws. An image of Tishomingo dominates the tribal seal and the flag.

The Chickasaw flag is indigo and bears a full-color representation of the seal of the nation (sample flag provided by the Chickasaw Nation, Tishomingo, Oklahoma). The orange (or gold) and light-purple bands encircling the seal symbolize the purity and honor of the Chickasaw people. The warrior, besides depicting the beloved Tishomingo, stands for all Chickasaws ("The Great Seal of the Chickasaw Nation," undated, unsigned letter from the Chickasaw Nation Headquarters). Around the outside of the seal, outlined by a yellow corded band, are the words "THE GREAT SEAL OF THE CHICKASAW NATION."

Chief Tishomingo carries two arrows, which stand for the two historical divisions of the Chickasaws, the forest dwellers and the town dwellers. The chief wears four head feathers, representing the four prime directions of the compass. The bow, traditionally made of hickory, symbolizes the hunting prowess of the Chickasaw warrior and his willingness to defend his people. The quiver, made of deerskin and decorated with white fur, reinforces the same ideals. Stretching across Chief Tishomingo's shoulder

31

is a warrior's mantle, traditionally made of swan feathers. His deerskin shield represents the protection that Chickasaw warriors offer their people. The deerskin kneestraps represent the fleetness of the warriors (*NAVA News* [March/April 1989]: 6).

The river in the background recalls the Mississippi, a Chickasaw word meaning "without source." The foliage represents the flora found along the Mississippi, the ancient homeland of the Chickasaws.

Although the Chickasaws have lived in Oklahoma for more than 160 years, their hearts still lie along the banks of the Mississippi. Their tribal seal and their flag recall their days in the Southeast, when their heritage blossomed and their history, pride, and glory achieved their zenith—a time that they will not forget. (The Confederate States of America apparently created flags for each of its allies in the "Five Civilized Tribes"; unfortunately the design presented to the Chickasaw Nation is not known.)

Choctaw Nation
of Oklahoma

The Choctaws of Oklahoma were the first of the "Five Civilized Tribes" to accept expulsion from their native lands in what is now the southern half of the states of Mississippi and Alabama and move to Indian Territory (now Oklahoma) in the early 1830s (*ENAT*, 61–63). Along the "Trail of Tears"—this long march from the the their homelands—the Choctaws lost almost a quarter of their people to disease, starvation, and attacks by whites.

When the Civil War broke out in 1861, the Choctaws—along with most tribes forced into Indian Territory—sided with the Confederacy. During this alliance the Choctaws became the first United States tribe to adopt a flag. It is documented as a light-blue flag bearing a red circle edged in white in the center (*FBUS*, 256–58). Within the red circle are a sacred pipe, a bow, and three arrows representing the three subdivisions of the Choctaw Nation. These subdivisions are named for three chiefs: Apuckshenubbee, Pushmataha, and Mosholatubbee ("The Great Seal of the Choctaw Nation," *Oklahoma Chronicles* 33:4 [Winter 1955–56]: 357–58). That design is the basis of the Choctaw national seal to this day. A replica of this flag is displayed in the Oklahoma Historical Museum in Oklahoma City. It was used only in 1861–64, but it has continued to inspire flags for the Choctaws in Oklahoma. A variant of this flag exists in the Oklahoma Historical Society (Joseph H. Chute, *Emblems of Southern Valor* [Louisville, Ky.: Harmony House, 1990], 108–9).

In the 1970s Paramount Flag Co. of San Francisco filled an order for Choctaw Nation flags. This reappearance of the Choctaw flag followed exactly the pattern of the first of the earlier flags but drastically altered the colors. The field became dark red, the ring around the central disk became light blue; the disk changed to a deep yellow; and the bow, arrows, and sacred pipe were in natural colors.

The current flag (sample flag provided by the Choctaw Nation, Durant, Oklahoma) follows this basic design but adds more detail. The inner circle remains deep yellow, but the sacred pipe and bow and arrows are now white, edged in black. The pipe has black smoke coming from it. The light-blue ring is edged by two light-green cords (a very narrow inner one and a wider outer one). The blue ring bears a legend in black: "THE GREAT SEAL" above and "OF THE CHOCTAW NATION" below. The deep red field has been changed to purple.

This flag seems to have been inspired by the drawing of the Choctaw flag carried by the Choctaw Confederate Troops as depicted in a 1958 sheet from the Oklahoma Historical Society entitled "Fourteen Flags over Oklahoma" ("Official Seals of the Five Civilized Tribes," *Oklahoma Chronicles* 18:4 [December 1940]: 430–31). It resembles a flag shown in old postcards depicting the "Flags of the Five Civilized Tribes" based upon gift flags from the State of Alabama. The postcard, however, shows the flag as a bluish-purple ("Fourteen Flags Plaza," *Oklahoma Today* [Summer 1968]: 14–16). This flag is the only other one that includes writing around the seal.

The changing colors of the Choctaw flag may be an attempt to replicate a mistaken perception of an earlier flag's color. Usually only flag manufacturers and scholars are concerned with the impact of light and time upon fabric as the color fastness of the dye is lost. For example, blue dyes tend to transform slowly into maroon and then into purple; white will turn yellow; red will fade to purple and eventually to pale blue. It is possible that the variations seen in the Choctaw flag reflect the vagaries of time upon fabric.

Special thanks to Dr. Whitney Smith, Flag Research Center, for much of the historical documentation on the Choctaw flag.

Citizen Potawatomi Nation— Oklahoma

"Potawatomi" means "People of the Place of the Fire" in Algonquin. This term refers back some four hundred years, when the Potawatomis were united with the Ojibwe and the Ottawa Nations. In those days the land of the Potawatomis and the other two nations was what is today Ontario. When the three groups moved southward, they split up, forming the three distinct nations. The Ojibwes moved west to what is now Wisconsin and Minnesota; the Ottawas moved to the lands around Lake Huron; and the Potawatomis moved onto the Lower Peninsula of Michigan (*ENAT*, 197–98). When the Potawatomis moved, they took with them the original "Council Fire" that had been used by the three groups when united. From this is derived their name: they are now called the "Keepers of the Fire."

Today the Potawatomis span an area from Michigan through Oklahoma. The largest band of modern Potawatomis is the Citizen Potawatomis, formerly the Citizen Band, found in Oklahoma. They received that title because—after being ejected from Kansas and settling in Oklahoma—they accepted the United States government's offer of citizenship and allotments of land. The Citizen Potawatomis control only the 4,400-acre Tribal Historic Area in Oklahoma; but the vast majority of them live on private property, as is true with virtually all of Oklahoma's Native American peoples.

The original flag of the Citizen Band of the Potawatomi Nation was white and bore the tribal seal in the center. At the top of that seal are a crossed sacred pipe and tomahawk, signifying skill and strength in war bonded with a strong historical reputation as a peace-loving people. In the center is the great "Council Fire" from which they get their name. The fire is a symbol of warmth and friendship as well as the wisdom derived from the "Great Council Fire" (*Potawatomi Seal*, undated pamphlet). Below that are two crossed red-oak leaves. The acorns of the red oak were a source of food for the Potawatomis, and the leaves were widely used in Potawatomi beadwork designs. The seal was ringed by the legends "GREAT SEAL OF THE POTAWATOMI INDIANS" and "PEOPLE OF THE PLACE OF THE FIRE." As a money-saving device, the seal on the flag was represented solely in red outline.

With a change in tribal government in the mid-1990s came a change in name and flag. The newly renamed Citizen Potawatomis now employ a bright blue flag bearing the seal in full color. The wording encircling the seal is now in black on a red ring. The other elements of the seal still appear upon a white disk in the center. Across the top of the flag is the new name "CITIZEN POTAWATOMI OF OKLAHOMA" in white letters.

Cocopah Tribe
of Arizona

 In southwestern Arizona lies the home-
land of the Cocopahs, who call themselves
"Xawitt Kunyavaei" ("River People").
The Cocopahs once shared the Cocopah
Reservation with the Yuma and Maricopa
Tribes; but the Maricopas and Cocopahs withdrew, leaving the reservation
in the hands of the Yumas. The Cocopahs, however, still live in and around
the town of Somerton, Arizona (*TDAI*).

The Cocopah flag is white with a full-color image of the tribal seal in
the center (unsigned letter dated 17 November 1994). The seal shows a
Cocopah man spear-fishing in the Colorado River, which was essential to
the life of the Cocopahs. At his feet are several salmon-colored fish and in
the background is a stand of corn, both staples of the Cocopah diet. Also
in the background are a wikiyup (the traditional house) and a ramada (a
shelter from the hot desert sun), both in gray. Purple hills, a yellow sun,
gray desert rocks, and green plants complete the picture. The overall
design shows the traditions of this desert-dwelling nation, dependent on
the Colorado River. Around the edge of the seal are the words "THE
SOVEREIGN NATION OF THE COCOPAHS" above and "Xawitt Kunyavaei" below.

Coeur d'Alene Tribe—Idaho

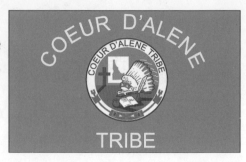

 French *voyageurs* in the days before the acquisition of the immense Louisiana Territory dubbed the Indians who lived just beyond the edge of that territory "Coeur d'Alene" ("Awl-Hearted") because they were sharp traders and hard bargainers. Those Indians referred to themselves as "Schitsu'umsh," meaning "Discovered People" or "Those Who Are Found Here." They still are called the "Skitswish" as an alternative to the name imposed by the Europeans. The Coeur d'Alenes inhabited an area stretching from present-day Montana to the Spokane River in Washington and from roughly the Canadian border south to the Snake River.

The modern Coeur d'Alenes occupy a reservation covering some 345,000 acres (under 70,000 acres as recently as 1995) in western Idaho along the border with Washington. Both the Coeur d'Alene River and Lake Coeur d'Alene are at least partly within the boundaries of the modern reservation, although the city of Coeur d'Alene, Idaho, lies beyond its northern border. The current enrollment of the tribe is nearing 4,000 members.

Symbolizing the modern Coeur d'Alenes is a circular seal proudly displayed on most of the tribe's common buildings from the headquarters in Plummer to a large back-lit image surmounting the main entrance to the Coeur d'Alene Casino/hotel complex just north of the town of Worley. Over fifteen percent of the tribe is employed at the complex.

The seal is surrounded by a white ring bearing the name "COEUR D'ALENE TRIBE" in black letters in the top half and two stylized Coeur d'Alene arrows pointing downward (usually considered a sign of peace) below. The arrows are brown with accents of red and blue and yellow tips edged in red.

Within the outer ring, the inner portion of the seal is divided horizontally into an upper blue and a lower brown half. In the left of the blue area is a white rectangle bearing a green outline map of the state of Idaho. The green reflects the abundant pine forests that cover the panhandle, in which the Coeur d'Alenes live. To the left of the map is a Christian cross that can be depicted in various colors (brown, gray, or light blue), but it is brown on the flag. It casts a shadow onto the lower section. The shadow—gray, brown, or black (as on the flag)—can lean to the left or right depending upon artistic interpretations; on the flag it leans to the left. In the right half of the seal, overlapping the top and bottom halves, is a Coeur d'Alene chief's headdress with a blue band and red-tipped feathers. The outer red-tipped feathers are sometimes depicted with yellow streamers, as on the flag, and the blue band that would fit around the forehead frequently has yellow and black triangular accents. The headdress signifies the leadership of the chiefs in governing the Coeur d'Alene people and the authority that stems from them.

The lower half of the seal contains a yellow quill pen in an inkwell, a sacred pipe, and an open book. The pen, inkwell, and book all reflect the importance the tribe places upon education. The pipe recalls "important occasions for prayers" (Coeur d'Alene Tribe, *Seal of the Coeur d'Alene Tribe*, undated informational handout).

When employed on the tribal flag, the seal is placed on a royal-blue background. Arcing over the seal in golden-yellow is the name "COEUR D'ALENE" and below the seal the word "TRIBE." The flag kept indoors at the tribal headquarters in Plummer includes a gold fringe. Exterior flags do not employ the fringe.

With income from their various business enterprises, the Coeur d'Alenes have managed to create "concrete" reinforcements of the ideas that their symbols embody. They have established a $5 million school complex, a Tribal Wellness Center as part of the Benewah Medical Center, a college degree program in cooperation with Idaho's Lewis and Clark State College, and classes in the Schitsu'umsh language.

With the increase in the size of the reservation and the investments in the reservation's future to improve the lives of the tribal members, the modern business acumen of the Coeur d'Alenes shows that the French *voyageurs* named them very appropriately.

Thanks to Richard James Mullen, Tribal Council Preservation officer of the Coeur d'Alene Tribe, for taking the time to explain the flag to Healy's cousins Neal and Kathy Rosia, who live not far from the reservation.

Colorado River Indian Tribes (CRIT)—Arizona and California

The Colorado River Indian Reservation stretches along the river border between California and Arizona. The river runs like a spine through the entire length of the reservation of some 278,000 acres—home to 2,400 members of four distinct tribes: the Mohaves, Chemehuevis, Hopis, and Navajos. An 1865 act of Congress originally created the reservation for just the Mohaves and Chemehuevis. In 1945 the Bureau of Indian Affairs relocated some Hopis and Navajos to the reservation from their homes in northeastern Arizona.

The largest of the four nations on the reservation is the Mohaves; their name comes from the term *aha-makave,* meaning "beside the water." The Chemehuevis, whose name comes from a Mohave term dealing with fish, call themselves "Nu Wu" or "the People." They are closely related to the Southern Paiute people of Nevada (*ENAT,* 95–98). Their traditional homelands stretched along the Colorado River between Nevada and Yuma, Arizona.

The Hopis are from northern Arizona, where their reservation is totally surrounded by that of the Navajos (see Hopi Tribe of Arizona). The Hopis were village dwellers with homes built atop mesas for defense. Hopis and

Navajos have now lived on the Colorado River Reservation for more than fifty years. Their skills in farming under arid conditions have helped them and the reservation thrive.

Today the four tribes maintain and observe their traditional ways and unique religious and cultural identities but function as one political unit. The Colorado River Indian Tribes (CRIT) adopted a flag on 4 January 1979 from a design by tribal member Margie McCabe. The design contest called for a flag that would uphold the tribal traditions and indicate the uniqueness of the four nations living and working together as one. CRIT Flag Day, on 4 January of each year, is a celebration and appreciation of the unity of the four peoples (Colorado Indian Tribes Museum, undated pamphlet).

The flag has three horizontal stripes. The top stripe is light blue with an orange sun, whose rays represent the endless rising and setting of the sun on the land and water of the reservation. The central stripe is tan or light brown, symbolizing the earth from which the tribes reap their food and build their dwellings. The bottom stripe is dark blue with two white wavy lines, representing the Colorado River, which gives life to the earth and people of the reservation. Centered on the tan stripe and extending to the sun are four white feathers tipped with black, one for each tribe. Below them appears the acronym "CRIT" in black.

Comanche Indian Tribe— Oklahoma

The Comanches, the "Lords of the Plains," once dominated an area that included much of present-day Texas, New Mexico, Oklahoma, Kansas, and northern Mexico. The fiercest of fighters and among the last tribes to submit to reservations (*ENAT*, 68–71), they were excellent equestrians, keeping large herds and introducing the horse to neighboring tribes after acquiring it from the Spanish. Today the Comanche Nation is centered at Lawton, Oklahoma, where the modern Comanches engage in farming and earn income from leasing mineral rights.

The flag of the Comanche Nation celebrates its historical status as the dominant tribe of the south-central United States. The field is divided vertically, with blue on the left, red on the right. (Two versions of the flag exist; and one is double-sided, with blue on the left and red on the right on both sides.)

The seal of the Comanche Nation also always has the blue portion on the left. According to the Public Information Office of the Comanche Tribe, the flag may date to 1991. The seal is a Comanche battle shield divided roughly in half (seal provided by the *Comanche News*, newsletter of the Comanche Nation, Lawton, Oklahoma). The left portion is blue; the right portion is yellow and bears the image of a Comanche warrior on horseback in red to represent the name given to all Native Americans by the European settlers—the "red man" (Jamesena Stops, editor, *Comanche News*). The undulating border between the halves represents a snake moving backward. According to their legends, the Comanches were once known as the "Snakes." The blue represents loyalty, while the yellow recalls the brightness of the sun and a state of happiness.

The blue and red colors are derived from a British wool trade blanket, the wrap preferred by the Comanches when riding the Plains over a century ago. The blanket recalls the Comanches' life without boundaries, a time when they were the true rulers of the Plains. A critical element in many Comanche ceremonies, the blanket also boasts of the riding prowess of the Comanches. Four feathers appear on the shield when it is used as the seal of the Comanche Nation. As with many other tribes, they recall the sacred number four.

The Comanches are using their seal and flag with increasing zeal. In April 1995 they issued license plates for vehicles registered to tribal members and based upon tribal lands ("Comanche Tribal License Tags Are Here," *Comanche News* [July 1995]: 1). The central element of the new plates is the seal of the Comanche Nation. In July 1995 the Comanches officially opened their Comanche Veterans Memorial in Lawton ("Comanche Veterans Memorial Dedicated," *Comanche News* [August 1995]: 1). Two central flagpoles fly the American and the Comanche flags.

A version of the flag with a variant seal flies at the Flag Plaza in Oklahoma City. A yellow circle replaces the serrated edge of the shield. Across the top of the circle in black is "COMANCHE NATION," with "LORDS OF THE SOUTHERN PLAINS" in slightly smaller letters below. The seal is divided in half, blue on the left and red (not yellow) on the right. The Indian on horseback is shown in yellow and greatly enlarged to provide more detail.

Confederated Salish and Kootenai Tribes of the Flathead Reservation— Montana

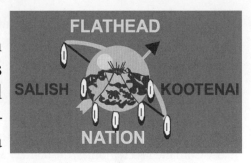

The Flathead Reservation covers almost 620,000 acres of western Montana. This land is home to two separate tribes functioning as a single unit, the Confederated Salish and Kootenai Tribes (*GAI*, 193). A small contingent of the Kalispel Nation and some Spokanes, both Salish tribes, also live there.

The Salish were called "Flatheads" by white settlers, due to their appearance and connection to the Coastal Salish people, who tied padded boards to their foreheads to shape their heads. They now call themselves by their original name, however. The Kootenais live both in the United States and Canada, where their name is spelled "Kootenay" (*ENAT*, 113–14). After countless generations of supporting themselves by fishing, the Kootenais obtained horses around 1700 and transformed themselves into a tribe of the Plains, pursuing the buffalo and using tipis.

Today these two tribes celebrate their former Plains lifestyle on their flag (sample provided by the Office of Property and Supply, Confederated Salish and Kootenai Tribes, Pablo, Montana). Centered on the red background is a blue disk bearing a tan tipi decorated with bear prints and a buffalo in dark blue. These two emblems reflect hunting and fishing—the buffalo as a major game animal and the bear as a skilled fisher. Behind the tipi in blue stand the Rocky Mountains, which transverse the land of the Salish and Kootenais, and above them on the left is a yellow sun. The sky and the mountain snow are light blue.

Crossed behind the central disk, which symbolizes an Indian shield, are a traditional bow and arrow, the hunting weapons of the Plains Indians. From the bow and shield hang seven white-and-black eagle feathers, representing the seven members of the Flathead Council. The bow and arrow are tan and dark blue. Above the disk is the name "FLATHEAD" and below it the word "NATION" in yellow; on the left is "SALISH" and on the right "KOOTENAI" in dark blue. In recognition of the difficulty that writing causes on a flag viewed from the back, two versions of the flag of the Flathead Nation exist: the formal flag is double-sided, with the writing appearing properly on both sides; the common flag is single-sided.

Confederated Tribes and Bands of the Yakama Indian Nation— Washington

YAKAMA INDIAN NATION
TREATY OF 1855

Located in south-central Washington State is the 1,130,000-acre reservation that is home to the Yakima or Yakama Indian Nation (*AIDD*, 39). That reservation was granted to the Yakamas in a treaty signed in 1855 by Governor Isaac Stevens of the Washington Territory and representatives of the Cayuse, Umatilla, Walla Walla, Nez Percé, and Yakama Tribes.

Although the treaty called for a period of two years to allow the various tribes to migrate to and resettle on their new reservations, Governor Stevens declared Indian lands open for white settlers a mere twelve days after the treaty was signed (*ENAT*, 253–54). A Yakama chief, Kamiakin, called upon the tribes that had been duped to oppose this declaration forcefully, but not before they had built up their strength. Things moved too quickly, and shortly thereafter a series of raids, counter-raids, and reciprocal atrocities began. These uprisings became known as the "Yakima Wars."

The war continued until 1859, when the last phase (known as the "Coeur d'Alene War") ended. The Yakamas accepted their reservation and still dwell there today. Some Paiutes and a few members of other tribes also reside on the Yakama Reservation.

The flag of the Yakama Nation, which is about 6,300 strong (*AIDD*, 39), shows the reservation in white, outlined in gold, against a sky-blue background (sample flag provided by Elmer's Flag & Banner, Portland,

Oregon). Within the map is a depiction of Mount Adams, an impressive mountain that lies partly within the reservation, which is sacred to the Yakamas. Soaring above the mountain is an eagle depicted in full color. Not only is the eagle sacred, but it shares a livelihood with many Yakamas, who earn their living fishing for salmon in the waters of the Columbia River and its tributaries.

Above the eagle is the "morning star," a symbol of guidance and leadership; and arcing around Mount Adams are fourteen gold stars and fourteen eagle feathers honoring the bands of the Yakama Nation. The feathers represent the fourteen chiefs who signed the treaty of 1855, while the fourteen stars represent the Confederated Tribes and Bands of the Yakama Indian Nation. At the bottom of the map are the name of the nation and "TREATY OF 1855."

In 1955, the centennial of the treaty signing, members of the "Old Toppenish Long House" ("Toppenish" is the Yakamas' name for themselves) adopted a flag to represent the people of the Yakama Reservation ("As Long as the River Flows," *Akwesosne Notes* 3:4 [May 1971]). The flag adopted at that time was similar to the present flag of the Yakama Nation but did not include the reservation map; nor did it have writing on it. It is obvious that the flag adopted in 1955 was the basis for the current flag.

In the mid-1990s the Yakima Nation renamed itself "Yakama," more closely reflecting the proper pronunciation in its native language. A new flag was adopted at that time; it is simply the old flag with the new name spelled properly.

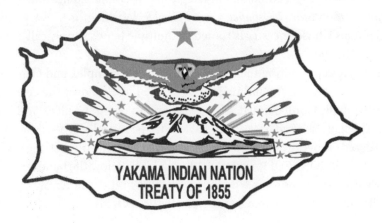

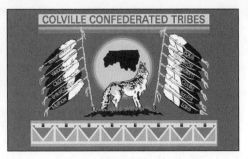

Confederated Tribes of the Colville Reservation— Washington

Sprawling across a million acres in northeast Washington is the Colville Reservation—larger than Rhode Island. Home to eleven tribes, it is named for Fort Colville, a British outpost established in the 1820s (*Who Are the Colville Indians?* [Colville Tribal Museum, Grand Coulee, Washington]). It was created in 1872 and fully populated by the 1880s.

The first tribes were the Nespelem, San Poil, Okanogan, and Lake Nations. They were soon joined by others—the Wenatchee, Entiat, Chelan, Methow, Moses-Columbia, and Palouse Tribes—making up the original ten bands. Chief Joseph's Band of the Nez Percés arrived later, following his people's unsuccessful attempt to flee to Canada. Because of the large number of bands on the reservation, the federal government started referring to all eleven tribes simply as the Colville Indians ("What Is the History of the Native People of This Region?" in *Grand Coulee Dam Area Visitors Guide, Star Newspaper,* Grand Coulee, Washington). Today those individuals whose ancestry is rooted in multiple bands simply call themselves "Colville."

The flag representing the Colville Indians is a complex and elaborate banner-like design. A handmade copy of the flag flies over the entrance to the Colville Confederated Tribe's Museum in Grand Coulee, Washington. The flag has a red background. Close to the top edge is a yellow band (bordered above by a green stripe and below by a blue stripe) with "COLVILLE CONFEDERATED TRIBES" in blue. Below the band a yellow disk with narrow borders (the inner one blue and the outer one green) recalls the tribal shield used by warriors. In the center is a map of the reservation in black. Below this disk and overlapping its lower portion is a wolf, facing right and standing on a green grassy mound. The wolf—baying at the moon—is shown in natural colors. On the flag at the museum, the wolf is made from actual fur, possibly wolf or coyote. The use of appliquéd fur appears to be unique among Native American flags, and this may be the only such flag in existence.

Below the wolf runs a yellow band with a geometric pattern in blue, green, and black. Flanking the disk and wolf are two yellow lances. The left lance bears five large white-and-black eagle feathers extending to the left. The right lance has six similar feathers extending to the right. On each feather is the name of one of the bands on the reservation in capital letters. Thus on the left feathers (starting at the top) are the names of the Moses-Columbia, Palouse, Okanogan, Entiat, Chelan, and Methow Bands; on the right feathers are the names of the Nez Percé, Wenatchee, Nespelem, Colville, San Poil, and Lake Bands. (This addition of the names and the real fur are probably peculiar to the handmade flag and not found on regular copies of the flag.)

The flag's design was altered for commercial manufacture in 1996, with one major addition and many subtle changes. The major addition is a broad light-blue stripe crossing slightly above the base of the flag but not reaching either edge. It contains a number of complex geometrical elements in green, red, and black on yellow. This new stripe may signify the bridge at Grand Coulee Dam, the major entrance from the south and a gateway for tourism, a major economic boon to the town of Grand Coulee and the entire reservation.

The yellow stripe across the top of the flag is now about equal in length to the new "bridge" stripe; its green and blue edges have been replaced by band of light blue over light green just below it; the lettering on that stripe is red. The wolf is white, yellow, and black; the grass has a black base; the blue and green throughout have been changed to light blue and light green. The feathers with the names of the individual tribes have been enlarged, and the names of the tribes are now printed in light blue, edged in white.

Confederated Tribes of the Grand Ronde Community of Oregon

While Native Americans had lived in the Pacific Northwest for several millennia, by the mid-nineteenth century pressure from settlers arriving over the Oregon Trail led to unbearable friction. In 1856 the federal government removed more than twenty Indian bands from their homelands and relocated them to 69,000 acres on the Grand Ronde Reservation on the Oregon coast. Although many Native Americans, despite their seminomadic traditions, became homesteaders, the U.S. government later declared that their lands could not be used for farming or tree-growing. As a result, many sold their land for as little as US$1.10 per acre and moved away. By 1901 the Grand Ronde Reservation had dwindled to 440 acres.

The 1934 Indian Reorganization Act, which decreased federal control of Indian affairs and increased Indian self-government and responsibility, allowed the tribe to purchase land for subsistence and farming sites, raising tribal acreage to 977 by 1936. Eighteen years later, however, a new federal law terminated the mantle of federal protection for the tribe. The Grand Rondes increasingly became a landless people in their own land—in 1975 their territory had been reduced to a 5-acre cemetery plot. In 1983 Congress reinstated federal recognition and today (according to the Confederated Tribes of the Grand Ronde Community of Oregon) the reservation owns 10,300 acres.

The tribe's flag resulted from a contest held after the Grand Rondes regained federal recognition; the winner received US$50. Although the seal appears prominently on tribal publications and letterheads, the flag has not yet been adopted by tribal council resolution.

A black-and-white seal, centered on a white field, combines historic, geographic, and spiritual aspects of the Grand Ronde Confederated Tribes. A unifying black outer ring encircles the main image of the seal. The multiple compass points immediately inside the ring allude to the twenty-three bands and tribes, drawn from all over the Oregon Country, that form the confederation. The five main tribes (Umpqua, Molala, Rogue River, Kalapuya, and Shasta) are honored by the five white-and-black eagle feathers hanging below the outer ring.

Inside the compass points is a wider black ring with "THE CONFED-ERATED TRIBES" above and "OF GRAND RONDE" below in white. In the center of the seal, according to the tribes, "is Spirit Mountain where our people went on their Vision Quests, or to seek their Tomanawis, or 'spirit.'" The mountain holds deep symbolic and spiritual significance for a people emerging from a difficult 150-year odyssey during which their fate often hung in precarious balance. The Grand Rondes have named their new casino "Spirit Mountain."

Thanks to Jackie Whisler, administrative assistant at Grand Ronde tribal headquarters.

Confederated Tribes of the Siletz Reservation— Oregon

Some two hundred years ago the United States Corps of Discovery, under the leadership of Captains Meriwether Lewis and William Clark, reached the mouth of the Columbia River, the modern boundary between the states of Oregon and Washington. Until that event, the Native American population of the area had experienced minimal contact with Europeans and European-Americans. An occasional ship would anchor at the mouth of the Columbia to trade and take on supplies, and a rare visitor from the forces of Imperial Spain or a British trading company might venture into that remote region of North America. The Lewis and Clark expedition was followed by a constant and ever-increasing stream of trappers, traders, and others hoping to strike it rich with the most valuable resource the region had to offer—the beaver pelt.

While the "pelt rush" was on, it brought to the Indian population other aspects of European-American culture—most devastatingly, smallpox. Within twenty years thousands of coastal Indians had died from the disease, against which they had no immunity. In fifty years so many of the coastal people had been killed that many tribes were forcibly "confederated" because their populations had shrunk to such sad numbers.

It should be noted that the term "tribe" as usually employed to describe large amalgams of closely related clans with a common language, culture, and heritage does not always work when referring to the tribes in the northwestern United States. According to Robert Kentta of the Confederated Tribes of Siletz Indians (CTSI), there are differing opinions on "what constitutes a tribe" and whether politically autonomous villages

should be listed separately or whether they should be grouped together by linguistic affiliation.

In 1855 the Siletz or "Coast" reservation was established for all tribes and bands of western Oregon, according to Mr. Kentta. Today the Siletz Tribes still have represented among their tribal membership all (or virtually all) tribes, bands, and villages that existed in western Oregon at the time of removal. One common count is that the Siletz people have twenty-seven distinct tribal entities, including some linguistically related northern California groups like the Shastas and Tolowas. There are even a few Klickitat families represented on the reservation, descendants of Klickitats who began living in the Willamette Valley in the 1820s. The Siletz people number about 2,000, and under 1,000 actually live on the reservation, which is located along the northwest coast of Oregon.

The tribes (with bands in parentheses) most commonly included on the list of those who were removed to the Coast Reservation and whose descendants are today members of the Confederated Tribes of Siletz Indians are the Alsea (Yaquina and Alsea); Chinook (Upper and Lower); Coos (Hanis and Miluk); Kalapuya (Yamhill, Santiam, Yoncalla, etc.); Lower Umpqua; Molala; Shasta (Rogue and Klamath River); Siuslaw; Takelma

(Dagelma, Latgawa, and Cow Creek); Tututunne (all southwest Oregon Athapascan groups: Upper Umpqua, Upper Coquille, Euchre Creek, Flores Creek, Pistol River, Port Orford, Yashute, Mikonotunne, Applegate River, Galice Creek, Chetco, Chasta Costa, Tolowa, etc.); and Tillamook (Siletz, Salmon River, Nestucca, etc.).

The CTSI flag was designed around 1995 or 1996 by two tribal members, Robert Simmons and Sharon Edenfield, and was formally adopted by a tribal resolution at about the same time. The flag is white and bears the tribal seal in the center. The upper and lower borders of the flag are edged with designs inspired by the basketry of the Siletz people. According to Natasha Kavanaugh from the CTSI Office of Public Information, Ms. Edenfield is credited with incorporating the black basket design elements.

The seal that dominates the center of the flag pictures a salmon, the main source of sustenance for the Siletz people over the centuries. The salmon seems to "float" over a sandy beach, through which a small blue creek meanders. Behind the salmon lie the ubiquitous northwestern conifer forests, over which towers the snow-capped Uchre Mountain. Outside a narrow black band encircling the seal is the official name in dark-blue letters: "CONFEDERATED TRIBES" above and "OF SILETZ INDIANS" below.

Ms. Kavanaugh reports that in the originally approved logo the circle of the seal appeared on a staff. "The one we have now is a recent rendition of that original design."

Thanks to Robert Kentta of the Siletz Tribe and to Diane Rodriguez and Natasha Kavanaugh from the Office of Public Information of the CTSI.

Confederated Tribes of the Umatilla Reservation— Oregon

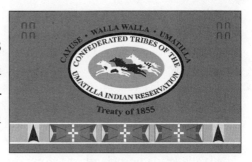

Three tribes closely related for hundreds of years—the Cayuses, the Umatillas, and the Walla Wallas—constitute the Confederated Tribes of the Umatilla Reservation. The tribal enrollment is in excess of 2,200 and includes both reservation residents and nonresidents. The reservation, situated in northeastern Oregon, also serves as home to nearly 2,000 non-Indian residents and about 1,000 Indians from the Yakama, Nez Percé, and Warm Springs Tribes.

All three tribes are considered to be part of the "Plateau Culture." As such the modern term "tribe" is very misleading. Before the arrival of Europeans, according to "History & Culture of the Cayuse, Umatilla and Walla Walla Indians" on the reservation's website (http://www. umatilla. nsn.us/hist1.html): "What is called a tribe today was actually just a large grouping of family bands which frequented a common area, spoke a common dialect and wintered in a common location." No single leader controlled the whole group. Each family band had a spokesman to represent it in council, whose only means of control were "persuasion and group pressure. If a headman or an individual had a disagreement with the group consensus, he merely moved elsewhere." The names "Umatilla" or "Walla Walla" and others like them "usually designated the location of one of these large encampments." Although each group lived in one general area, they all associated freely and could cross the others' territories. "All friendly bands were permitted the privilege of use of the others' lands" (ibid.).

Historically, the Cayuse people associated more closely with the Nez Percés—and the most famous of all Nez Percés, Chief Joseph, was actually

Nez Percé and Cayuse. The Cayuse people were great traders and special-ized in woven mats and animal pelts but also traded horses. Horse trading became so associated with the tribe that today the term for a domesticated Indian pony is "cayuse."

The Umatillas were great salmon fishers, an industry that is still an inte-gral part of their culture. The salmon played a significant part in the diet and economy of the Umatillas, as it did for all tribes that lived near the beautiful Columbia River.

The Walla Walla homeland was along the banks of the Walla Walla River and in the vicinity of the juncture of the Snake and Columbia Rivers. From their initial contact with white trappers until the 1850s, the Walla Wallas—like their fellow confederation members—were friendly. Due to land grabs by white settlers and treaty violations, the tribes of the region all partici-pated in the "Yakima Wars" of 1855. One of the most important Walla Walla chiefs was Peo-Peo-Mox-Mox, who was murdered by the whites he had come to meet to discuss peace. His murder sparked a continuation of hos-tilities for another three years.

In the modern Confederated Tribes, each tribe has one or more cere-monial chiefs. The current Umatilla chief is Raymond Burke "Wish-low-too-la-tin"; the Cayuse chief is Jesse Jones "Uma-pie-ma"; and the Walla Walla chiefs are William Burke "Wet-yat-muss-till-lie-la-kop-pit" and Carl Sampson "Peo-Peo-Mox-Mox" (the name of the great chief of 150 years ago). Under their ceremonial leadership, five years of debate and various design alternatives culminated in the adoption of the flag of the Confed-erated Tribes of the Umatilla Reservation in 2001. It was first hoisted in May 2002.

The flag is red, with the tribal logo slightly above the center line. The logo is a golden oval depicting three horses—cayuses—racing to the left across a green patch of grass. The lead horse is a brown and white pinto, the middle horse is solid black, and the third horse is a white Appaloosa with black spots on its hindquarters. The horses represent the three tribes.

This oval is surrounded by a wide white band (edged in black on the outside) with "CONFEDERATED TRIBES OF THE" on the top in black and "UMATILLA INDIAN RESERVATION" on the bottom. Above this entire logo are the names of the three tribes in black: "CAYUSE," "WALLA

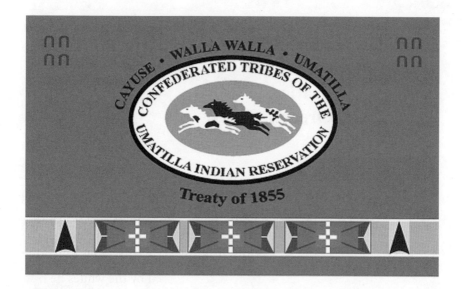

WALLA," and "UMATILLA," separated by black dots. Below the logo is the phrase "Treaty of 1855" in black.

The upper-left and upper-right corners of the flag each contain a set of four dark-blue horseshoes. Across the full length of the flag slightly above the base runs an elaborate design of pink, red, white, light blue, dark blue, and golden yellow. It repeats several geometric patterns, including triangles, trapezoids, crosses, and rectangles. This design is symbolic of the artistic beadwork of the tribes.

The ceremonial hoisting was led by U.S. military veterans who were also tribal members, including Chief William Burke. At the ceremony, Chief Carl Sampson expressed the wish that "this flag will turn the lives of our people around. That it will have true meaning" (*East Oregonian,* 25 May 2002, 3A).

Chief Sampson's remarks speak volumes about the power of a symbol. They reflect the importance of understanding these embodiments of a people's hopes and history. His wish for his tribal flag is the essence of this entire volume.

Thanks to NAVA Member Harry Oswald for providing detailed graphic information about the flag.

Confederated Tribes of the Warm Springs Reservation of Oregon

Located in north-central Oregon, just south of Mount Hood, is the Warm Springs Reservation, home to eight bands from three separate tribes that function as a unit. The Warm Springs Indians lend their name to the reservation and are made up of the Taih (Tygh), Wyam, Tenino, and Dock-spus Bands. The Wascos are from the Dalles, Dog River, and Ki-gal-twal-la Bands. The remaining tribe is a band of the Northern Paiutes (*GAI*, 183). The 3,000 residents of the reservation engage in farming and logging through a modern industrial corporation. They also maintain the Kah-Nee-Ta vacation resort in the hilly, northern part of the reservation. The flag of the Confederated Tribes of the Warm Springs Reservation flies prominently at this modern resort complex.

The banner-like flag is light blue (sample flag provided by Elmer's Flag & Banner, Portland, Oregon) with a yellow ribbon across the top with "THE CONFEDERATED TRIBES OF THE" in red and a similar ribbon across the bottom with "WARM SPRINGS RESERVATION OF OREGON." Between the ribbons are two flying eagles in brown and white, approaching the center from either side. They recall the most sacred of all animals to Native Americans as well as the abundance of wildlife on the reservation. A central yellow disk forms a traditional shield, with seven eagle feathers hanging below to symbolize the protection and safety that the three tribes find within their sovereign boundaries. The shield contains a map of the reservation in red outline, including a depiction of Mount Hood in dark green with a white snowcap. Three brown tipis below the mountain and three yellow stars on a blue sky above it represent the three tribes and their lands' proximity to magnificent Mount Hood, the highest peak in Oregon.

Coquille Tribe
of Oregon

The Coquilles have lived in the same general vicinity for more than 6,000 years. In the nineteenth century they were ravaged by malaria, smallpox, and an invasion of gold miners in the 1850s that reduced their population from 8,000 to a few hundred scattered survivors. Although declared extinct in 1954, the Coquilles were granted federal recognition in 1989. Since then they have reemerged as a vital and thriving community and an economic asset to the Coos Bay region of southwestern Oregon, becoming a major employer in an area devastated by a decline in the timber industry.

A white flag with the tribal seal in maroon or wine-red flies over the Mill Casino and over the headquarters of the 650-strong Coquille Indian Nation of Coos Bay (Don Macnaughtan, "Lost and Found Heritage: Recovering American Indian Tradition at the Coquille Tribal Library, Bandon, Oregon," *New Zealand Libraries* 48:1 [March 1995]: 11–14).

The flag of this now-thriving nation dates from the early 1980s, according to the Dene-Miluk Cultural Center Library. "Dene" is the traditional name employed by the Athapascan people; the Navajos, for example, continue to call themselves "Diné" or "the People"; "Miluk" is the traditional name for the Coos Bay Indians, the immediate ancestors of the Coquilles; and both the Coos Bay and Coquille people still employ the name "Dene" for themselves.

The maroon seal, on a white background, celebrates the history and culture of the Coquille people. In the center is an Oregon Coast "plank house," the traditional style of Native American housing in southwestern Oregon. Behind the house is UmnatL QwLai (Grandmother Rock), a

sacred tribal site at the mouth of the Bandon River. While the rock itself was destroyed by the federal government in the nineteenth century, the site is still sacred and the rock remains on the seal. A conifer tree to the left of the rock and others behind the house recall the forest and the timber industry, which have long been elements in Coquille life. Behind the seal, protruding from the top, is a Coquille fishing spear. Fishing has been vital to the Coquilles' existence for millennia.

Encircling the seal are the words "COQUILLE" on the upper right and "INDIAN TRIBE" at the bottom. A distinctive arrangement of large and small maroon triangles surrounds the seal, representing the tattoo markings that the people of the southwestern coast of Oregon used to measure strings of dentalium—the local shell money of the ancient Native American population.

Thanks to Don Macnaughtan, former tribal librarian at the Dene-Miluk Cultural Center Library, for the information contained in this section.

Coushatta Tribe
of Louisiana

Recognized by the federal government in 1973 after a long campaign by the Coushatta people, the Coushattas of Louisiana first came into contact with the Europeans in 1540 when the Spanish explorer Hernando De Soto trekked through what is now Alabama, Mississippi, Louisiana, and Texas. In traditional European style, De Soto pillaged the Coushatta lands around the Tennessee River region of present-day Alabama and held the chief and tribal elders hostage. In typically diplomatic fashion, he threatened to burn the hostages alive should the Coushattas oppose his continual robbing of their villages. The initial encounter with the explorer set the tone for European/Indian relations for almost 500 years. The last major blow to the Coushattas came as a result of the Creek War of 1813–14, when many tribes were decimated and shipped off to Indian Territory (now Oklahoma).

Today's Coushattas are based in the small town of Elton, Louisiana, with additional tribal holdings around the towns of Kinder and Sulphur. Approximately 300 tribal members reside on the small reservation. They arrived in the late 1700s following a chief called Red Shoes, "King of the Alabamas and Coosades" (www.coushattatribela.org/history.html). He led a band of some 80 to 100 Indians to what is now Louisiana and settled the lower reaches of the Red River. Hundreds more Coushattas followed Red Shoes and his people. Soon the tribe established itself firmly within the area. According to the Coushattas, the tribe's name may have one of several origins. One theory is that the name originally meant "white-reed brake" and came from the swamp cane that grew in the areas where the tribe usually settled. The cane was used in traditional basket weaving and for arrows and blowguns. A second and more popular legend is that a wandering band of Coushattas came upon a group of white men, who asked who they were. They misunderstood the question and answered "koashatt," meaning that they were "lost"—thus the name "lost tribe" stuck. It is, however, accepted among tribal members that the traditional name for the tribe is "Koasati," which disposes of the popular legend.

The Coushattas of Louisiana use a plain white flag bearing a round tribal seal in the center. Above the white core of the top half of the seal is a series of concentric rainbow-like half-rings (yellow, orange, red, then black at the top). On the lower half is the name "Coushatta Tribe" in red on a black background with the words "of Louisiana" appearing below in small white letters. Crossing both halves is a garfish in natural colors, jumping out of the water symbolically formed by the black portion of the seal. The garfish extends beyond the central circle into the writing surrounding the seal: the phrase "SEAL OF THE" on top and "SOVEREIGN NATION" on the bottom in black, separated by red ovals.

Each element of the Coushatta Tribe emblem has a traditional meaning. The garfish, once used for food and jewelry, represents courage, wisdom, strength, and discipline. The colors, which reflect the traditional clothing of the Coushatta people, also symbolize the changing colors of the day and night. Each color has its own meaning: black is for night, white for day, red for life-giving blood, orange for discipline, and yellow for the sun. The colors also include the four sacred colors of most Native American tribes in North America—red, white, yellow, and black.

After 500 years of interaction with the Europeans, the Coushattas may have finally achieved the peace, prosperity, and stability that disappeared so long ago.

Cow Creek Band of Umpqua Indians of Oregon

Only in 1982 did the Cow Creek Umpquas receive federal recognition as an Indian nation. They had been initially recognized as a result of the Treaty of 1853, but in 1956 they officially disappeared as a recognized nation.

Since being recognized again, a fight that took almost sixty years, the Cow Creek Umpqua Nation has returned to the banks of Cow Creek in western Oregon. Today the Umpquas run a bingo parlor, a hotel/casino complex, and several other businesses just northwest of Crater Lake National Park.

Unlike many tribes in the Pacific Northwest, the Umpquas are not a Salish-speaking group. They are a Takelma-speaking people inhabiting the lands drained by the Umpqua River between the Cascade Mountains to the east and the coastal mountains to the west.

The Cow Creek Band employs a flag of light blue bearing a full-color representation of the tribal seal in the center. The seal is round and is dominated by a naturally colored bald eagle holding a fish in its talons. The eagle here, as with other northwestern tribes, represents the strength of the Umpqua people and their skill in fishing. The fish recalls the vital role of fish as a primary food source for centuries for the Native American population. Behind the eagle are the green slopes of the Cascade Mountains and coastal range. The mountains identify the traditional homelands of the Umpquas.

Surrounding the seal is a band of light blue edged in black. The top of the band contains the words "COW CREEK BAND OF" and the bottom "UMPQUA TRIBE OF INDIANS," the official name of the tribe.

Below the seal are two dates: "1853" recalls the treaty that initially recognized the sovereignty of the Cow Creek Band, while "1982" celebrates
the restoration of its status as a federally recognized tribe that had been
lost in 1956. Outside the two years are flowering sprigs of huckleberry. The
huckleberry is one of the most common fruits in the Cascade region and
has long been a major food source for the Umpquas.

Crow Creek Sioux Tribe— South Dakota

The Crow Creek Reservation, located along the north shore of the Big Bend stretch of the Missouri River in South Dakota, was established in 1889 as a result of the Treaty of 1868. The flag of the Crow Creek Sioux is white (photograph provided by the United Sioux Tribes, Pierre, South Dakota), with the tribal seal in the center. The seal is a blue disk: three tipis in white with black accents meet at the center, representing the three districts that form the reservation.

Encircling this central disk is a golden-yellow ring with the words "CROW CREEK SIOUX TRIBE" in black above and the treaty year "1868" below. Outside the gold ring are the names of the three districts in Dakota with the English names outside in brackets. On the left is "KAHMI TANKA [BIG BEND]"; on the right is "KANGI OKUTE [CROW CREEK]"; and at the base is "CUNKICAKSE [FORT THOMPSON]"—the reservation's capital. Separating the three district names are blue swatches, as if white lozenges were placed over a blue circle to form an outer ring. When the seal is used alone, the district names appear in white directly upon the blue circle and the name at the top of the gold ring is prefixed by "SEAL OF."

Tipis are used on the seal and flag of the Crow Creek Sioux as a unifying symbol of the Sioux peoples. Almost all Sioux flags and seals use the tipi, evoking the history of the Sioux as the dominant nation of the northern Plains, following the buffalo and living in dwellings made from its hide. The tipi is a symbol of home: the reservations of the various Sioux nations are their modern homes, even to those who have left for cities. The tipi is also a symbol of welcome, especially when depicted with open flaps—as are the tipis on the seal and flag of the Crow Creek Sioux (see Rosebud Sioux Tribe and Yankton Sioux Tribe of South Dakota).

Crow Tribe
of Montana

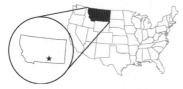

In their own language, the Crow Tribe of southeastern Montana call themselves "Absaroka" ("Bird People"). The early French explorers and *voyageurs* called the Crows the "Handsome Men" because of their beautifully worked garments and their long flowing black hair, which sometimes reached all the way to the ground. The name "Crow" came from crudely translating the term "Absaroka" into "Crow People" instead of "Bird People" (*ENAT*, 76–78).

The flag of the Crow Tribe is light blue and bears the tribal seal in the center. This is one of only a half-dozen flags originally reported by Dr. Whitney Smith in his *Flag Book of the United States.* Like the flags of two other tribes, the Cherokees and the Seminoles, the current flag differs from the one reported some twenty-five years ago. The current seal bears many symbols, starting at the bottom with the sacred pipe.

The pipe was traditionally offered as a first placating step in any significant petition of the Crow people, an offer not to be refused. Above it is the "Sacred Medicine Bundle" (see also Cheyenne River Sioux Tribe). This bundle contains sacred tobacco seeds, tobacco being the only significant crop of the Crows. These particular seeds are believed to be the original supernatural blessing of the Crows that led them to their present home (Lloyd Old Coyote, *Crow Tribal Emblem,* undated pamphlet).

Next in line is a sweat lodge, a place of purification for both mind and body frequently employed prior to any major undertaking by the Crows (this use of the sweat lodge is widespread among Indians from the Northeast to the Southwest). The perfectly symmetrical tipi represents the values of a good home and the home of the Crows (ibid.).

Behind the tipi are three mountain ranges, the Wolf Mountains, the Big Horn Mountains, and the Pryor Mountains. The rays of the sun represent twelve of the original thirteen clans of the Crows. The thirteenth, the

"Greasy Mouth" clan (commonly referred to as the sun worshipers), is represented by the sun itself (Frederick Turnsback, director of procurement, Crow Nation, letter dated 15 November 1994).

On each side of the central tipi is a Crow war-bonnet (originally the left one was larger, but in modern versions both headdresses tend to be identical in size). One represents the clan chiefs on the mother's side, the other the clan chiefs on the father's side. Both lend guidance, inspiration, and protection to all tribal members.

The changes in the flag over the last thirty years are slight. In the current flag there is a definite heavy black border separating the seal from the field of the flag—an artistic license not mandated by the official description. At the base of the seal that appeared in Dr. Smith's book (*FBUS*, 258) was a single white star, which is now gone. The four lodge poles that represented the four seasons and four winds in Lloyd Old Coyote's design are now missing (but should be present); and the "Big Dipper" constellation, which symbolized the "carrier of messages," has been removed. Despite these changes, the flag of the Crows continues to be one of the most striking examples of Native American flags.

Yet another flag is closely associated with the Crow Nation: that of Chief Plenty Coups. Plenty Coups was a realistic and intelligent member of the tribe who quickly rose to the rank of chief, emerging as a leader whose forceful advocacy of change brought him fame and made him a figure of controversy among his own people.

Enemy tribes such as the Sioux and Cheyennes surrounded the Crows in the 1880s. To ensure the safety of his people, Chief Plenty Coups allied his people with the white traders and the U.S. military. The Crows provided scouts for the U.S. Cavalry and fought in some battles alongside them. As a symbol of the military's gratitude for the support of Plenty Coups and the Crows, he was awarded a special personal flag.

The flag was based upon the military flags employed by the U.S. Army in the late 1800s but had a red background. It also bore the chief's name in white capital letters below the seal of the United States. This is one of the few examples of Native American leaders employing flags in the nineteenth century and one of only two such flags awarded by the United States government or its agents, the other being the flag of the Paiute chief Winnemucca (see Reno-Sparks Indian Colony).

Thanks to Jim Ferrigan of Flag Services of Reno, Nevada, for the information on the flags of both Plenty Coups and Winnemucca.

Delaware Nation (formerly Delaware Tribe of Western Oklahoma)— Oklahoma

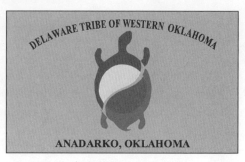

DELAWARE TRIBE OF WESTERN OKLAHOMA

ANADARKO, OKLAHOMA

The Delawares are named for the river that flows through their old homelands in the present states of Delaware, New Jersey, New York, and Pennsylvania. The river was named for Lord De La Warr, the colonial governor of Virginia, who never saw the colony or river bearing his name. In the Algonquin-based tongue of the Delawares, they are the Lenni Lenapés ("True People").

The Delawares had three major divisions, the Munsees (Wolf clan), the Unamis (Turtle clan), and the Unalactigos (Turkey clan) (*ENAT*, 78–80). These main groups were further divided into many different bands. Over time they lost lands in present-day New York, New Jersey, Pennsylvania, Delaware, Ohio, Indiana, Missouri, and Texas. They had been pushed out of Texas into what is now Kansas by 1835 and later into Indian Territory (Oklahoma).

Outside of Oklahoma, Delaware people now live in Pennsylvania, New Jersey, Wisconsin, Colorado, Idaho, and Ontario. In Oklahoma the Delawares are divided into western and eastern groups (see Delaware Tribe of Indians).

The Western Delawares use a light blue flag. The name "DELAWARE TRIBE OF WESTERN OKLAHOMA" forms an arch of black letters across the top of the flag (it is unknown whether the flag has yet changed to represent the new name). Across the bottom in black letters is "ANADARKO, OKLAHOMA," the Western Delawares' capital, home to the area office of all Western Oklahoma tribes and the American Indian Hall of Fame.

A Tulamokom is centered on the flag (*Tulamokom*, undated pamphlet). This design—which represents a turtle, one of the three main clans of the Delawares— serves as the tribal logo (copy of seal provided by Annin & Co., Roseland, N.J.). Tulamokom (Grandfather Turtle) symbolizes the grandfathers of the Delawares, their parents, and the current generation of Delawares (*Tulamokom*). The upper portion of Tulamokom's body is blue for the sky and represents tomorrow. The lower red portion of the turtle stands for yesterday and surrounds the moon of last night. The red also tells of the Delawares' past: the blood of ancestors spilled on the very lands they walk upon today. The sun at the center— divided into yellow and brown—is for the promise of a new tomorrow. Tulamokom, the embodiment of past and future, was designed by Delaware Jim Van Deman, a great-great-grandson of Black Beaver, the famous Lenni Lenapé chief.

Delaware Tribe of Indians— Oklahoma

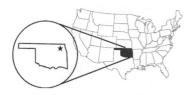

The Lenni Lenapé or Delaware Indians are divided into two distinct tribes in western and eastern Oklahoma. The western Delawares are based in the town of Anadarko (see Delaware Nation [formerly Delaware Tribe of Western Oklahoma]). The Delawares (formerly the Eastern Delawares) in the northeastern corner of Oklahoma still use the Algonquin name "Lenni Lenapé," which means "True People." Its three main divisions are the Unalactigos, the Unamis, and the Munsees. The Lenni Lenapé flag is white with the tribal seal in red, white, and black (copy of seal provided by Annin & Co., Roseland, N.J.). Near the center of the seal is a traditional Delaware mask, red on the left and black on the right. Mask-making is common among indigenous peoples on all continents and was widely practiced by Native Americans.

This mask represents Mesingw, the Masked Spirit of traditional Lenapé legend ("The Indians of the Delaware Valley" exhibit, Mercer Museum, Doylestown, Pennsylvania). Mesingw is the guardian of forest creatures, which were the main source of food for all eastern tribes, much as the

buffalo was for the nations of the Plains. In front of the mask are a sacred pipe and a fire starter.

Surrounding these central images, placed at the four points of the compass, are symbols relevant to the Lenni Lenapés. At the north is a Christian cross, representing the current religion of the people. The other images represent the three clans: on the east is a turkey claw for the Unalactigos; on the south is a turtle for the Unamis; on the west is a wolf paw print for the Munsees.

Around the seal are "SEAL OF THE DELAWARE TRIBE" above and "LENNI LENAPE" below in black. Separating the central emblems from the wording are a series of bars or sticks bearing various designs. These sticks are simply decorative and do not represent the legendary Walum Olum ("red score"), a pictograph carved on wood and used to record the Lenni Lenapés' legends, history, and migrations (*ENAT*, 78–80).

Eastern Band of Cherokee Indians of North Carolina

The Eastern Band of Cherokees lives along the border of North Carolina and Tennessee. With a population over 7,000, the Eastern Band of Cherokees is the largest federally recognized Native American tribe in the eastern United States. The band members use the same seal as their Oklahoma cousins (see Cherokee Nation) with minor artistic modifications. This is the sole instance where two bands of the same tribe employ the identical symbol, though separated by hundreds of miles and governed by different executive and legislative branches. It unifies the Cherokee people symbolically, if not geographically.

On the flag the tribal seal, edged in green, appears on a white (or buff) background. While the Cherokees in Oklahoma use a central star with each point divided half-orange, half-yellow, the Eastern Band uses a solid yellow star with a double black outline. The star and wreath lie on a light-blue circle (rather than gray), with a red rather than orange band around it.

Thanks to NAVA member Glenn Nolan for a copy of the flag.

Eastern Shawnee Tribe of Oklahoma

The ancient homelands of the Shawnee Nation covered an area that today includes the states of Ohio, West Virginia, Kentucky, and Tennessee. The Shawnee people were nomadic, and some attribute their merging of distinctive Native American beliefs, ceremonies, crafts, and lifestyles to this constant movement and interaction with other tribes and bands.

The Shawnees gave Native Americans one of their greatest leaders, Tecumseh. A man of compassion and wisdom, Tecumseh was a brilliant military strategist. He sided with the British against the Americans in the War of 1812 in the hope of securing a true nation for the Indians west of the Appalachians. Under the leadership of Tecumseh, the fort at Detroit fell to the British. But when an advancing American army forced the British to flee to Canada, the Americans' superiority in numbers and weaponry sealed the fate of Tecumseh's forces and led to his death in 1813.

Today the Eastern Shawnees have a historic tribal area of just over 1,000 acres in Oklahoma. Despite the small size of their landholdings, the Shawnees continue to prosper through a mix of old and new ways.

The flag of the Eastern Shawnees is red, bearing their tribal emblem in the center (copy of seal provided by Annin & Co., Roseland, N.J.). The emblem is encircled by the words "EASTERN SHAWNEE TRIBE OF OKLAHOMA" in black. The emblem consists of a light-blue disk representing a warrior's shield. Across the center of the shield is an Indian spear pointing to the right. Above it is a black panther, a rare variation of the now nearly extinct Florida panther or cougar, which once roamed the old

lands of the Shawnees. The panther was respected for its ingenuity and ferocity. On the seal it also represents the great Tecumseh, whose name in Shawnee means "panther." Below the spear is a swan—a graceful, majestic bird epitomizing tranquillity, peace, and beauty. These two animal totems represent attributes desired by the Shawnee people.

Four eagle feathers hang from the round shield, denoting the prime directions of the compass. This use of four feathers is a recent modification to the flag. It formerly bore five feathers, one for each of the five ancient clans of the Shawnees when they lived near the Ohio River.

Eastern Shoshone Tribe—Wyoming

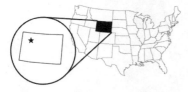

The lands of the Shoshones cover much of the American West, spreading through present-day Nevada, Utah, southern Idaho, and Wyoming. The Shoshones, once known as the Snakes, were one of the great buffalo-hunting tribes of the western Plains and some of the greatest equestrians. One of their ancestors now adorns the 2000 dollar coin: Sacajawea.

In modern times, the Shoshones are divided into three separate entities—the Shoshone-Bannocks of southern Idaho, the Western Shoshones in Nevada, and the Eastern Shoshones located on the Wind River Reservation in central Wyoming. One of the great chiefs of the Eastern Shoshones has been chosen to represent the state in the National Statuary Hall in the U.S. capitol rotunda—Washakie. Chief Washakie is one of only three indigenous Americans depicted in the entire collection, the other two being Sequoyah, representing Oklahoma, and King Kamehameha I from Hawaii.

Washakie, whose name means "Shoot the Buffalo Running," was chief of the Eastern Shoshones for some sixty years and died in 1900. His face dominates the logo of the Eastern Shoshones, which also features the Grand Teton Mountains and the prairie rose.

The flag of the Eastern Shoshones may honor Washakie, because the central element is the head of a buffalo. The buffalo was also the mainstay of the life of the Eastern Shoshones, as it was for all the tribes of the Great Plains. The buffalo's head appears in the center of a golden yellow flag and is flanked by depictions of the prairie rose, what may be medicine bundles, and a pair of coup sticks. The coup sticks, each trailing six eagle

feathers (the number of members on the tribal council), are emblems of courage since they were employed in displays of bravery by warriors. The coup stick was used to touch an opponent without harming him. Proving that he had the skill and courage to get close enough to his opponent added to a warrior's reputation, and "counting coup" was a measure of status and courage. Above the buffalo's head is a sacred pipe, and at the top is an eagle with wings outstretched. All these items are shown in natural colors.

This emblem is contained within two concentric circles of green zigzag patterns reminiscent of the beautiful beadwork designs of the Shoshones. Between the two rings in red lettering are the words "EASTERN SHOSHONE TRIBE" at the top and "SHOSHONE RESERVATION" at the base. While it is commonly recognized that the Wind River Reservation is home to two tribes, the Eastern Shoshones and the Northern Arapahoes, the two tribes are both governmentally and geographically distinct. All 2,700 Eastern Shoshones occupy the northern and western parts of the Wind River Reservation and have their headquarters at Fort Washakie. It is this portion of the Wind River Reservation that constitutes the Shoshone Reservation.

Thanks to Carolyn Shoyo of the Eastern Shoshones for e-mailing an electronic image of the tribal flag.

Flandreau Santee Sioux Tribe of South Dakota

The Flandreau Santee Sioux Tribe is the smallest of the Sioux tribes in South Dakota, with a population below 300 and landholdings of 3,200 acres (*AIDD*, 43), yet Santees lent their names to the states of North and South Dakota. Sioux nations to their west were known as Nakotas or Lakotas, but the Santees called themselves Dakotas.

The Santees include the Sisseton, Wahpeton, Wahpekute, and Mdewakanton Bands. The first two bands live on the Lake Traverse Reservation in South Dakota and the Devil's Lake Reservation in North Dakota (see Sisseton and Wahpeton Sioux Tribe). The last two bands are scattered on several small reservations in Minnesota, Nebraska, and South Dakota. One of these small reservations is the colony outside the town of Flandreau, South Dakota (United Sioux Tribes, Pierre, South Dakota, *Presenting the Flandreau Santee Sioux,* undated pamphlet).

The Flandreau Santees, a mix of Wahpekutes and Mdewakantons, derive their name from the Dakota "Isanyati," a shortening of "Mde Insanti," the Dakota name for the Mille Lacs region of Minnesota, the historic Santee homeland. "Isanyati" thus essentially means "People of the Mille Lacs Region."

The Flandreau Santees settled in their current location after the "Minnesota Wars" of 1862 and adopted the lifestyle of their surrounding European-American neighbors. Until 1994 the Flandreau Santee Sioux flag was dark blue with a white circle in the center. Arching across the top of this circle was "FLANDREAU" in black; across the bottom was "SANTEE." The circle was crossed by a pair of sacred pipes representing the Mdewakanton and Wahpekute Bands. From each pipe hung two feathers, for a total of four—the mystical number in Native American symbolism and the number of bands in the Santee Nation.

The sacred pipes on the flag had special significance. The Santees mined the red stone used to carve the heads of the pipes employed by many tribes throughout North America. Santee miners still take this sacred rock from a quarry now protected by the federal government as Pipestone National Monument in southwestern Minnesota (see Iowa Tribe of Oklahoma). The Santees also carve elaborate pipe heads and make handsome pipes for sale.

In 1994 the tribe adopted a dramatically different flag, perhaps influenced by its entry into the gaming industry. The new flag is white, edged with light blue. Near the center is a disk with light-blue edging and divided vertically, with orange on the left, red on the right; the two colors may recall the two bands that make up the Flandreau Santees. Superimposed on this disk is the head of a bald eagle, the powerful messenger between the Great Father and humans and the creature atop the hierarchy of totems in Native American beliefs. The stylized eagle's head is shown in brown and white, edged in light blue.

Emanating from the disk to the right are five sun rays of orange, yellow, red, yellow, and orange. A brown sacred pipe crossing behind the disk bears two feathers, again perhaps referring to the Wahpekute and Mdewakanton Bands. Along the upper edge of the pipe in the upper-left corner is "APRIL 24, 1936," the date when the Flandreau Santee Sioux Tribe adopted its constitution. Along the top of the lower part of the pipe is "WAKPA IPAKSUN," the Wahpekute band's name in its native language. In an arc along the top of the disk is "MDE AKANTON," the name of the Mdewakanton band in Dakota. Arching behind the head of the eagle are the words "FLANDREAU SANTEE SIOUX TRIBE, FLANDREAU, SOUTH DAKOTA." All lettering on the flag is black.

Forest County Potawatomi Community of Wisconsin Potawatomi Indians — Wisconsin

KEEPER OF THE FIRE

Nearly 1,000 members strong, the Forest County Potawatomis possess a 12,000-acre reservation in northern Wisconsin near the border with the Upper Peninsula of Michigan. The tribe was formed in 1913 and received federal recognition in 1937.

As with nearly all contemporary Potawatomis across the country, the Forest County Potawatomis celebrate their ancestral role as the "Keepers of the Sacred Fire." Long ago the Ojibwes (Chippewas), the Ottawas, and the Potawatomis were united. The Ojibwes were the "Keepers of the Faith"; the Ottawas were the "Keepers of the Trade"; and the Potawatomis had the duty of maintaining the fire around which the tribes would assemble.

The flag of the Forest County Potawatomis emphasizes this traditional role. The flag is white, with the seal of the tribe in the center. The seal represents a medicine wheel, also called the circle of life. That wheel is subdivided into quadrants, four being a sacred number to most Native Americans. The upper-left quadrant is black, which represents the end of life and the direction west. The upper-right quadrant is white, which stands for the north and hibernation or dormancy. The lower left is red for the south and rebirth or rejuvenation. The lower right is yellow for the east and new life. These four colors are frequently associated with the four seasons and the four human races as well.

Superimposed on the circle of life is a gray outline image of a warrior tending a campfire—the "Keeper of the Sacred Fire." Hanging from the circle are three eagle feathers in black and white.

Forming a semicircle over the tribal seal is the name "FOREST COUNTY POTAWATOMI NATION" in black; and underneath the seal is the sobriquet "KEEPER OF THE FIRE," also in black.

Fort Belknap Indian Community (Assiniboine and Gros Ventre)— Montana

Sharing the 589,000 acres of the Fort Belknap Reservation in northern Montana are the Assiniboine and the Gros Ventre Tribes. The Assiniboines, whose name in Algonquin means "Those Who Cook with Stones," were once part of the Yanktonai Sioux. They lived in the region around Lake Superior—today's northern Minnesota and northwestern Ontario. The Assiniboines split off from the Sioux in the 1600s and migrated westward to what is now Manitoba, Saskatchewan, North Dakota, and Montana.

The name "Gros Ventre," meaning "Big Belly" in French, derived from the hand motions used to describe this tribe in the sign language of the Plains. The Plains Indians used sign language to bridge the different spoken languages of the many tribes of the region. The sign for this group (who called themselves "Ah-ah-nee-nin," "White Clay People") was to pass both hands in front of the abdomen to show that they were big eaters. The Gros Ventres, decimated more by European diseases than by war, were moved to the Fort Belknap Reservation in the 1880s, joining the Assiniboines.

The flag used by these two nations is green, a rare color in Native American flags, with the reservation seal in the center. The seal represents a traditional Indian shield, which illustrates the protection of the two nations in the past, present, and future from loss of tribal identity, culture, and land (*Seal of the Fort Belknap Reservation,* undated pamphlet). The shape of the shield refers to the circle of life, a frequent concept in Native American beliefs, according to which everything in life depends upon every other thing. Seven feathers in red, white, and black hang from the shield. Six feathers stand for the twelve elected council members who represent the three districts of the reservation. The seventh and central feather stands for the tribal chairperson.

The shield bears many symbols. The four directions and the four seasons are recalled by the use of the four main colors: red (actually a reddish-orange) for summer, yellow for fall, white for winter, and green for spring. The central buffalo skull, divided into brown and white parts yet remaining one figure, symbolizes the coexistence of two tribes functioning as a whole. Across the forehead of the skull is a jagged line representing the Milk River, a tributary of the Missouri, which flows through the reservation. Two arrowheads facing each other emphasize strong ties with the past.

Above the skull in green is Snake Butte, a landmark known throughout the region. Because Indians often seek visions there, Snake Butte is considered sacred by many Plains tribes; one of the few natural springs in the area rises there. Across the top of the shield in black is "SEAL OF THE FORT BELKNAP RESERVATION" and in the bottom part "GROS VENTRE," on the left, "ASSINIBOINE" on the right, and "FOUNDED 1889" below, referring to the date of the formal establishment of the Fort Belknap Reservation.

Fort Mojave Indian Tribe—Arizona, California, and Nevada

Located where Nevada, Arizona, and California meet, the Fort Mojave Indian Reservation encompasses over 32,000 acres. This is the principal home of the Mojave Nation, which gave its name to the Mojave Desert and the Mojave River. The climate of the Mojave land is one of the harshest in the United States. The Mojaves have coped with the temperature extremes and aridity by settling along the bottomlands of the Colorado River, where the soil is enriched by the annual floods from mountain runoff and the sun is partially blocked by the hardy piñon pines that can survive on the river's moisture.

The Mojaves first encountered the Spanish (under Hernando de Alarcón) as early as 1540 (*ENAT*, 143–44). The Mojave flag was inspired by this early and lengthy contact with the Spanish. It is white with a blue fringe. On most flags the fringe is simply decorative, but on the Mojave flag the combination of white cloth and blue fringe recalls the blue and white beads that the Spanish traded with the Mojaves.

Centered on the flag is the circular tribal seal, with peaked yellow scallops around the outer edge signifying the sun, so dominant in the life of a desert people. Within the sun, on a brown ring, is "FORT MOJAVE INDIAN TRIBE" in black. Within the ring a reservation map shows three states and the Colorado River: California (the Golden State) in yellow, Arizona (the Copper State) in a brownish orange, and Nevada (the Silver State) in blue. The states are labeled in black: "CALIF.", "ARIZ.," and "NEV." The Colorado River is light blue. At the junction of the three states lies the reservation in dark brown. At the left (on California) are a decorated lance, a bow, and an arrow, all in natural colors. At the right (on Arizona) is the head of a Mojave man in natural colors.

Fort Sill Apache Tribe of Oklahoma

Geronimo! No other name in all Native American history as readily brings to mind heroism, bravery, and devotion as does Geronimo's. He was a chief of the Chiricahua (Chirakawa) Band of Apaches living on the San Carlos Reservation in Arizona in 1881 when an Apache medicine man, Nakaidoklini, was killed by a detachment of U.S. Cavalry. The medicine man had been preaching a new Native American religion that claimed dead warriors would return and drive the white people from Arizona. When the soldiers were sent to arrest Nakaidoklini for his preaching, fighting broke out and he was killed.

The Chiricahua, Warm Springs, and other Apaches fled the reservation. Under Geronimo's leadership they conducted raids throughout Arizona until a cessation of hostilities brought them back in 1884. Shortly afterward, another dispute broke out when the military banned the use of the Apache ceremonial alcoholic drink, *tiswin*. Again Geronimo and several followers fled the reservation and escaped into Mexico. The U.S. Army relentlessly pursued Geronimo and his outnumbered band. By 1886 Geronimo and his warriors had surrendered, suffering from exhaustion and starvation (Junie Gooley, letter dated 15 February 1995).

After Geronimo's death in Oklahoma in 1909, his followers received permission to return to the San Carlos Reservation, which most did in 1914. Those who stayed behind, the Chiricahua and Warm Springs Bands of Apaches, are still called Chief Geronimo's Apaches and now reside near Fort Sill, Oklahoma.

The flag of the Fort Sill Apache Tribe salutes their great leader of the past and recalls the lands the Chiricahua and Warm Springs Apaches once

called home. On a yellow field, the seal (copy of seal provided by Annin & Co., Roseland, N.J.) bears an image of Geronimo in black, holding a rifle and surrounded by natural elements not of Oklahoma but of southern Arizona, including a large green saguaro cactus. The outer white ring, edged in red, bears the official name "THE FORT SILL APACHE" in red above and their new home, "OKLAHOMA," below, with black symbols separating the two.

Gila River Indian Community (Pima and Maricopa)— Arizona

South of Phoenix, Arizona, lies the 372,000-acre Gila River Reservation, one of two central Arizona homes to the Pima and Maricopa Indian Nations. The other, north of Phoenix, is the Salt River Reservation. The Gila River community dates to 1939 and has more than 12,000 people; its main source of revenue is agriculture.

The name "Pima" is derived from the phrase "Pi-nyi-match," which means "I don't know," the response that Pimas gave when questioned by early Spanish explorers. Their own name is "Akimel O'odham" (Ah-kee-mult-o-o-tam), which means "River People" (*ENAT*, 186–87). The Pimas are divided into two distinct groups, the Upper Pimas and Lower Pimas. The Upper Pimas are treated here; the Lower Pimas are residents of the Mexican state of Sonora.

The Gila River community has adopted a flag; only three copies are known. One hangs in the office of the community's governor, another in the office of the lieutenant governor, and the third in tribal headquarters in Sacaton, Arizona.

The flag has a white field with a simplified brownish-copper outline map of Arizona (the Copper State). On the map is a white Native American shield bearing seven stylized black feathers, one for each of the seven districts that make up the reservation. Arching above the shield in black is "GILA RIVER INDIAN COMMUNITY"; below it, "PIMA MARICOPA." Overlapping the shield is a reservation map in beige, with black lines indicating the seven districts and the Gila River. Both maps are shown with a heavy black edging ("Symbols of the Pima & Maricopa Indian Nations," *NAVA News* [November/December 1990]: 8).

Above the reservation map, yet within the shield, is a small black stick figure known as the "Man in the Maze." This figure is a recurring character in Pima art and is usually depicted at the top of a circular maze in Pima baskets, cloth work, and other art of the region. The "Man in the Maze," shown complete with his traditional maze, is the basis of the seal of the other Pima and Maricopa community in Arizona (see Salt River Pima-Maricopa Indian Community).

In a unique historical flag note, the Pima soldier Ira Hayes was one of the six U.S. servicemen who raised the American flag atop Mount Suribachi on Iwo Jima in World War II, thus creating one of the great icons of modern flag usage.

Hannahville Indian Community of Wisconsin Potawatomi Indians of Michigan

Having lived in the area of what is now Michigan since the mid-1600s, the Potawatomis were forcibly evicted by the federal government in the 1830s. Like the famous Cherokee "Trail of Tears," the Potawatomis remember their eviction as the "Trail of Death." Not all Potawatomis were successfully rounded up and pushed westward. Some of those who avoided the federal removal became the Hannahville Potawatomis of today.

Located on the sparsely populated Upper Peninsula of Michigan, the Hannahville Potawatomis recall a happier time in their history. Almost five hundred years ago the Ojibwes (Chippewas), the Ottawas, and the Potawatomis were one great people—each having separate responsibilities toward the group as a whole.

The Potawatomis bore the sacred fire around which the three groups would assemble. Thus they were dubbed the "Keepers of the Sacred Fire." It is that name that the Hannahville Potawatomis celebrate on their flag.

The flag is white, with a black-and-white image of an Indian man (who faces toward the flagpole) tending a fire. The fire is shown in red and yellow with a jagged arc behind the flame. The title "KEEPER OF THE FIRE" in red arches along the left side of this emblem from the edge of the firewood to the feather on the man's head. Below this entire logo is the name "POTOWATOMI" in large light-blue letters.

Ho-Chunk (Winnebago) Nation of Wisconsin

The Ho-Chunks' present name means "sacred language" or "master language," a term based upon the name of their Siouan-based language, Hocak Wazijaci, which is unique in the Great Lakes region. For a long time their name for themselves was "Hochungara" ("People of the Big Speech"). They were saddled with many different names, several unflattering. Centuries ago the neighboring Sac and Fox Tribes called them "Winnebagos," meaning "People of the Filthy Waters." The name "Hotcangara" was poorly translated as "Fish Eaters"; but "Winnebago" endured. The return to their native language for the tribe's name is part of a larger effort to revive and save the Hocak Wazijaci language.

The area that is now Wisconsin has been the home of the Ho-Chunk people for centuries, their traditional lands being on the Door Peninsula separating Green Bay from Lake Michigan. (A branch of the tribe still calling itself Winnebago is located in Nebraska, but it has no flag.)

The Ho-Chunk flag was adopted in 1992 (*Tribal Flag*, undated pamphlet). It is white with a green border and bears an ornate horizontal stripe across the middle with the tribal seal in the center. The flag's five basic colors —red, white, green, blue, and black—represent specific animals in the kinship system, in which each clan is associated with a particular animal and hopes to gain its admirable qualities. These colors also have special meanings in sacred tribal stories, which are recalled by their use in the flag.

The seal, adopted in 1984 (ibid.), is white with black edges. It includes two of the most important animals in Native American beliefs, the thunderbird and the bear. The thunderbird, depicted as a brown eagle, represents the six upper clans from which all Ho-Chunk chiefs must come; it grasps a pipe (with yellow feathers and a red pipe head) for the peace enforced by the upper clans. Below it is the bear, in black, representing the six lower clans and the "Chief of the Earth" in Ho-Chunk belief. In Ho-Chunk society the members of the Bear clan maintain order, providing the soldiers and the police. A brown war club separates the thunderbird from the bear. This design was common among the many tribes in the western reaches of the Great Lakes.

These images are superimposed on a green outline map of Wisconsin encircled by a ring with the legend "THE GREAT SEAL OF THE HO-CHUNK NATION" arching across the top in black.

Hoopa Valley Tribe—California

The sovereignty of modern Native American peoples in the United States is something they hold very dear. It is a recognition of their unique cultural heritage; their historic links to the land that now constitutes the United States; and their rights to their ceremonies, laws, traditions, beliefs, and artifacts. No tribe in the United States cherishes its sovereignty more than the Hoopa Tribe of northern California. The valley of the Trinity River, called the Hoopa by the neighboring Yurok Tribe, has been their home for centuries; and their strong ties to that land reinforce their love of their sovereign status. The Hoopas even have a holiday called Sovereignty Day to celebrate the sovereignty of all Native American peoples within the United States.

Located northeast of the city of Eureka, the Hoopa Valley Reservation, with more than 86,000 acres, is the largest in California. It is home to almost 2,500 tribal members.

On Sovereignty Day in 1994 the Hoopas unveiled their tribal flag. Like the flags of many other tribes, it is white and bears the tribal seal in the center. That seal recalls three facets of the heritage of the Hoopa people: basket weaving, their plank-style homes, and their beloved valley of the Trinity River.

The center of the seal shows a plank house in a clearing along the banks of the Trinity River. Beyond are the hills that form Hoopa Valley. Directly behind the house are three trees, while three birds fly in the blue sky that forms the backdrop of the scene. Although this is not specified, the recurrence of the number three may point to the close-knit relationship between the Hoopa people and their neighbors, the Yurok and Karuk Tribes. All items in the scene appear in natural colors.

This bucolic setting is surrounded by a black design similar to that used in Hoopa basketry. Outside this pattern, the seal, which is outlined by a very narrow red ring, bears the legend "THE GREAT SEAL OF THE" above and "HOOPA VALLEY TRIBE" below.

With the adoption of a tribal flag, the Hoopas now celebrate their sovereign status with the ultimate modern symbol of sovereignty—the flag.

Hopi Tribe
of Arizona

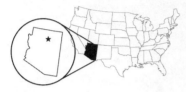

The Hopituh ("Peaceful Ones") or Hopi Indians of northeast Arizona are considered by many to be the people who live most like their ancestors, continuing the traditional way of life in all its facets. They embody a philosophy called the "Hopi Way," which Carl Waldman defines as encompassing "religious beliefs, relationship to nature, behavior towards other people, craftsmanship and survival" (*ENAT*, 95–98). The story of the flag of the Hopi people reflects both their traditionalism and the Hopi Way.

The modern Hopi people still reside in pueblos dotted across their 1-million-acre reservation. The 8,500 or so Hopis are considered to be descendants of the mysterious Anasazis or "Ancient Ones," who disappeared from history around 700 years ago. The Anasazis, like their modern relatives, were pueblo dwellers. The long ties between the pueblo and the Hopi people are reflected in the Hopi logo, which depicts the corner of a pueblo with a ladder leaning against one wall.

. The concept of a tribal flag was long alien to the Hopi traditionalist culture, and only recently did the tribe finally adopt a design that had been proposed years earlier. In a January 2002 article appearing in *Tutuveni* (the newspaper of the Hopi Tribe), Leigh Kuwanwisiwma, director of the Hopi Cultural Preservation Office, states: "The discussion of a tribal flag came about in 1993 at the request of former Chairman, Vernon Masayesva." A conceptual design was presented in the newspaper, and comments from tribal members were solicited. Mr. Kuwanwisiwma began to develop the final idea from this effort in 1993, which culminated in the formal adop-

tion of "Naatoyla" (the Hopi flag) in the spring of 2002—an identity for a Hopi way of life.

The Hopi flag has three vertical stripes: *sakwa* (turquoise or blue/green), *qootsa* (white), and *sikyangpu* (yellow), with a device centered on the white stripe. According to an official description supplied by the Hopi Cultural Preservation Office and authored by the designer, Mr. Kuwan-wisiwma, the turquoise stripe (closest to the pole) represents "Natwani . . . or all the traditional food crops of the Hopi people." The Hopis generally refer to this as *saqw'tala* or a "place of green plants." The stripe symbolizes continuance of all life, the lifeblood of the Hopis—the rain, water, rivers, and moisture. It also stands for "the duty of a Hopi male to provide for his family . . . and to submit to the way of the corn and humility."

The white stripe "represents the beginning of life" or *qastiyayngwani*. It signifies "purity and life in balance at the time of creation" as well as the "tranquility of creation and the perfect path of life laid out for all living things."

The yellow stripe represents the "gift from nature and the spiritual domain." These are the elements that sustain the Hopi people, especially food from the earth. The Hopi word for this is *si'tala* or "many flowers," which means "when plant life is rejuvenated, the land is blessed with renewed spirits."

Centered on the white stripe is a black ring, divided (north-south and east-west) into four quarters by a black cross. Within each of the quarters is a black dot. Below this Tuuwaqatsi or earth symbol is a depiction of mountains in brown. Two stalks of corn, the main food of the Hopis, emerge from the corners of the mountains. Arcing over this entire symbol is the word "HOPI" in a black serif typeface.

Tuuwaqatsi reminds the Hopi people that "through their clan duties and responsibilities, [they] carry out [their] stewardship of the earth." It reinforces the relationship between humans and the whole earth across all time. The division of the earth into quarters represents the "four eras" of human life. The upper-left quadrant stands for the first Hopi life experience, sometimes called the "first world" (the Hopi creation legend describes three cavelike worlds through which the Hopis and all the animals traveled until they emerged into the fourth world—the present earth—via the Grand Canyon). The dot symbolizes that the Hopis experienced this first world. The lower-left quadrant stands for the second world, the bottom-right for the third world, and the upper-right for the present or fourth world. This "fourth quarter completes the human experience and completes [their] knowledge of the past and present."

The green corn stalks or "Natwani" represent the sacred Hopi Way, a "final covenant with [their] guardian spirit Ma'saw," and their "commitment to endure in [their] harsh environment." The two plants symbolize the human body, rooted in the earth. There are six ears of corn (clockwise from the upper right): purple, gray, red, beige, blue, and yellow, representing the six cardinal directions (north, south, east, west, up, down) "from which the cloud priests come to bless the Hopi people and the earth."

The flag is always fringed in red, which indicates that "[l]ife will always be difficult, one of hardship, sometimes conflict." Hopis say that "this domain of hardship is always around us, but . . . [it] reminds us of a proper way of life so that we will not repeat our mistakes."

This newest symbol of the Hopi people, although recently adopted, encompasses many aspects of Hopi culture and belief that date back to the Anasazi people, some two thousand years ago.

Hualapai Indian Tribe— Arizona

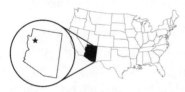

The Grand Canyon outshines all other scenic wonders in Arizona, cutting a mile-deep gash through the northern part of the state. Until modern engineering overcame this immense chasm, it served as a physical barrier for migration. As the Hualapai people sought to avoid the U.S. Cavalry back in 1875 and return to their ancestral homes in the northwestern part of Arizona, they came upon the barrier of the Grand Canyon. Because of this obstacle, the Hualapais now inhabit a nearly 1-million-acre reservation south of Grand Canyon National Park.

The modern Hualapais were one band of the Pie (sometimes spelled Pai) people, the Hwal Bay Ba'chja. According to their creation story, the Pies (meaning "the People") are said to be the only true humans. Both the Hualapai creation story and the natural wonders of their lands—as well as a touch of the Arizona state flag—inspired the seal of the Hualapai Tribe.

The Hualapai seal is a series of three rings. The outermost ring bears the legend "GREAT SEAL OF HUALAPAI TRIBE" in black letters arcing over the top half and the name of the reservation capital in the lower portion: "PEACH SPRINGS ARIZONA." Inside this ring is a narrower band with thirty-seven small images of the piñon pine, the historic food source of the Hualapai people. At the base of this band is the year of the reservation's founding in black: "1883."

The innermost ring (bordered in black) contains the essence of the seal. The heads of two Hualapais (a woman on the left and a man on the right) face each other, with their black hair curving downward and coming together to form a perfect arc. Both wear a single feather in their hair.

Behind them, occupying the upper half of the seal, is a rising sun emitting gold and red rays, just like those on the flag of Arizona. A black outline map of the current reservation is superimposed on the central five sun rays. The lower half of the inner seal is dominated by two medium- to light-blue panels depicting an imposing purple canyon. The panels are separated from the top portion and from each other by a light-blue "T"—representing the Colorado River (vertical bar) and its tributaries (horizontal bar)—bearing a series of coyote paw prints. Sometimes these paw prints are shown arcing outside the canyon, paralleling the curve of the hair.

According to Loretta Jackson, manager of the Department of Cultural Resources, there are two acceptable and interchangeable versions of the flag. The tribal flag can have either a bright-yellow or medium-blue background:

> Both colors are important symbols to the Hualapais: yellow refers to life-giving corn, pollen, and sun, while blue alludes to the equally life-sustaining waters, especially to the numerous springs and the mighty Colorado River, Ha Yiðaða—water spine—the backbone of the Pies. All fourteen original Pie bands incorporated in their name the word "Ha," meaning water. Blue is also the color of the sky, the universe, the origin of all life.

On the yellow-background version the seal is outlined by a medium-blue band with two inscriptions in black: "GREAT SEAL OF HUALAPAI TRIBE" on top and "PEACH SPRINGS ARIZONA" on the bottom. Another blue ring separates the inscriptions from the ring of green pine trees.

According to Sharon Muñoz of Hualapai Tribal Headquarters, the symbolism of the seal is as follows:

> The Great Spirit created Man and Woman in his own image. In doing so, both were created as equals. Both depending on each other in order to survive. . . . The connection of the hair makes them one person; for happiness and contentment cannot be achieved without each other.
>
> The canyons are represented by the purples in the middle ground, where the people were created. These canyons are Sacred, and should be so treated at all times.
>
> The reservation is pictured to represent the land that is ours, treat it well. The reservation is our heritage and the heritage of our children yet unborn. . . .
>
> The sun is the symbol of life; without it nothing is possible—plant don't grow—there will be no life—nothing. The sun also represents the dawn

of the Hualapai people. Through hard work, determination, and education, everything is possible and we are assured brighter days ahead.

The tracks in the middle represent the coyote and other animals that were here before us.

The green around the symbol is pine trees, representing our name Hualapai—PEOPLE OF THE TALL PINES.

Joe Powskey, the artist who designed the seal in the late 1970s, adds: "This artist wants his People to gaze upon their seal with pride, dignity, and beauty. To realize that we are a special People. We all have the will and talent to be whatever we want to be, and to be successful in whatever we choose to do. To include God in our daily lives and also to give thanks for each and every day. Be proud to be a Hualapai!" He also explains one design element that is difficult to see: "Seven tears on each of their faces remind us of the imprisonment of the Hualapai Tribe and the inhumanity that was committed [against them] during that time," especially during the "March of Tears of the Pie."

Thanks to Loretta Jackson, Sharon Muñoz, and Joe Powskey for the information they provided.

Iowa Tribe of Oklahoma

The Iowas, pronounced "I-O-Ways," get their name from the Sioux "Ayuhwa," meaning "Sleepy Ones." According to legend and tribal history, the Iowas once lived in the lower Great Lakes region and were one nation with the Otoes, Missourias, and Winnebagos. The Winnebagos stayed behind when the other three tribes followed the buffalo herds to the mouth of the Iowa River. Later the Otoes and Missourias split off from the Iowas and headed west, while the Iowas remained in the area where the Iowa River meets the Mississippi (*ENAT*, 102–3).

Even before white settlers appeared, the Iowas were forced to move north because of pressure from other tribes. By 1700 the Iowas lived in present-day southwestern Minnesota near the site of Pipestone National Monument—a major source of catlinite, the soft, carvable red stone used for pipe tips for calumets. Trade in this precious material extended from the quarry region to both coasts even as early as the Iowas' arrival. With the influx of white settlers, the Iowas moved south to what is now Kansas and Nebraska. Some Iowas remain in those two states today. In 1883 the bulk of the Iowa Nation was moved to the Indian Territory (now Oklahoma).

The flag of the Iowas that reside in Oklahoma is red and bears the tribal seal in the center (copy of seal provided by Annin & Co., Roseland, N.J.). On top of the seal in black is the legend "IOWAS OF OKLAHOMA." Within the white seal are two symbols common to many Native American peoples: the headdress, which appears in light blue, red, white, and black;

and the sacred pipe, in black with a yellow streamer. Below these two images is an old plow in black, recalling the agricultural basis of tribal life in Oklahoma. The circular seal represents an Indian shield; from it hang four white-and-black eagle feathers, which allude to the four cardinal directions. Behind the shield and extending slightly from either side is a ceremonial lance decorated with yellow streamers.

The flag uses the four primary colors in Native American art: black, yellow, red, and white. These colors are said to represent the four human races and the four directions of the compass (see Miccosukee Tribe of Indians of Florida).

Iroquois League— New York

Of all Native American flag symbols, none has a longer history of representing its people than does Hiawatha's Belt of the Iroquois League—over 400 years. Six nations make up the famous confederacy, located in the northeastern United States and southeastern Canada.

Formed around 1570, the Iroquois League (or Iroquois Confederacy) originally included five tribes, from east to west: the Mohawks, Oneidas, Onondagas, Cayugas, and Senecas. A sixth tribe, the Tuscaroras, migrated from what is now North Carolina to the border regions between New York and Pennsylvania in the early 1700s and united with the original five tribes in 1722.

Known among themselves as the "Hodinoshone" ("People of the Long House"), the members of the Iroquois League dominated their neighbors, drawing strength from their unity (*ENAT*, 103–7). From earliest times, this unity was symbolized by a wampum belt fashioned in a pattern that has become known as "Hiawatha's Belt." (Wampum are beads made from whelk and clam shells strung on twine made from plant fiber and sinew. Either as individual strands or fashioned into belts, wampum was valued highly and given as gifts or exchanged ceremonially.) Each tribe in the confederacy had a unique wampum belt. For example, the Tuscarora belt was white and bore four stripes of blue-purple shells (*Map of Iroquois*

Lands, n.d.). Hiawatha's Belt depicted five figures (*AIDD,* plate 18). In the center was what to some is a heart; to others it is a great or sacred tree under which the Iroquois met in council. On either side of the central device were two different-sized squares or rectangles, connected to one other and to the central device by a narrow band. The belt records the Native American interpretation of the league's formation.

The five devices symbolize the five original tribes: the Senecas, "Keepers of the Western Door"; the Cayugas, "People of the Marsh" and "Keepers of the Great Pipe"; the Onondagas, "Name Bearers" who kept the wampum belt that contained the history of the Iroquois; the Oneidas, "Stone People" symbolized by the Great Tree; and finally the Mohawks, "Keepers of the Eastern Door."

In the last thirty years, the unity of the Iroquois Nations has grown stronger. Several confrontations between Iroquois people and the governments of Québec and New York have increased Iroquois self-awareness, leading to the reemergence of "Hiawatha's Belt" as a symbol of the nation. Thus, in modern times, what was once a wampum belt has been reborn as a flag. Seen in both Canada and the United States, the blue or purple flag bearing the symbol of the unity of the five nations (in white) has become a rallying symbol for Iroquois of all tribes (Karoniaktajeh [Louis Hall], "Ganienkeh," *Flag Bulletin* 16:4 [July/August 1977]: cover and 108–11).

Jamestown
S'Klallam Tribe
of Washington

One of the smallest tribes with a flag is the S'Klallam Tribe of the 11-acre Jamestown Reservation in western Washington, with 216 members in 1995 (*Indian Service Population and Labor Force Estimates,* U.S. Dept. of Interior, Bureau of Indian Affairs). In their own language, "S'Klallam" means "Strong People."

The Jamestown S'Klallam tribal seal serves as a major element of their flag. Like the seals of many other Pacific Northwest Coast tribes, their seal uses a traditional artistic motif. It features stylized representations of an eagle intertwined with a salmon, on a gray circle.

According to Annette White of the Jamestown S'Klallam Tribe, the eagle symbolizes "strength, power, freedom, and an enduring vision of the past and future that surveys his domain and is one with the Earth." The salmon stands for "life, continuance, perpetual adaptation, and the pulse of the Earth." Both elements appear in black and gray with red-ochre highlights.

The seal appears on the left side of the flag's dark-blue background, superimposed on a narrow red band just below the midpoint that extends the full length of the banner. Above the band in white on the right is the name "JAMESTOWN S'KLALLAM TRIBE" and below the band the legend "The Strong People." Only one copy of the flag is known.

Jatibonicu Taino Tribal Nation of Borikén— Puerto Rico

According to Cacike Pedro Guanikeyu Torres, principal chief: "The Jatibonicu Taino of Puerto Rico (Puerto Rico is 'Borikén' in the Taino language and means 'Land of the Valiant and Noble Lord,' which refers also to the Great Spirit or Creator) are descendants of the original twenty-four tribal bands that settled in Puerto Rico." Their ancestors are the Central American Indians and the Arawak Indians of South America, who had migrated north in the early centuries of the second millennium and colonized the islands of the Caribbean where Tainos can be found today: Puerto Rico, Santo Domingo/Haiti, Jamaica, Cuba, the Bahamas, and Florida, which has some fifteen bands (see Jatibonicù Taino Tribal Band of New Jersey).

"Jatibonicu" means "Great People of the Sacred High Waters" (waterfalls), whereas "Taino" is a name first used by the Spanish invaders. It derives from the answer that the indigenous people gave to the Spanish when asked, "Who are you?" The Jatibonicu people simply answered "Taino," which means "Good and Noble People," in order to distinguish themselves from some of the more warlike southeastern tribes such as the feared Caribs and Waibs.

The first contact with Europeans signaled the beginning of the end—as it later did for other Native Americans throughout the hemisphere—for an estimated 3 to 8 million Tainos, who had spread throughout the Caribbean Islands and Florida. It occurred on 12 October 1492, when Christopher Columbus landed on the island of Guanahani (San Salvador in the Bahamas). He later departed for Spain with six Borikén Taino women and one thirteen-year-old boy named Gueycan (Center of the Sun) and paraded them before the royal court of Ferdinand and Isabella in Madrid.

When Columbus returned on his second voyage in 1493, he brought the six women and the young Taino boy with him. On seeing the outlines of Puerto Rico on 18 November 1493, the overjoyed women shouted "Borikén," jumped overboard, and swam for shore. On 19 November, a Sunday morning, Columbus and his men landed on the shores of the island of Borikén (today Puerto Rico).

The flag of the Jatibonicu Taino Tribal Nation of Borikén (whose tribal motto is "Like a Mountain We Stand Alone") derives from the prophecy of a Great Three-Colored Rainbow and a later vision that a Jatibonicu Tribal Elder had in the late 1960s while he stood in the ceremonial center during a vision quest in Caguana (named after the Fertility Mother of the Taino Tribes) in Puerto Rico. The vision contained all the elements currently shown in the central element of the flag, on a field of yellow. The green and red stripes were added later. Red stands for tribal blood spilled during the tragic years following European contact, as reflected by *maga*, a red flower indigenous to the region. Green signifies Bibi Atabey (Mother Earth). Yellow is for Baba Guey (Father Sun) and indicates the reflection of the rays of the sun—a symbol of great illumination and wisdom— upon the wings of the *colibrí* (hummingbird), which is the totem of the Jatibonicu Taino Tribe.

The relative ratios of the stripes and detailed specifications for the central image were worked out during March and April 2001 by Chief Guanikeyu (Noble Bird of the White Earth) Torres, who was assisted with computer graphics by Peter Orenski. The outer ring symbolizes the men's sun circle—and hence Baba Guey—while the inner circle is the women's moon circle—or Atabeira, Grandmother Moon. The outer ring is surrounded by twenty-four leaves of the sacred cohobana tree, whose seeds are essential for tribal sacred ceremonies. The number of leaves stands for the nation's twenty-four original clans or tribal bands in Puerto Rico.

Contrary to first impression, the elements inside the moon circle do not represent a human face, just as the outer leaves do not represent sun rays. Rather, the three circled dots inside the moon circle are a reflection on water of the Sacred Mountain (note the tribal motto cited above); hence the top of the mountain appears at the bottom in the reflection.

The three elements that denote the Cemi (totem) of the Sacred Mountain symbolize three spirits. Yaya, at the bottom of the image, is the Spirit of Spirits or Great Spirit or Creator. The right circled dot symbolizes the Spirit of the Living People or Goiz, while the circled dot on the left is the Spirit of the Ancestors or Hupia. It is important to avoid calling Hupia "Spirit of the Dead," because the Jatibonicu Taino people do not believe in death. The curved lines of the central symbol symbolize the sacred Snuff Pipe in which crushed seeds from the Cohobana tree are snuffed during sacred Cohoba visionary ceremonies.

The motto associated with the new flag is "One People, One Nation, One Destiny," because the flag also represents the three confederated Taino tribal bands in Puerto Rico (Jatibonicu Taino Tribal Nation of Borikén), Florida (Tekesta Taino Tribal Band of Bimini, Florida), and New Jersey (Jatibonicù Taino Tribal Band of New Jersey). These confederated Taino tribal bands form the central Grand Council of the Government of the Jatibonicu Taino Tribal Nation.

Thanks to Cacike Pedro Guanikeyu Torres, principal chief, for information provided to Peter Orenski, used by permission of the Jatibonicu Taino Tribal Nation of Borikén.

Kaibab Band of Paiute Indians— Arizona

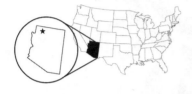

The Paiutes as a people spread over a vast area of the Far West, from present-day Idaho and Oregon in the north down to Arizona and California. The southernmost reservation of the Paiutes is the Kaibab Reservation along the northern border of Arizona, near the town of Fredonia. In addition to the approximately 250 band members, the reservation is home to Pipe Springs National Monument, an 1860s-era fort built over the main spring. The fort, called "Winsor Castle" after the first ranch manager, was built by the Mormon Church to be the headquarters of a large cattle-ranching operation. This isolated outpost served as a way station for people traveling across the Arizona Strip, the part of Arizona separated from the rest of the state by the Grand Canyon. Today this corner of Arizona is still quite isolated, yet the Paiutes continue to live and grow in the area as they have done for at least a thousand years.

During their centuries of living in this land north of the Grand Canyon, one of the main sources of nutrition for the Paiutes was the pine nut from the piñon pine. Gathering, shelling, processing, and cooking the pine nuts was an activity that involved the entire family. The importance of this staple food crop is remembered on the modern flag of the Kaibab Band of Paiute Indians.

The flag is a medium blue, similar in shade to the flag of the United Nations. In its center is the seal of the tribe in white line art, enclosed in a narrow white band. Arcing over the top of the seal and encompassing about three-quarters of the length of the flag is the name "Kaibab Band of Paiute Indians" in an elaborate script. Below the seal is the word "Arizona" in smaller letters.

The seal itself depicts a mother and child returning from a pine-nut harvesting venture, bearing baskets of pine nuts in their arms and on the mother's back. In the foreground, a male (presumably the father) is kneeling, starting a fire by rubbing sticks. By his legs lies a large, flat basket. This type of basket was used by many tribes, including the Paiutes, to shake the shells away from the actual pine nuts. At the man's feet lies a pottery jug, recalling another of the ancient Paiute art—pottery making. When the seal is used on stationery and other media, the date "June 11, 1923" frequently appears below the state's name. This may represent either the date of the founding of the reservation or the date of incorporation of the band.

Until recently, there was only one copy of the tribal flag in existence. It even missed the grand entry to the tribal powwow one year during the 1990s because it was needed at a tribal funeral occurring the same day. A second copy was ordered in 2002 for display by the Inter-Tribal Council of Arizona, thus doubling the number of Kaibab Paiute flags in existence.

Kalispel (Pend d'Oreille) Indian Community— Washington

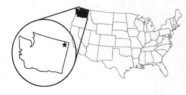

The Kalispels are inland members of the Salish people. Their 4,500-acre reservation outside Usk, in the northeastern corner of Washington, is home to some 215 members (*NAA*, 285; *REAI*, 34). Their name means "camas," the Salish word for a local plant whose roots served many northwestern Indians as a food source. They have also been called the "Pend d'Oreille" (French for "earring") people. "Pend Oreille [*sic*]" is the name of the county in which they live and of the Idaho lake at the center of their traditional homelands.

The Kalispel flag depicts a tableau of their Pacific Northwest homeland as seen at night. At the bottom a dark-blue stripe less than one-quarter the height of the flag recalls the fields and valleys of eastern Washington. Above that, a light-blue stripe up to about the center of the flag depicts a lake or river and may actually stand for the Pend Oreille River or Lake Pend Oreille, the main waterways of their former lands.

In the top half of the flag are dark-blue hills topped by dark coniferous forests against a light-blue sky. Centered in the top half, a bright golden circle representing the moon bears a camas plant with light-blue flowers. On the water stripe two people in a canoe fishing appear in dark blue, and two white stripes represent sparkles of white moonlight.

Karuk Tribe of California

California is home to more tribes than any other state. They range the full length of the state from suburban San Diego all the way to the border with Oregon. One of the northernmost groups of California's Native Americans is the Karuk Tribe. The Karuks are one of three Indian nations that reside along the Klamath River, the others being the Hoopa Valley Tribe and the Yurok Tribe. All three have shared similar lifestyles for centuries, dwelling in cedar-plank houses, living off the bounty of the river, and gathering acorns. While their neighbors built canoes, the Karuks were distinctive in that they traded for canoes when they needed them instead of making their own.

The modern Karuks are centered in the town of Happy Camp and employ a distinctive flag that celebrates one of the great artistic expressions of all California (and most other) tribes—basket weaving. The design is based upon typical patterns found on Karuk baskets, both ancient and modern.

The flag of the Karuk Tribe has three vertical stripes, with the central red stripe being approximately three and a half times as wide as each of the white stripes. Elements of basket designs are featured on all the stripes.

The two white stripes mirror one another. Both are divided in half by a narrow black stripe. On the outer portion of each of these subdivided stripes are three groups of black triangles evenly dispersed from top to bottom, with their bases pointing outward and the tips pointing toward the center. The inner half of each white stripe bears two sets of the three-triangle pattern, with the points of each triangle facing the edge of the flag. These two groupings are offset from the outer sets, forming a zigzag pattern.

The central red stripe is accented at the extreme left and right by narrow yellow bands, with even narrower red edging separating them from the white stripes. In the very center of the flag is a ring of three white eagle feathers, each bearing a white bead at its base from which two black strings dangle. The feathers all have black tips extending about halfway down their length. Within the feather ring is the tribe name "KARUK" in an attractive font.

The recurring emphasis upon the number three may recall the three related tribes of the Klamath River, but this has not been stated with any confidence. The flag was designed by Karuk tribal member Lonna Dexter.

Kaw (Kanza) Nation— Oklahoma

The Kaw Nation of Oklahoma gave its name to the Kansas River and thus to the state of Kansas (*ENAT*, 108–9). "Kaw" means "People of the Wind"; "Kanza" means "People of the South Wind." The Kaw people of today still call themselves the people of the wind.

In 1873 the federal government moved the Kaw people from their homelands in Nebraska and Kansas to a small reservation in Indian Territory (now Oklahoma). The Kaws live there today, next to their kin the Osages. In 1887 the tribe divided the reservation into privately held parcels, with the tribe retaining only a 20-acre Historic Trust Area.

The Kaw Nation's flag is white, with the tribal seal in the center (JoAnn O'Bregon, Kaw Executive Council, letter dated 11 November 1994). The seal bears a full-color representation of two Kaw warriors on horseback on the Great Plains, their traditional homeland. One of the warriors, with hands outstretched, holds a medicine bundle and prays to the Great Spirit. The other holds an upright lance. The seal sometimes depicts three warriors, not two. Arching over the top of the seal in black is the legend "SOVEREIGN NATION OF THE KAW" and at the bottom "KANZA."

A Kaw was elected to the highest office ever held by a Native American. From 1929 to 1933 Charles Curtis, a Kaw, served as vice-president of the United States under President Herbert Hoover. Earlier he had been credited with helping to pass the Citizenship Act of 1924, which granted U.S. citizenship to all Native Americans.

Kialegee Tribal Town (Creek)— Oklahoma

The modern Creeks of Oklahoma have formed what is called the Creek Confederacy. It unites the four parts of their nation now found there, far from their original lands in present-day Alabama. The four constituent parts of this confederation are the large and well-known Muscogee Nation and three smaller segments, the Alabama-Quassartes, the Thlopthloccos, and the Kialegees (*ENAT,* 74–76). The Kialegees actually constitute what is officially called a "tribal town" as opposed to the broader-based tribe.

Over the Kialegee Tribal Town flies a flag that reflects their past and the Creek culture. The flag is blue, like the flag of Oklahoma, and bears the seal of the tribal town in the center (sample flag provided by the Homer Miller Co., Oklahoma City).

The seal consists of a light-blue circle dominated by a pair of stickball sticks. Stickball was a major game for centuries among the Creek people, who are credited with its invention long before Europeans reached North America. The sticks divide the seal in four quadrants, four being the sacred number among many Native Americans. Although the sticks may remind one of a lacrosse stick, lacrosse was actually influenced by tribes of the Northeast, not by the stickball game of the tribes of the Southeast. One stick is used in lacrosse, but two are used in the game of stickball. The lacrosse stick is fairly large-cupped in comparison to the stickball stick.

In the upper quadrant is a black Christian cross for the faith of the modern Creek people. The right quadrant bears a bald eagle shown in

natural colors, this being both the preeminent animal in Native American lore and symbol of the United States. The left quadrant contains a traditional tool for the grinding of corn, the staple of the Creek people throughout their history. The bottom section has a representation of the ancient ceremonial lodge found in Creek towns. This lodge, up to twenty-five feet high, was made of clay walls and had a bark-covered, cone-shaped roof. The lodge is shown in natural shades, upon a green hillock. In olden days this building served not only as a place for religious rituals but also as a shelter for the elderly and homeless (*ENAT*, 74–76).

Surrounding this entire seal is a yellow ring containing the official name "KIALEGEE TRIBAL TOWN" in blue letters around the top and "ESTB. 1939" (the year the town was founded) at the base.

The flag of the Kialegee Creeks acts as a reminder of the long tradition of town dwelling by the Creek people and reinforces their link with that past as it continues in the Kialegee Tribal Town.

Thanks to John Timothy II, director of the Ataloa Lodge Museum and former cultural resources officer at the Five Civilized Tribes Museum in Muskogee, Oklahoma, for information on Creek culture.

Kickapoo Tribe
of Oklahoma

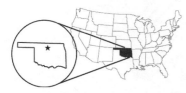

The Kickapoos' history (*ENAT*, 109–10) begins in what is now Wisconsin, although their legends and prayer sticks indicate that they may once have inhabited parts of Michigan. They are closely related to the Sac and Fox people who lived in the same general area. In 1769 they joined six neighboring tribes in a war against the Illinois Indians and moved into lands in what is now Illinois and Indiana. By 1832, with the influx of white settlers and the defeat of many tribes in the Black Hawk War, the Kickapoos were forced into Missouri. Later still, they were pushed into Kansas and finally—after branching into two groups—settled in the Indian Territory (now Oklahoma) and Mexico. A small Kickapoo band still lives in northeast Kansas.

The many moves of the Kickapoo Nation seem to have been foretold by their own name. "Kickapoo" is a corruption of the phrase "Ki-we-ga-paw," meaning "He moves about, standing now here, now there."

The flag of the Kickapoo Nation of Oklahoma features the tribal seal in black on a cream or buff field. The seal (copy of seal provided by Annin & Co., Roseland, N.J.) contains a tribal meeting house on an oval shield, behind which appears a Kickapoo arrow. From the shield hang three white-and-black eagle feathers, recalling the subgroups of the Kickapoo people. A band surrounding the shield bears the legend "GREAT SEAL OF THE KICKAPOO NATION" across the top and "OKLAHOMA" below in black.

While the flag's field has been described as "cream," it may be buff, as produced by certain flag manufacturers in the United States and as used in the flag of the Navajos. Or it may actually be white, the most common background color in Native American flags, but faded over time by chemical reactions in the aging fabric (see Choctaw Nation of Oklahoma).

In early 1996 the State of Oklahoma dedicated a flag plaza to the Native American peoples currently living within its boundaries. Thirty-six flagpoles bear thirty-five flags—the pole for the Kickapoos is bare. Their religious beliefs discourage the display of such symbols, even though they have a flag in their tribal offices (see also Tolowa Tribe).

Kiowa Indian Tribe
of Oklahoma

The historic tribal area of the Kiowas, established in 1867, covers 234,000 acres in what is now southwestern Oklahoma. This last homeland for the Kiowas came after a long history of migrations dating to the early 1600s. The Kiowas originated in present-day western Montana and over the centuries worked their way east and then south (*ENAT*, 110–12). The tribal name comes from the Kiowa name "Ka'i-gwu," meaning "Main People."

The pale-blue flag of the Kiowas bears the tribal logo in the center (Charlotte Redbird, tribal administrative secretary, letter dated 15 February 1995). The logo shows a Kiowa warrior of the Plains surrounded by a ring of ten white-and-black eagle feathers representing the ten Kiowa Medicine Bundles (seal provided by the Kiowa Tribal Headquarters).

The ten feathers also recall the Principal Dogs or "Ten Bravest" warrior society (*Kiowa Tribe of Oklahoma*, undated pamphlet). When the Principal Dogs went into battle, the leader stood next to a lance bearing his sash of leadership and encouraged the rest of the tribe onward. From that spot, the head Principal Dog fought and protected his sacred sash. He could not desert his position until replaced by another of the "Ten Bravest." This use of the Principal Dog's sash flying from the head of a lance is one of the earliest uses of flaglike objects (or vexilloids) by a Native American people.

At the base of the logo is a small circle (green on the left and yellow on the right) with a silhouette of a buffalo head in black. The warrior rides an Appaloosa, a breed developed by the Salish Tribe of Idaho and Montana in the traditional homeland of the Kiowas. This horse has a painted lightning bolt on his front left leg, suggesting the voice of thunder heard each spring. (This bolt is also represented on the Great Drum of the Ohoma Society, where it is held in the talons of an eagle.) The warrior wears a Spanish officer's red cape, a red headband, and a bone breastplate. These, as well as the sky-blue circle that acts as a backdrop for the warrior, are part of the Koitsenko warrior tradition.

The warrior holds a shield depicting the Rainy Mountain of Oklahoma, a burial ground sacred to the Kiowas and considered the "end of the Great Tribal Journey" (Kiowa Tribe, *Seal of the Kiowa Tribe* information card). The recurring circular patterns in the sky, the feathers, and the small shield at the base of the logo recall the sun and the moon. These two celestial bodies are important in Kiowa ceremonial dance rituals such as the Skaw-Tow or Sundance, the Feather or Ghost Dance, and the peyote religious service of the Native American Church. The entire logo is encircled by "KIOWA TRIBE" above and "OF OKLAHOMA" below in black.

Lac du Flambeau Band of Lake Superior Chippewa (Ojibwe) Indians— Wisconsin

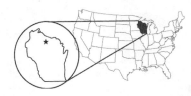

A distinctive design element in the traditional dress of the Ojibwe (Chippewa/ Anishinabe) people is the use of floral patterns, especially in beadwork. The Ojibwes were distinctive among most Native American nations in their dependence upon wild rice as a staple of their diet. They were extensive users of the bark of the birch tree (*ENAT*, 57–60), which served as a building material for their wigwams and the exterior of their canoes and was molded into various containers for food, water, and other items.

All three items—the floral pattern, wild rice, and birch bark—can be found in the flag of the Lac du Flambeau ("Lake of Flaming Torches") Ojibwes of northern Wisconsin. The reservation is located in northernmost Wisconsin just south of the border with Upper Michigan. It is home to approximately 2,500 tribal members and covers some 144 square miles.

The white flag of the Lac du Flambeau people bears in each corner a floral device reminiscent of the beadwork patterns of Ojibwe traditional costumes. These designs represent the wild rice plant found in the myriad lakes in the lands of the Ojibwes—Wisconsin, Minnesota, Michigan, and Western Ontario. In the center of the flag is a stretched hide shield with a Wisconsin landscape of green fields and conifer forests. Rising over the forest is a red sun, while dominating the foreground is an intricate motif merging the head of an eagle with the head of an Ojibwe man, including a pair of gold earrings and two feathers as a headdress. All elements of the central device appear in natural colors. Just below and to the right of this element is an Ojibwe sacred pipe.

From the shield hang six beaded feather ornaments; the shield itself is bracketed by a pair of birch-bark torches. These torches recall the use of such devices by the ancestors of the modern Ojibwes, who tended to do their fishing at night. Arching over the shield is the reservation name "LAC DU FLAMBEAU" and below it the words "OJIBWE NATION." This caption is unusual in that most Anishinabes ("First People") in the United States accept the name "Chippewa" for official purposes. In Canada, "Ojibwe" or "Ojibway" is the preferred version. The Lac du Flambeau Ojibwes are one of the few United States Anishinabe groups officially to adopt the name "Ojibwe" over the name "Chippewa."

Leech Lake Band of Chippewas (Ojibwes)— Minnesota

Commonly called "Chippewas" in the United States and "Ojibways" in Canada, the Ojibwes of Michigan, Minnesota, Wisconsin, the Dakotas, and Ontario prefer to call themselves "Anishinabes," meaning "First People." They accept "Ojibwes," but many intensely dislike "Chippewas," even though some bands include it in their official name for recognition by the wider world. "Ojibwe" (or "Ojibway") is an Algonquin word that refers to a unique style of puckered seam on the moccasins of the Anishinabes. "Chippewa" is considered a poor attempt by early French explorers to say "Ojibwe" (*ENAT*, 57–60).

The Ojibwes are one of the largest tribes in the United States, third only to the Navajos and Cherokees, according to most surveys. The Ojibwes, however, so widely intermingled with European-Americans that by the middle of the twentieth century it was thought that a pure-blood Ojibwe no longer existed.

Rather than flying a single flag for the Ojibwe Nation in the United States, each band decides whether it wants a flag and what the design should be. The flag of the the Leech Lake Band, which lives on the 28,000-acre Leech Lake Reservation in Minnesota, is white and bears the tribal seal in the center (flag provided by Advertising Flag Co.).

The seal has a red ring, with "LEECH LAKE RESERVATION" in black, around a white central disk. Within it a yellow equilateral triangle points upward, its corners touching the ring. Outside the triangle are (left) symbols of nature—pine trees and a soaring eagle; (right) symbols of education—a diploma and a mortarboard; and (below) a symbol of justice and law—the scales of justice. Within the triangle are a sacred pipe and two crossed brown feathers representing the Ojibwe people. The yellow triangle recalls the birchbark wigwams that were the traditional dwellings of the Ojibwes and unifies the other symbols to show that the Ojibwe people have a home on the Leech Lake Reservation where they can prosper under the rule of law, through education, and in harmony with nature.

Lower Brulé
Sioux Tribe—
South Dakota

 The Kul Wicasa or Lower Brulé people form part of the Sicangu Band of the Teton Sioux. Their lands were one of six reservations established by the Fort Laramie Treaty of 1868 (see Cheyenne River Sioux Tribe, Crow Creek Sioux Tribe, Oglala Sioux Tribe, Rosebud Sioux Tribe, and Standing Rock Sioux Tribe of North and South Dakota). The Lower Brulé Reservation originally encompassed some 446,500 acres but has been reduced to 139,000 acres (*NAA*, 284).

Approximately 95 percent of the Kul Wicasas live around the community of Lower Brulé on the southern shore of the Missouri River. The Lower Brulé Tribe became administratively distinct in 1971 when the Crow Creek Reservation separated from it. They had been a single administrative unit since 1883 (*Presenting the Lower Brulé Sioux* [Pierre, South Dakota, n.d.]).

The Lower Brulé flag is sky-blue, with the tribal seal in the center. As on most Sioux tribal flags, the tipi occupies a key place in the seal: for the Lower Brulé people, a black-and-white tipi with red trim appears on an outstretched buffalo hide of light tan against a sky-blue background. Both symbols recall the great days of the Sioux people as the masters of the northern Plains, living in tipis and following the enormous herds of buffalo. A sky-blue band (edged in red on both sides) encircles the seal, with "LOWER BRULÉ SIOUX TRIBE" in red across the top and "LOWER BRULÉ, SOUTH DAKOTA" across the bottom.

Thanks to the staff at the United Sioux Tribes for a photo of the flag of the Lower Brulé Sioux.

Lower Elwha Tribal Community (Klallam)— Washington

In the early 1800s, before intensive encroachment by American and British fur traders and before missionaries were established, the Klallam people were approximately 10,000 strong. Their many villages dotted the Strait of Juan de Fuca along the northern coast of present-day Washington State, neighboring the Makah lands in the west and the Skokomish Tribe of Puget Sound in the east (*Elwha Klallam History* provided by Barbara Lawrence of the Lower Elwha Tribal Office). Like other Coastal Salish of the Olympic Peninsula (see Makah Indian Tribe, Quileute Tribe, and Quinault Tribe), the Klallam people—whose name in their native language means "Strong People"—lived up to their nickname, "Fish-Eaters." They skillfully secured life-sustaining catches of salmon, herring, trout, sturgeon, and other small fish (*Indians of the Northwest* [n.p.: Petra Press, Running Press Book Publishers, 1997], 15).

Like the other tribes along the Northwest Coast (see Quileute Tribe), the Klallam people stalked whales but were mainly content to obtain valuable meat, bones, and oil from whales that were caught in shallows or beached by storms (ibid., 19).

In the 1840s, following the large-scale arrival of fur traders and missionaries who slowly decimated the Native American populations with epidemics of smallpox, flu, and tuberculosis (to which indigenous people had no immunity), the ranks of the Klallam people decreased dramatically. Today they occupy three reservations with a total tribal enrollment of about 1,700 people, of which some 650 are members of the Elwha community. The 572-acre Lower Elwha Reservation is located six miles west of the city of Port Angeles at the mouth of the Elwha River, about midway along the northern Washington shoreline that marks the Juan de Fuca Strait (see also Jamestown S'Klallam Tribe of Washington).

According to Barbara Anne Lawrence, cultural resources specialist for the tribe (*Elwha Klallam History*), the Lower Elwha flag was created in 1995 by 25-year-old Alfred Charles, Jr., who responded to an invitation for tribal members to design a flag. Starting from design elements such as the thunderbird and killer whales already present in the seal of tribal stationery, Mr. Charles simplified and sharpened these elements, placed them on a white background, and thereby produced the striking flag that the Lower Elwha people display today. According to tribal member Brenda Masocol, the logo or tribal seal was originally made by Billy "White Shoes" Charles.

The symbolism of the flag—from the light-blue background evoking water; to the thunderbird, by whose spirit the earth is watered and the harvest from sea and field is gathered; to the respectful regard for the whale as protector rather than prey—reflects the Elwha Klallam people's ancient fishing tradition. Ms. Lawrence describes the symbols as follows (*Elwha Klallam History*): "The thunderbird represents the protection of our people. The lightning bolts it is throwing come from a story about the thunderbird flying up a river and throwing lightning bolts at the water to ensure a good fish harvest. The black fish are killer whales. They are the protectors of our people when traveling by canoe or water."

The circular seal is bordered by a heavy black ring; inside it the English words "ELWHA KLALLAM TRIBE" arch across the top in black; beneath them in black (spelled in international phonetics) is their translation into the Klallam language. In the center of the seal is a thunderbird in black with white highlights. The lowest two tail feathers are red bordered in black, and the wings are red with black borders and black and white elements. Two yellow lightning bolts with black borders rise above its wings. Beneath the bird are two killer whales facing each other, in black, white, and red. The whales' lower bodies are marked by horizontal yellow "Y" shapes containing a white dot. The tails are black, each containing a red disk and white accents. The upper fins are yellow bordered in black and contain three black dots each, whereas the lower fins are solid black.

The Lower Elwha Klallam flag is an example of a strong, balanced design that remains faithful to the mythology as well as the historic and artistic tradition of its people.

Loyal Shawnee Tribe— Oklahoma

LOYAL
SHAWNEE TRIBE

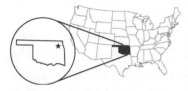

One of America's newest federally recognized tribes is the Loyal Shawnee Tribe of Oklahoma. President Bill Clinton granted it recognition in January 2001 shortly before leaving office, after years of legal wrangling. In 1866 the Loyal Shawnees signed a treaty with the Cherokee Nation and were absorbed into the larger tribe. Although they retained their culture and tradition, they were considered legal members of the Cherokee Nation.

The last few years of the effort to separate and obtain recognition began in 1996. At that time, according to the *Indian Observer*, a Cherokee tribal newspaper, "Leaders of the Loyal Shawnee Tribe presented a resolution to the Cherokee National Tribal Council executive and finance committee, at a July 25 meeting, seeking to dissolve the 1869 treaty which made their Tribe a part of the Cherokee Nation. The request comes after the Cherokee council rejected the Shawnees' proposal to build a bingo hall and casino during their regular meeting July 15." Principal Chief Joe Byrd denied that the desire to separate was caused by that rejection.

The Loyal Shawnees merged into the much larger Cherokee Nation of Oklahoma over 130 years ago as a matter of survival. Their separation can be viewed as the latest effort in that survival. The separation from the Cherokees has been relatively smooth, even though the Cherokees opposed the idea. According to Loyal Shawnee member Greg Pitcher, the major hurdle to separation was moot, because "[w]e are not expecting to have a land base in Oklahoma or anywhere else." Since the Shawnees would not be requiring the Cherokee Nation to relinquish tribal lands, the Cherokees could more easily let them go.

In 1998 the *Tulsa World* reported that "[the Oklahoma] State Senate passed a joint resolution, Monday [2 March 1998], unanimously, 48–0, stating the state of Oklahoma recognizes the Loyal Shawnee as a separate Nation." It was subsequently approved by the State Assembly and became law later that year.

On 3 January 2001 *Indian Country Today* noted that "more than 130 years after the Loyal Shawnees became a part of the Cherokee Nation, the United States Congress has finally given them federal recognition. It came as Title VII of the Omnibus Indian Advancement Act recently passed by Congress." By this time, the Cherokee Nation of Oklahoma had become a supporter of the effort by the Loyal Shawnees. *Indian Country Today* reported: " 'We have worked with the Shawnees for years to achieve this,' Cherokee Principal Chief Chad Smith said. 'They are proud of their heritage as Shawnees, and proud of the dignified way they have gained their federal recognition. Over the preceding four years, the Cherokee Nation passed two, separate resolutions which supported the Loyal Shawnee bid to be restored as a separate, federally recognized tribe.' "

With restored federal recognition, the Loyal Shawnees adopted a tribal flag, which is light blue with a white rectangle slightly above the center. The rectangle is edged in red except for two small openings on either side. Within the rectangle are twelve four-pointed yellow stars (the bottom points are longer than the other three) in two staggered rows of six over six. In the center of the rectangle is the bottom point of a much larger thirteenth star that extends well into the light-blue field, almost reaching the top edge of the flag.

Below the rectangle are two leaves (plant species unknown) pointing toward the base of the large star. Below them in black is the tribe's name: "LOYAL" centered above "SHAWNEE TRIBE." Unfortunately, the symbolism of the stars, rectangle, and leaves is not known. This new flag, however, does make a distinctive emblem for an ancient and newly emerged nation. Long may it wave!

Lummi Tribe— Washington

LUMMI NATION

TREATY OF 1855

Located in northwest Washington State is the Lummi Reservation, home to the Coastal Salish Lummi people. They share this 7,678-acre homeland with the Nooksack Nation, another branch of the Coastal Salish people (*NAA*, 285). The Lummis number about 1,000 and have lived there for hundreds of years, developing—along with their Salish cousins—a culture rich in art and design that recalls their sophisticated heritage of coastal seamanship (*ENAT*, 164–66). Their flag reflects a tradition among the Coastal Salish nations of uniting their distinctive art with their long association with the fishing industry (Cu-Se-Ma-At [Cathy Ballew], letter dated 16 June 1995) (see Quinault Tribe and Upper Skagit Indian Tribe of Washington). The white flag has "LUMMI NATION" across the top in black and "TREATY OF 1855" across the bottom. The violations of that treaty, signed by most tribes in what today is the state of Washington, led to the long "Yakima Wars." The black-edged oval seal of the Lummi people, centered on the flag, depicts an eagle in traditional Salish style in black, white, yellow, and red (seal provided by the Lummi newspaper *Squoi Quoi*). Central to many Native American cultures, these colors recall the four cardinal directions and are frequently associated with the four human races (see Miccosukee Tribe of Indians of Florida).

A closer examination of the eagle, a symbol of strength and freedom, reveals a compelling reference to the traditional fishing lifestyle of the Lummis. Its upward-pointing wings form two Salish-style orcas or killer whales, for centuries an important food source for the Lummis and an equally important focus of their tribal fishing heritage.

Makah Indian Tribe— Washington

MAKAH INDIAN NATION

DIAHT, WAÁTCH, OSETT, TSOO-YESS, BAADAH

The westernmost tribal lands in the continental United States belong to a people speaking a dialect of the Wakashan language, the Makahs (*ENAT*, 121–22). Although different from their Coastal Salish or Haida neighbors, the Makahs share many elements of culture, art, and living conditions with them and include some of these in the Makah flag.

The flag is white, with a red and white thunderbird with black accents in the center. The depiction of the thunderbird recalls the artistic style of Pacific Northwest Coast Indians. The Makahs, like many of their neighbors in western Washington, carved totem poles (see Lummi Tribe and Upper Skagit Indian Tribe of Washington).

The thunderbird, one of the most powerful creatures in Native American lore, holds a black whale in its talons. The whale recalls the Makah heritage as expert whalers: unlike many northwestern tribes who used only beached whales, the Makahs actively hunted them. In October 1997 they were granted the right to resume an annual gray whale hunt.

To each side of the thunderbird is a black-and-white serpent with a red tongue. Arching over the central device in red is "MAKAH INDIAN NATION"; beneath it in black are the names of the five villages of the Makah Nation: "DIA'HT, WA'ATCH, OSETT, TSOO-YESS, BAADA'H" (Leonard "Bud" Denney, letter dated 24 March 1997). The flag dates to the 1960s.

Thanks to the Makah tribal secretary, Neah Bay, Washington.

Mashantucket Pequot Tribe of Connecticut

The Pequot Indians have lived in the southern New England area for centuries. They frequently fought the neighboring Niantics and Narragansets for control of territory and in turn received a fitting name: "Pequot" or "Pequod" means "Destroyers" (*ENAT,* 184–85). Herman Melville named Captain Ahab's ship the *Pequod* in his novel *Moby-Dick.* The Pequots fought the British in the 1630s in the Pequot War, with disastrous consequences: the Pequots were massacred and enslaved. The few remaining members of the tribe were freed in 1655 and settled near Mystic, Connecticut, just south of the present-day Foxwoods Reservation of the Mashantucket Pequots.

The Pequot flag is white, with a round seal in the center depicting a prominent knoll with a lone black tree silhouetted against a green-blue sky. The knoll and tree represent Mashantucket, the "much-wooded land" where the Pequots once hunted and where they kept their identity alive for hundreds of years. A white fox stands in front of the tree—in their native language, the Pequots are known as the "Fox People." The combination of fox and tree recalls the name of the reservation: Foxwoods. On the black knoll beneath the tree is a glyph—the sign of Robin Cassasinnamon, the Mashantucket Pequots' first leader after the massacre at Mystic Fort in 1637 (*The Mashantucket Pequot,* undated pamphlet).

Today, with earnings from their Foxwoods casino complex, the Mashantucket Pequots may well be the most commercially successful Indian nation in the United States. In 1994 the Pequots generously donated US$10 million to the Smithsonian Institution for the planned National Museum of the American Indian on the National Mall in Washington, D.C. This was the largest contribution ever received for that project ("How a Decimated Tribe Turned to Casino Profits," *Times* [Trenton, New Jersey], 19 March 1995).

Menominee Indian Tribe of Wisconsin

The Menominees of Wisconsin, a tribe terminated by the federal government in the 1950s and restored in the 1970s, control about 222,000 acres (*AIDD*, 44). Their name derives from the Algonquin term *manomin* ("good berry"). The English understood it to mean "Wild Rice People," from their harvesting of the wild rice growing in the lakes of the region.

Today the Menominees celebrate their lands and culture on their tribal flag, which bears the circular seal of the Menominee Nation on a white background (seal provided by Tribal Headquarters of the Menominee Nation). The seal depicts a red thunderbird, one of the paramount creatures in Native American lore. The thunderbird is often drawn as an eagle, but the Menominees use a more traditional design. A white upward-pointing arrow splits its tail, as a symbol of the bright future facing the Menominee people.

Two other images in black appear over the thunderbird's shoulders. To the left is a map of the reservation, showing a pine forest. To the right is a cross-section of a log. Both the pine forest and the log symbolize the timber industry, which sustains the Menominee way of life.

In a white ring around the outside of the seal in black are the words "GREAT SEAL OF THE" above and "MENOMINEE NATION" below. The seal is edged with a narrow red band to separate it from the white field of the flag.

Miami Tribe of Oklahoma

The Miamis originally lived in the southern Great Lakes region that is now Indiana and Ohio. By 1840 they had been pushed west of the Mississippi River into what is today the state of Kansas. These lands were confiscated by the United States government, and the Miamis were moved to a small parcel of land in modern-day Oklahoma.

The name "Miami" may come from the Ojibwe word meaning "People of the Peninsula," referring to their midwestern homelands. One other possibility is the Miamis' own word for "pigeon." The Miamis originally referred to themselves as "Tightwees," which means "Cry of the Crane."

Beginning in 1887, under a process called allotment, the remaining land of the Miami Nation was assigned to individual tribal members, thus eliminating any tribal homeland. Today the Miamis are without any reservation lands or any trust lands but not without their culture or heritage (*ENAT*, 132–33). Many individuals of the tribe still own private property within what used to be their final reservation.

The flag of the Miami Tribe of Oklahoma is white, with the tribal seal in the center (Barbara Nichols, assistant librarian, Miami Tribe, letter dated 14 November 1994). Actual flags repeat the tribe's name underneath the seal in black letters. The dark-blue seal bears the name of the tribe in stylized red letters that simultaneously form two tipis (sample seal provided by the Miami Tribal Headquarters). Above this tipi motif is the Miami word "mamaque," which means "together." Below the tipi motif is the word "pehkokia," which means "peace." Circling the blue disc is a black band bearing the legend "THE GREAT SEAL OF THE MIAMI OF OKLAHOMA." All the lettering is metallic gold. Due to artistic license, the dark blue may range all the way to light blue, the metallic gold elements may be yellow or white, and a narrow white edging may separate the black ring from the central blue disk.

Miccosukee Tribe of Indians of Florida

The Miccosukees are a south Florida tribe closely related to their neighbors, the Seminoles. They officially number under 150 and control some 75,000 acres (*AIDD,* 44). The Miccosukee Reservation lies just west of Miami and borders the upper reaches of the Everglades, the huge swamp that served them for many years as a source of food, clothing, and shelter and as a refuge from federal forces during the long Seminole Wars. The Miccosukees have never signed a peace treaty with the United States and never renounced their claims to much of southern Florida.

The flag of the Miccosukees is one of the few well-known Native American tribal flags (*FBUS,* 257–59). It has four horizontal stripes: white over black over red over yellow. As with many other Native American tribal flags with four elements, the four stripes symbolize the four major directions: white for south, black for north, red for west, and yellow for east. Many tribes also see these four colors as standing for the human races. These colors are imbued with a magical essence in the eyes of many Native Americans. In the television special *The War against the Indian* (Discovery Channel, 5 February 1995), actor Graham Greene, an Oneida, explained the four colors: yellow is for the Asian, with whom the seas are associated; black for the African, who protects the air; white for the European, the keeper of the fire; and red for the Indian, who safeguards the earth.

The seal of the Miccosukee Nation (which does not appear on the flag) depicts a chickee, the traditional dwelling of the tribes of the Everglades. Both the Miccosukee flag and seal bear a strong similarity to those of their cousins and fellow Everglades dwellers, the Seminoles (see Seminole Tribe of Florida).

Mille Lacs Band of Chippewas (Ojibwes)— Minnesota

The Mille Lacs Reservation, located about 100 miles north of Minneapolis, is home to the Mille Lacs Band of the Chippewa (Ojibwe) Nation (see Leech Lake Band of Chippewas [Ojibwes]). The Mille Lacs Ojibwes pioneered a potent aspect of their claim to nationhood. All vehicles registered on their reservation display license plates of the Mille Lacs Band, not of the state of Minnesota. This demonstrates that the land and the people of this small reservation are outside the purview of the government of Minnesota and answer solely to the United States. A few other tribes, such as the Comanches, the Spokanes, and the Colvilles, have subsequently adopted their own license plates; but the Mille Lacs Chippewas appear to have been among the first. This small band also possesses a flag, with at least two copies known (one is at the Mille Lacs Band Tribal Headquarters).

The flag is blue, with a blue disk in the center ringed in white. The white ring bears the words "MILLE LACS BAND" in black at the top and "OJIBWE" at the bottom. The blue disk contains a white silhouette map of Minnesota; approximately centered on that map is a smaller blue disk for the Mille Lacs or "thousand lakes" of the reservation. (Minnesota itself is known as the "Land of Ten Thousand Lakes.") Crossing the horizontal axis of the larger blue disk is a brown sacred pipe. Above it an orange sun rises over the waters of the lake, radiating three rays upward and symbolizing a new life and beginning for the band. Below the pipe is a green wild rice plant, the source of sustenance for the Ojibwes and a symbol of life and independence.

Minnesota Chippewa (Ojibwe) Tribe

Minnesota is home to more bands of the Ojibwe or Chippewa Nation than any other state. All but one of the seven federally recognized Ojibwe reservations (the Red Lake Reservation) have come together as the Minnesota Chippewa Tribe. The tribe is composed of the Bois Forte (formerly Nett Lake), Fond du Lac, Grand Portage, Leech Lake (which is actually two bands, the Mississippi and Pillanger Bands), Mille Lacs, and White Earth Chippewas. These seven groups on six reservations total nearly 13,000, making the Minnesota Chippewas one of the largest single bodies of one tribe.

Each reservation has its own distinctive flag, but there is also a separate flag employed by the Minnesota Chippewa Tribe. That flag is white and bears the seal of the Minnesota Chippewa Tribe in the center. The seal depicts a sunrise over the lakes of Minnesota and traditional elements of Ojibwe life along the shore. These include a typical Ojibwe home of the eighteenth century and a birchbark canoe. Many of the individual elements found in the seal of the Minnesota Chippewa Tribe can be found in the seal employed by its constituent bands. The rising sun, for example, is featured in the flag of the Mille Lacs Band, while the conifer tree can be found in the flag of the Leech Lake Band (see Leech Lake Band of Chippewas [Ojibwes]).

Surrounding the seal is a yellow band bearing the words "MINNESOTA CHIPPEWA TRIBE SEAL" across the top and repeating the tribe's name in the Anishinabe language of the Ojibwes at the base of the seal. The founding date of the Minnesota Chippewa Tribe, "June 18, 1934," appears below the Anishinabe name. Encircling the seal within the yellow band (running clockwise from the beginning of the Anishinabe name to the end of it) is a thin black arrow.

Mississippi Band of Choctaw Indians

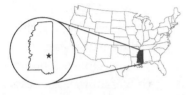 When the Choctaws were forcibly evicted from their traditional homelands in Alabama and Mississippi in the 1830s, some remained in hiding in the woodlands and swamps of southern Mississippi. Today descendants of those Choctaws who refused to leave form the federally recognized Mississippi Band of Choctaw Indians. In 1945 the federal government accepted the constitution of the Mississippi Choctaws. They also run their own school system, operate industrial sites and resorts, and maintain autonomous law-enforcement units. In December 1994 the Mississippi Band of Choctaw Indians adopted the flag that flies outside the tribal office and the casino ("MBCI Tribal Flag Now Official," *Choctaw Community News* [December 1994]: 16). The colors of the flag reflect Choctaw political ties over the last 500 years. The red, white, and blue vertical stripes refer to the Mississippi state flag, the colors of the United States, and the flag of France (a long-time ally of the Choctaws before their land came under British and American control). The red stripe and yellow ring around the seal derive from the red and gold of Spain, recalling the early contact with the Spanish through the explorations of Hernando De Soto in 1540.

The seal of the Mississippi Choctaw symbolizes their progress and survival in the face of adversity. Within a blue circle surrounded by a yellow band, a drum and drumsticks invoke the voice of the people. The hickory stickball sticks and white ball signify their strong will to survive and prosper. On the yellow band in black, separated by red stars, is the legend "MISSISSIPPI BAND * OF * CHOCTAW INDIANS * 1945."

Modoc Tribe of Oklahoma

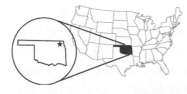

In 1873, when California's "Modoc War" ended, 153 Modoc men, women, and children were sent to the Quapaw Agency in Indian Territory (now Ottawa County, Oklahoma) as prisoners of war. The years following removal were difficult for the Modocs, who were provided little food, clothing, or medical care. It is a tribute to their courage and determination that the Modoc people at the Quapaw Agency survived, despite the poor living conditions. In 1909 the U. S. government finally felt that the Modocs had been punished enough and allowed those who chose to return to the Klamath Agency, Oregon (Act of 3 March 1909, 35 Stat., 751). Several did return; however, a few families chose to stay in their new home. The descendants of those who remained were recognized as the Modoc Tribe of Oklahoma in May 1978. Twenty-nine Modocs were reported to have returned to the Klamath Reservation in Oregon, according to a letter dated 24 May 1911 from Acting Commissioner C. B. Hawke to Senator George E. Chamberlain. Some of these twenty-nine were known to have returned to Oregon prior to 1909.

The history of the Modocs of Oklahoma as a distinct entity begins in November 1873, when they arrived at the Quapaw Agency. Of the nearly forty tribes now based in Oklahoma, only the Modocs have roots on the West Coast.

Today the Modocs of Oklahoma use a flag that closely associates them with their new homeland. As described by Chief Bill G. Follis:

The flag of the Modoc Tribe of Oklahoma is medium blue, as is the flag of Oklahoma, bearing the name "MODOC" across the top in yellow and "OKLAHOMA" also in yellow across the bottom. Between these two words appears the great seal of the Modoc Tribe of Oklahoma.

The seal is round, edged in white. From the seal hang ten feathers in black and white with tufts of yellow and red. The central design of the seal is an eagle in natural colors flying over a dark blue ocean with a coastline appearing at the bottom of the seal. To the left, a patch of brown and gold coastline symbolizes the original homeland of the Modoc people in southern Oregon and northern California.

The colors black, white, yellow, and red are found in many tribal flags and are considered the four primary colors in Native American art, with several spiritual and sacred meanings. Although these feathers had been reported to symbolize the ten clans of the Modoc people, tribal historian Patricia S. Trolinger notes that the Modocs did not have clans; so this is incorrect.

This flag became the official flag of the Modoc Tribe of Oklahoma in 1978. Chief Follis is the ultimate authority on the flag, since he designed it. He became the third chairman of the Modocs of Oklahoma in 1972, when the tribe was not yet federally recognized. Federal recognition did not come until May 1978. After the Modocs were terminated with the Klamath Tribe (in Oregon) in 1954, all tribes in the northeastern corner of Oklahoma banded together to establish the Inter-Tribal Council, Inc., of Northeastern Oklahoma. At that time, the Modocs formed an unofficial tribal government. This is when the term "chairman" came into use by the Modocs. Chief Follis was the first federally recognized chief of the Modocs in Oklahoma since the death of Bogus Charley in 1880. Several Modoc chiefs at the Quapaw Agency after Bogus were only recognized as such by the Modoc people.

Thanks to Chief Bill G. Follis and Modoc tribal historian Patricia Scruggs Trolinger for providing and correcting the information on the Modoc Tribe of Oklahoma.

Mohegan Indian Tribe of Connecticut

One of the latest tribes to achieve federal recognition, the Mohegan Nation (improperly pronounced Mo-hi-can) spans many centuries of interaction with European-Americans. "Mohegan" means "Wolf People." The tribe is most famous for its fictional extinction at the hand of James Fenimore Cooper in *The Last of the Mohicans* (*ENAT*, 142–43). The tribe did not die out. In fact, it continued to thrive in Lower New England long after Cooper's romantic novelization. Now, with the opening of a casino, it has adopted a new flag.

The Mohegan flag is white with a royal-blue border around the outer edge. In the center is the new tribal seal with the words "THE MOHEGAN TRIBE" arching over the seal in black and "MUNDU WIGO" below. "Mundu Wigo," a favorite expression of Fidelia Fielding, one of the last fluent speakers of the Mohegan language, means "The Creator is good" ("What Our Symbol Means," unattributed clipping).

The seal is a black circle ringed in red. Within it is a complex figure based upon an ancient Mohegan motif. A red dot in the center circled by thirteen smaller white dots is enclosed in a white narrow border, forming a square. Attached to each side of the square is a royal-blue semicircle edged in white. At each corner of the square a diagonal white line aims outward, ending in two lines that curve back toward the center.

The four semicircular domes pointing to each of the four sacred directions represent the back of "Grandfather Turtle upon whom the earth was

formed" and the shape of the old wigwam dwellings of the Mohegan people. The four diagonal lines symbolize four sacred trees and represent a "branching out towards future generations" (ibid.).

The thirteen white dots recall the thirteen moons in a lunar year, the thirteen sections on a turtle's back, and thirteen generations since Uncas, the great leader of the Mohegans (ibid.). The central red dot is the "Sacred Center Circle" of the spiritual life force felt throughout the universe.

An interim flag was previously adopted in 1994 before the casino was built (Shirley M. Walsh, Tribal Office manager, letter dated 4 November 1994). It was blue, with the seal of the Mohegan Nation in the center—a blue disk, bearing a white wolf. Behind the wolf were mountains outlined in purple, while the paws of the wolf rested on tufts of green grass. Circling this disk was a red band bearing the words "MOHEGAN TRIBE" in black at the top and "THE WOLF PEOPLE" at the bottom.

Thanks to the Mohegan Tribal Headquarters, Uncasville, Connecticut, for information on the flag and seal.

Muckleshoot Indian Tribe— Washington

King County, Washington, which claims Seattle as its biggest city, also contains the Muckleshoot Reservation, the home of the Muckleshoot Indian Tribe. Like many of the tribes of western Washington, the Muckleshoots are members of the Coastal Salish people, who for over a thousand years have made a living from the salmon that filled the rivers. The "fishing wars" of the 1970s led to court intervention and to a significant expansion of Muckleshoot rights, land areas, and financial resources.

The tribal flag, adopted when the bingo hall and casino opened in 1993, has a turquoise-blue field bearing the tribal seal in full color. The seal is a circular yellow shield (edged by a narrow black ring), recalling traditional warrior shields. From it hang five eagle feathers with red tassels. Centered on the shield is Mt. Rainier, the dominant geographic element in the region and sacred to many local tribes. Behind the mountain is a two-colored sunburst—an inner burst of red and an outer one of orange. The rays of this outer burst shoot up into the name "MUCKLESHOOT" arching over the mountain in black; below the mountain in black are the words "INDIAN TRIBE." Above the entire shield is the legend "THE GREAT SEAL" in white. Two traditional sacred pipes in orange-brown overlap the seal from each side, with their bowls pointing inward.

According to the tribal office, three copies of the flag have been manufactured. One is displayed in the tribal council chambers, one is located in the president's office, and one flies outdoors. The seal when used alone does not usually depict the sunburst; nor does it have the legend "THE GREAT SEAL." This simplified seal is also seen in some modified forms, such as on tribal school T-shirts, which replace the words "INDIAN TRIBE" with "TRIBAL SCHOOL."

Thanks to NAVA member Harry Oswald for the photo of the Muckleshoot flag.

Muscogee (Creek) Nation—Oklahoma

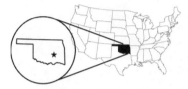

The Muscogees are the largest band of the Creek Indian Nation. They were one of the "Five Civilized Tribes" uprooted from their southeastern home by President Andrew Jackson (*ENAT*, 74–76). Following initial hardships and deprivation, the Creek Nation has thrived in Oklahoma. The tribe currently controls a small Tribal Historic Area there.

The Muscogees use a white flag (*Retrospect*, Creek Communications Department, Okmulgee, Oklahoma, 1983) bearing the latest rendition of the tribal seal (copy of seal provided by Annin & Co., Roseland, N.J.). This seal dates to the nineteenth century and has varied with changes in artistic styles. It has always depicted a traditional plow and sheaf of wheat, which appear in full color on the flag and refer to the agricultural base of the tribe since reaching Indian Territory in the 1830s (*FBUS*, 259). The latest version adds a large billowy red cloud, possibly alluding to the "Dust Bowl" hardships of the 1930s, edged in white on a blue sky.

This flag of the Muscogee Nation is nearly identical to one created by the Alabama Department of History in 1940 for the dedication of the Hall of Flags in Montgomery. At the time, the "Five Civilized Tribes" of Oklahoma—the Muscogees, the Seminoles, the Choctaws, the Cherokees, and the Chickasaws—were without flags; but as former residents of modern Alabama, they were included in the grand opening. To permit the participation of these nations in the ceremonies, special banners were created for the five tribes. Each was white and bore a full-color tribal seal in the center. The continued use of that design may be traced back to that event ("Official Seals of the Five Civilized Tribes," *Oklahoma Chronicles* [Oklahoma City] 17:4 [December 1940]: 357–59).

Almost 150 years ago the Muscogees (Creeks) flew another flag, also presented to them. The Creek Nation was given a flag by Miss Alice Leeper, daughter of the Confederate agent to the Creeks and other tribes (*True Democrat* [Little Rock, Arkansas], 29 August 1861). The Confederate Indian commissioner, Albert Pike, reported from the Wichita Agency on his mission to the Indians, calling the devices "new and appropriate" and describing the Creek flag as "a crescent and red star in a green union and upright bars of red  and white." The Confederate States of America apparently created flags for each of its allies in the "Five Civilized Tribes" (see Cherokee Nation, Chickasaw Nation, Choctaw Nation of Oklahoma, and Seminole Nation of Oklahoma).

Thanks to the Flag Research Center for information concerning the 1940 flags of the "Five Civilized Tribes."

Navajo Nation—
Arizona,
New Mexico, and
Utah

The Navajos are the largest resident tribe in the United States, constituting over 14 percent of the Native American population in the 1990 census and numbering more than 250,000 (*NAA*, 36–43). They occupy much of the Southwest, spreading across parts of Arizona, New Mexico, and Utah. The Pueblo Indians referred to the area from which the Navajos came as "Navajo" (*ENAT*, 154–58), while the Spanish called them "Apaches de Navajo," eventually shortened to "Navajos."

The Navajo flag, adopted on 21 May 1968 by the Tribal Council in Window Rock, Arizona, was designed by Jay R. DeGroat, a Navajo student from Mariano Lake. It was chosen from among 140 designs (*FBUS*, 259–60). The flag incorporates elements from the tribal seal designed by John Claw, Jr., of Many Farms and adopted on 18 January 1952.

The seal bears a ring of fifty arrowheads representing the states of the United States (the original seal had forty-eight; two were added when Alaska and Hawaii became states) and reflects the Navajo Nation protected by the United States. Within this ring of outward-pointing arrowheads are three concentric circles of turquoise, yellow, and red, open at the top. They represent the rainbow and the Navajo *hooghan* (hogan); the opening shows that the Navajo Nation's sovereignty is never closed. Within the circles are two green corn plants, the sustainer of life for the Navajos; their yellow tips represent pollen, used frequently in Navajo ceremonies. Within the corn are four sacred mountains surrounding a brown horse, red cow, and white sheep (livestock are a source of wealth for the Navajos). The mountains are white, turquoise, yellow, and black (clockwise from the top). Above them a yellow sun shines, and arching over all is

"GREAT SEAL OF THE NAVAJO NATION" in black ("The Symbols of the Navajo Nation," *NAVA News* [May/June 1988]: 4).

The Navajo flag is a pale buff color (perhaps representing sand), bearing a map of the Navajo Nation in the center. The original area of the 1868 reservation is dark brown, while the much larger current borders are copper (sample flag provided by the Office of Property and Supply, Navajo Nation, Window Rock, Arizona).

Elements from the seal appear on the flag. Surrounding the map are the four sacred mountains—black above, white on the right, turquoise below, and yellow on the left. These colors form a recurring theme in the legends of the Navajos, starting with the Navajo creation story. In it the world began as a black island floating in the mist. Above it were four clouds, black, white, blue (meaning turquoise), and yellow ("Mythology of the Navaho" [*sic*], *Hobbies Magazine* [November 1956]). The story describes the colored clouds as successive worlds and narrates the themes of birth, propagation, flood, escape, and continuing life. Arching over the mountains and map is the rainbow of red (outermost), yellow, and blue. Centered on the map is a white disk bearing the corn stalks and domestic animals from the seal, along with symbols of other aspects of the Navajo economy: a traditional hogan, oil-drilling equipment, and emblems of forestry, mining, and recreational fishing and hunting. All but the green and yellow corn stalks appear in black outline.

The overall image of the flag recalls an art form closely associated with the Navajos—sand painting. Many of the flag's details—and the sand-colored background—are frequently found in these temporary artworks, which initially served as altars in various healing ceremonies (traditional Navajos often object to the sale of actual sand paintings for this reason).

The orientation of the sacred mountains on the flag differs from that on the seal. The Navajos consider east (*ha'a'aah*) to be the place where everything begins; it signifies all things good and beautiful and is the location of the white mountain. On the seal, east and the white mountain are at the top; on the flag, they are on the right.

In 1995 the flag of the Navajo Nation became the first Native American tribal flag in space when astronaut Bernard Harris carried it aboard the space shuttle *Discovery* ("Navajo Flag Flies in Orbit Aboard Shuttle Discovery," *Plain Dealer* [Cleveland, Ohio], 9 February 1995). Dr. Harris is an African-American physician who lived on the Navajo Reservation as a child. When he asked the Navajos for a token to take into space with him, the president chose the flag. Navajo medicine men first blessed the flag by sprinkling corn pollen upon it and were assured that the *Discovery*'s flight path conformed to Navajo religious belief: it would fly in a clockwise direction. After its space flight, the flag was proudly flown over the Navajo National Capitol in Window Rock, Arizona.

Thanks to Peter T. Noyes, compliance officer, Navajo Nation, Historic Preservation Department, for relaying important aspects of the flag's description.

Nez Percé Tribe of Idaho

To many, the name "Nez Percé" immediately recalls Chief Joseph, the brilliant military strategist and leader of the Nez Percé people. His statement "I will fight no more, forever" was the title of a book and movie about the gallant fight and flight of his people across 1,700 miles through the Far West (ENAT, 158–61). They had attempted to escape the squalor and deprivation of an imposed relocation to the Nez Percé Reservation in Idaho and reach sanctuary in Canada.

Today the Nez Percé Tribe, still located on that reservation in north-central Idaho, honors Chief Joseph, who died in 1904 without being allowed to return to his native lands. At the center of the Nez Percé flag is the tribal seal, a black-and-white drawing of a bust of Chief Joseph ringed by "NEZ PERCÉ TRIBE" above and "TREATY OF 1855" (marking the founding of the reservation) below in black. The seal appears in the center of a black map of the reservation, edged in golden yellow. On the map are the rivers that cross the reservation, a salmon (a major source of food for the Nez Percé people), and a deer (also a traditional food source), all in gold.

Above the seal, edged in red, is a golden silhouette of an eagle, the bird sacred to many Native American people. Below and on the left of the seal, extending beyond the map, are four white-and-black eagle feathers edged in red. All these images are placed on a red field, which recalls the suffering and death of many Nez Percés in their fight for freedom (photo provided by All Nations Flag Co.).

The colors of the central design and the field bring together the four primary Native American colors: white, black, red, and yellow (Arthur Taylor, Nez Percé Cultural Resources Center, letter dated 19 December 1994). They symbolize the human races and the directions of the compass (see Miccosukee Tribe of Indians of Florida).

The tribal name, literally "Pierced Noses" in French, alludes to nose pendants that some Nez Percés wore when the French first encountered them (*ENAT*, 158–61). The Nez Percés call themselves "Nimipu," meaning "the People," while neighboring tribes called them "Sahaptin," a term that today refers to the native language of the Nez Percés.

The earliest standard flag attributed to any Native American (other than the Civil War flags designed for the "Five Civilized Tribes" by the Confederacy) was the flag of a Nez Percé. The shaman Smohalla, who founded the Dreamer cult (*ANAI*, 133) during the 1860s, flew a flag over his house and during ceremonies (J. W. Powell, "The Ghost Dance Religion and the Sioux Outbreak of 1890," in *14th Annual Report of the Bureau of Ethnology to the Smithsonian Institution*, part 2, 1892–93). Smohalla's flag was yellow for the grasslands all around, edged in green for the saltwater seas

 beyond. In the center was a red oval representing Smohalla's heart, edged in white, standing for the home or place where Smohalla dwelled. Together they symbolized "the center. I live there" (ibid., 126). Across the top was a blue stripe for the sky, on which was centered a single white star: ". . . the star is the North Star. That star never changes; it is always in the same place. I keep my heart on that star. I never change" (ibid., 126).

Northern Cheyenne Tribe—Montana

Since separating from the Southern Cheyennes (now simply the Cheyennes) in the 1830s, the Northern Cheyennes have stayed along the Upper Platte River; it is still the home of the people who call themselves "Tsistsistas" or "Beautiful People." Their Sioux neighbors named them "Cheyennes," meaning "Red Talkers" or "People of a Different Speech," because the Cheyenne language is Algonquin-based, while the Lakota Sioux speak a Siouan dialect.

The Northern Cheyenne homeland is a reservation in southeastern Montana, just east of their Crow neighbors. The Northern Cheyennes use a blue flag bearing the Indian glyph *wo'heh'hiv* ("morning star") in white (*FBUS*, 260–61). The symbol has been used for ages in Cheyenne art and decoration and painted on dancers in the religious ceremony known as the Sun Dance. It consists of a square set on one of its corners, with lines the length of its sides emanating perpendicularly from the center of each side.

The *wo'heh'hiv* recalls the great Chief Morning Star (also known as Dull Knife), who led his people to their current home after their defeat in the Indian wars of the Plains, and thus symbolizes hope and guidance. The flag was designed in 1964 by Hubert Bearchum during the administration of tribal president John Woodenlegs, who also chose "Wo'hih'hev" as his name for himself (Eugene D. Little Coyote, e-mail dated 11 May 1997). If the flag were to employ traditional coloration, the background would be a brownish-red, while the star would appear in black (ibid.).

Oglala Sioux Tribe—South Dakota

The Lakotas of the Pine Ridge Reservation in southwestern South Dakota (Oglalas) have one of the best-known Indian tribal flags. They have also given the Sioux, and the United States, two of the most famous Indian leaders: Chief Red Cloud and Chief Crazy Horse (*ENAT*, 222–28).

The Oglala flag's red field symbolizes the blood shed by the Sioux in defense of their lands and the very idea of the "red people." A circle of eight white tipis (tops pointing outward) represents the eight districts of the reservation: Porcupine, Wakpamni, Medicine Root, Pass Creek, Eagle Nest, White Clay, LaCreek, and Wounded Knee (*FBUS*, 260–62). When used indoor or in parades, the flag is decorated with a deep-blue fringe to incorporate the colors of the United States into the design.

The flag was first displayed at the Sun Dance ceremonies in 1961 and officially adopted on 9 March 1962. Since then it has taken on a larger role, perhaps because of its age, clear design, and universal symbolism. The Oglala flag is now a common sight at Native American powwows, not just Sioux gatherings, and is often flown as a generic Native American flag.

In the late 1960s or early 1970s another flag apparently represented the Oglala Sioux (clipping in the collection of the Flag Research Center). That flag had a light background bearing a red warrior's shield, which depicted what may be a thunderbird. Two upward-pointing spears crossed behind the shield, forming an "X." The name "OGLALA SIOUX" appeared above the shield and "NATION" below. (No other references to this flag have been found.)

Omaha Tribe of Nebraska and Iowa

Just as the modern city of Omaha, which is named for the tribe, acts as a sort of transition to the Great Plains, the former lifestyle of the Omaha people bridged the worlds of the sedentary tribes east of the Missouri River and the wandering tribes west of the river. The Omahas lived in permanent homes in permanent villages and maintained a farming culture. But each year, when the season of the great buffalo migration occurred, they would pack up and follow the herds. During the buffalo season the Omahas used tipis and lived like the tribes of the Great Plains, such as the Sioux and Cheyennes.

The Omahas are closely related to the Poncas and were at one times neighbors separated by the Niobrara River in Nebraska (*ENAT*, 167–68). The association with rivers was important in the delineation of tribal boundaries. They acted as natural, easily recognizable markers that separated the lands of one tribe from those of another. The significance of river boundaries is evident in the tribe's name. "Omaha," or more properly "Umonhon," means "Those Who Go Against the Current."

Today the Omahas possess a reservation in northeast Nebraska, some seventy miles north of the city that bears their name. A small portion of the reserve reaches into western Iowa—thus the official name. The current tribal enrollment is around 6,000 people. The native language of the Omahas is the Omaha-Ponca dialect of Dhelegi, a Siouan language. Dhelegi features prominently on the flag of the Omaha people.

The flag has a silver-gray background with a narrow black stripe across the base, with the translation of the Omaha name, "AGAINST THE

CURRENT," in white letters. Along both the inner and outer edges of the flag (tilted ninety degrees) is the phrase "HERITAGE FOR PEACE" in black. The words run from the bottom to the top along the left side and from the top to the bottom along the right side. Across the top in large black letters is the name "OMAHA TRIBE," with "OF NEBRASKA & IOWA" in smaller lettering directly underneath.

The center of the seal features an Omaha headdress in black (facing left) surrounded by a wide red ring, separated from the central circle by a narrow black band. From the red ring emanate eight rays (four each on the left and right). The ring bears seven words in the Dhelegi language, starting from the center left: "InKECABE," "THAIDA," "KOnCE," "MOnTHInKAGAXE," "HOnGA," "InTACUNDA," and "TAPA." No explanation or translation for these seven words has been found. Between the upper four words and the central device appears the phrase "UMONIHA TRIBE OF NEBRASKA & IOWA." All lettering on the red ring is in white.

Thanks to the staff at the Crazy Horse Memorial in South Dakota for providing a photo of the Omaha Nation flag.

Oneida Nation
of New York

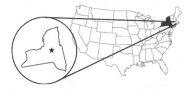

The Oneidas or Onyota'a ka were among the original members of the Iroquois League (see Iroquois League). The traditional lands of the Oneidas lay between those of the Mohawks and the Onondagas (*ENAT*, 168). The name "Oneida" means "People of the Boulder" or "People of the Standing Stone." This refers to a significant rock formation found on Oneida lands.

The Oneidas and the Tuscaroras were the only members of the league to side with the United States during the Revolutionary War. Today the Oneidas continue to seek the restoration of lost lands and an improving way of life for their kin. As part of their self-awareness, the Oneida people use their seal on a white flag.

Since the glory days of the Iroquois League, long before the formation of the United States, the symbol of the Oneida people has been a great tree (ibid., 169). The white pine was selected by Deganawidah the Peacemaker because its needles stay green forever (*The Oneida Indian Nation Seal*, n.d.). His vision of tribes coming together in peace under a "great tree" helped Hiawatha unite the Iroquois Nations in the sixteenth century (*ENAT*, 104). According to legend, the Peacemaker instructed the Iroquois to "bury their weapons of war under the sacred roots, and never unearth them again to use on each other."

The seal of the Oneida Nation is red, appearing frequently as a reddish-orange or even orange. It bears the great tree of the Oneidas in green in the center, and pictured upon it are three clan totems—a wolf, a bear, and a turtle—in black. The tree is topped by an eagle in black with outstretched wings. Below the eagle is a depiction of "Hiawatha's Belt" (*AIDD*, plate 18), the wampum symbol of the Iroquois League since its creation around 1570, in its original colors of white on blue. Around the seal on a white band edged in black appears the legend "ONEIDA INDIAN NATION" in black.

Oneida Tribe
of Wisconsin

Following the Revolutionary War, many Oneidas in upper New York State sold their lands. In 1838 a group of these Oneidas bought land from the Menominees in what is now northern Wisconsin (*ENAT*, 169). The Oneida Tribe of Wisconsin today is the largest concentration of Oneidas in the United States.

The Wisconsin Oneidas share the symbols utilized by the eastern branch of the tribe in New York (see Oneida Nation of New York). Both employ the great tree, the wolf, the eagle, the bear, and the wampum belt as symbols in their tribal seals. The seal of the Wisconsin Oneidas features the great tree standing atop the "turtle island" representing the earth. From either side of the tree appear the head of a wolf and the head of a bear, the two clan totems of the Oneida people. The inner circle in green forms the outline of an eagle's head at the top, above the tree. The eagle, an important creature in Native American beliefs, serves as the contact between the Great Spirit and humans. Below the turtle stretches the wampum belt of the Iroquois League (see Iroquois League) in purple, the natural color of the quahog shells that composed it. The outer part of the seal contains the legend "SOVEREIGN ONEIDA NATION OF WISCONSIN."

The seal appears in green outline on the white background of the flag. The Oneidas of New York and the Oneidas of Wisconsin demonstrate their common ancestry through the unity of their emblems, despite the 1,000 miles that separate them.

Osage Tribe—
Oklahoma

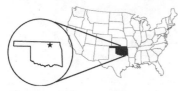

The Ni-U-Ko'n-Ska ("Children of the Middle Waters"), as the Osage people call themselves, came originally from what is now Ohio. They were members of the same nation that today includes the Kaw, Omaha, Ponca, and Quapaw Tribes. "Osage" is actually a corruption by the French of the name of the largest band, the Wazhazhe (*ENAT*, 170–71).

The Osages migrated from what is now Ohio to the area of modern-day Missouri and Arkansas; and by the early 1800s there were three distinct bands: the Great Osages, who settled around the Osage River; the Little Osages, who lived near the Missouri River; and the Arkansas Osages, who were part of the Great Osages until they broke off and moved to the region around the Arkansas River. Today the Osage Nation continues to thrive in Osage County, Oklahoma; its capital is the town of Pawhuska.

The flag (provided by the Osage Tribal Museum) is light blue, perhaps referring to the Sky People, one of the two clans into which the Osage people were traditionally divided (the other clan was the Earth People). Centered on the flag is the circular tribal seal (copy of seal provided by Annin & Co., Roseland, N.J.) in yellow with an outer band of gold. The seal depicts a large light-blue arrowhead pointing downward. Superimposed on it, also pointing downward, is a prayer fan composed of eagle feathers. The fan and feathers are white with black details; a small red band secures the feathers to the fan holder. A red sacred pipe crosses the arrowhead and fan diagonally. Above the arrowhead in black is "SEAL OF" and below it "OSAGE NATION."

The Osages have also influenced the state flag of Oklahoma, which bears an "Osage shield" of the great Osage chief Claremont (*The Seal of the Osage Nation*, undated flyer).

154

Otoe-Missouria Tribe of Indians— Oklahoma

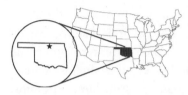

The Otoe-Missouria people were once part of a greater nation around the Great Lakes that included what are now the Ho-chunks (Winnebagos), the Iowas, and the two current tribal entities, the Otoes and the Missourias. As the ancient great tribe moved ever farther south and west from its original homelands, it broke apart, slowly forming the current nations. They were four separate nations by the time European-Americans arrived.

The final split occurred while the people lived along the banks of the Missouri. The Otoes separated from the Missourias after a quarrel between the chiefs of the combined tribes. The son of the chief of what would become the Otoes supposedly seduced the daughter of the other chief. Because of the son's actions, his tribe was driven away and became known as the Otoes or "Lechers" (*ENAT*, 172). Those who remained became the Missourias or "People with Dugout Canoes" (ibid., 136).

In 1829 the Missourias, after repeated attacks by nearby tribes, especially the Osages, rejoined their relatives the Otoes, forming the Otoe-Missouria Tribe of today (ibid.). The 1,250 members (*REAI*, 11) are currently based in Red Rock, Oklahoma.

The clan totems of the nation—the bear, eagle, beaver, bison, deer, owl, and pigeon—ring a prayer feather at the center of the tribal seal. All appear in natural colors on a white background. A serrated band of inner yellow triangles and outer red triangles rings the totems. Outside this in black is "SEAL OF THE OTOE MISSOURIA TRIBE." The words are highlighted by five thin black lines, two forming the outer edge of the seal and three running behind the words. At the top of the seal is a pair of feather decorations similar to those worn as warrior headdresses. A member of the tribe designed the seal, which appears on a white flag. Although the flag's legal status is not known, it has become the de facto flag of the Otoe-Missouria Tribe through common usage.

Ottawa Tribe
of Oklahoma

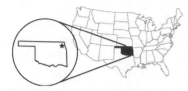

The Ottawa people lived along the shore of what is now Georgia Bay in Canada when the French explorer Samuel de Champlain first met them in 1615. A quarter-century later, pressured by the Iroquois (see Iroquois League), the Ottawas moved to Green Bay in present-day Wisconsin, spreading into northwestern Illinois and southern Wisconsin.

Culturally, the Ottawa people are Algonquin, the Chippewas (Ojibwes) and Potawatomis being their closest tribal relatives. Although they lived in villages and planted crops, the Ottawas were best known as traders, traversing the rivers of northeastern America as well as the Great Lakes in their canoes and following the "Moccasin Trail" well into what is now Florida. Their name derives from the Algonquin *adawe,* meaning to trade or barter (Joseph H. Cash and Gerald W. Wolff, *The Ottawa People,* vol. 34 in the Indian Tribes Series).

Supporting the French in the French and Indian War of 1754–63, the Ottawas—under Chief Pontiac—organized strong resistance to the British power in the Great Lakes area. During the American Revolutionary War, the Ottawas sided with the British but were still able to control most of what is now Ohio afterward. Increasing incursion by white settlers, however, forced the tribe to move steadily westward, first into Kansas and then onto a 12,000-acre tract of land purchased from the United States in the northeastern corner of Indian Territory (present-day Oklahoma), where they live today, 2,000 strong (ibid.).

The seal of the Ottawas, which appears on a white background on the flag, reflects their history. The evergreen tree (green with a brown trunk), which symbolizes the Tree of Life, and light-green grassy knoll in the center with a light-blue sky above recall their origins in the northeastern

woodlands. The light-brown canoe (with dark-brown trimmings and slats) in the foreground alludes to their trading skills and Algonquian name. It floats on medium-blue water highlighted with a dark-blue wave and light-green lily pads. At the right end of the canoe, on the grass knoll, stand a few cattails in dark brown with light-brown stems.

To the left of the central tree is a light-brown war club with dark-brown lines and cross-hatching (a typical weapon used in hand-to-hand combat and hunting). Toward its lower end a black-and-white eagle feather projects to the left, fastened with a dark-brown strap. To the right of the tree is a dark-brown otter with light-brown accents (looking to the left), recalling the Otter (Negig) Clan to which many of the Ottawas of Oklahoma belong and the basic religion of the Ottawa people—the otter skin or medicine-dance religion (*Seal of the Ottawa Tribe,* n.d.). The water on which the canoe floats represents the source of all life and is an important sacramental element in many Indian religions.

On a white band (outlined by two black rings) in black are the words "OTTAWA TRIBE" curving above the central seal and "OF OKLAHOMA" below. Below the tree on the central disk is the legend "UNITED WE STAND DIVIDED WE FALL" in black.

Thanks to Margie Ross, program director at the Ottawas' headquarters in Miami, Oklahoma, and to tribal member Claudean Epperson for information on the seal and flag.

Paiute Indian Tribe of Utah

Located in south-central Utah, the Paiute Tribe of Utah combines the Cedar, Koosharem, Shivwits, Kanosh, and Indian Peaks Bands. These five bands, numbering some 600 individuals, represent only a small portion of the Paiute Nation, which spreads across much of the West to include Arizona, California, Nevada, and Oregon as well as Utah (*REAI*, 33, 41). The name "Paiutes" has been translated to mean either "Water Utes" or "True Utes," alluding to their past union as one people with that tribe (*ENAT*, 174–76).

The flag of the Paiute Tribe of Utah is white, with the tribal seal in the center in red and white. That seal was adopted by Tribal Resolution 97-20 on 13 May 1997 and signed into law by Geneal Anderson, the tribal chairwoman. The seal already had been used on the floor of the tribal gymnasium and incorporated into the tribe's new headquarters in Cedar City, Utah.

On the seal (outlined by a ring of two lines) an eagle—symbolic of the deity—flies in front of a map of Utah. In the southwestern corner an arrowhead pinpoints the tribe's location (the Paiutes are especially known for their arrowheads). To the right of the eagle are a pair of gourd rattles, representing the Paiutes' Salt Song and Bird Song. To the left of the eagle is a hand-held drum, which represents the Circle Dance Song and the Hand Games Song. At the base of the map are three "hand game" sticks. The seal was designed by Paiute tribal member Travis Parashonts at the request of the Paiute Tribal Council.

Hanging from the seal, making it resemble a warrior's shield, are five decorated feathers for the five bands. Arching above the top is the official name "Paiute Indian Tribe of Utah." Inside the shield, below the "hand game" sticks, is "Federally Recognized April 3, 1980," showing the paramount importance of that event to the tribe.

Paiute-Shoshone Indians of the Bishop Community of the Bishop Colony—California

The Owens Valley Paiutes originally controlled a vast area along the Owens River in what is now eastern California. This area is nestled between the majestic Sierra Nevada range on the west and the White Mountains on the east, northeast of Sequoia National Park and north of Death Valley. Here the Bishop Paiutes control some 877 acres, upon which reside around 1,100 tribal members. The tribe is presently in the process of acquiring 250 acres of its traditional lands, restoring the Bishop Paiutes to their true home. Some 68,000 such acres in the area have been identified by the tribe for reacquisition over time.

The Bishop Paiute Tribe was created after a presidential order on 11 March 1912. This executive order set apart lands for the Bishop Colony. During this time tribal members made their livelihood from farming and ranching. In 1937 an act of Congress ceded all previously owned Indian lands to the City of Los Angeles in exchange for some city-owned land. This land exchange altered the way of life for tribal members, whose income would now come from nontraditional sources such as land leasing.

Today the Bishop Paiute Indians are revitalizing their culture and making progress toward economic self-sufficiency. The Bishop Paiute Reservation is located in Inyo County, a region famous for its spectacular landscape. It sits in a valley along snow-tipped mountains that rise four to six thousand feet from the valley floor. This scenery is celebrated on the seal of the Bishop Paiute Tribe today.

A medium-blue flag bears the tribal seal, which is pale blue, recalling the clear blue sky still found in eastern California. The sky rises over a

black mountain of the Sierra Nevada range, which dominates the lower half of the seal. Throughout the mountain run various blue lines, reminding the viewer of the source of the water for the Paiutes of the region. The mountain runoff is now the source for much of the water supplying thirsty Los Angeles.

Superimposed on the mountain is the name "BISHOP PAIUTE" arching above and "TRIBE" below in bold white letters, with a pair of white feathers dangling between the two phrases.

Pascua Yaqui Tribe of Arizona

Just outside Tucson, Arizona, lies a patch of desert, 1,150 acres. This is the Pascua Yaqui Reservation. It is one of five Yaqui communities in central Arizona. The others are Guadalupe in the Phoenix area, the Old Pascua Village in downtown Tucson, Barrio Libre in South Tucson, and Yoem Pueblo near Marana. The true name of the Yaqui people is "Yoeme," a Yaqui word meaning "the People"—a common way of referring to one's own tribe throughout North America (Pascua Yaqui Tribe, *Pascua Yaqui Tribe of Arizona—General Information,* undated pamphlet).

The Yoemes were dubbed the "Yaquís" by Spanish explorers who reached their lands along Mexico's Río Yaquí in 1533. The confusion between languages led the Spanish to assume the Yoeme word *hiaki* was the name of the people they had met. It actually meant "speech." *Hiaki* mutated into "Yaqui," and the name has been used ever since. In the 1880s many of the Yaquis fled ongoing persecution by the Mexican government and sought a haven in southern Arizona (ibid.).

The modern reservation, originally only 202 acres in size, was ceded to the Pascua Yaquis in 1964, and the tribe received federal recognition in 1978. Today the Pascua Yaquis number about 13,000 members (Pascua Yaqui Tribe, *Pascua Yaqui Tribe—Enrollment Department,* undated pamphlet). The entrance to the modern reservation is dominated by the Tribal Administration complex and the adjoining Casino of the Sun. These main buildings act as a backdrop for the display of both the tribal seal and flag.

The Yaquis settled in what is now the Old Pascua Village in northern Tucson. *Pascua* means "Easter" in Spanish and may recall the date of its settlement. The village was absorbed into the city in 1952. They also settled in the village of Guadalupe, near Scottsdale. Both these settlements still are centers of Yaqui culture.

Recalling the "Pascua" (Easter) portion of the tribe's name and the unique merging of Yaqui cultural tradition with their Catholic faith brought to them by the Jesuits, the tribal seal of the Pascua Yaqui Nation features a Christian cross. It bears the rising sun of Achai Taa'ah and, most significantly, the Deer Dancer, who was incorporated into Catholic celebrations to ease the adoption of the European-based faith by the Aztecan Yaqui people. The Deer Dancer is a major participant in the Palm Sunday festivities of the tribe, which is noted for its elaborate Easter celebrations. He is a traditional symbol of good in the Yaqui culture and originates "from a spiritual realm of bright, beautiful flowers that are empowered to destroy evil and bring out goodness" (Pascua Yaqui Tribe, *Seal of the Pascua Yaqui,* undated pamphlet). The seal also bears a crescent moon of Maala Mecha hanging over a landscape expressing the stark beauty of the Sonoran desert and the dominant plant feature—the saguaro cactus.

The flag combines elements of the seal, the colors of the United States, the land that gave the Yaqui people refuge, and the form of the flag of Mexico, their traditional homeland. The flag is composed of three vertical stripes: blue, white, and red (from left to right). The central white stripe is approximately one and a half times the width of the others.

The official explanation of the flag is as follows:

> The color red symbolizes the blood shed to protect our people, our land, our customs and our religion.
>
> The color white symbolizes the purity of our spirit.
>
> The color blue symbolizes the sky, where our mother, Maala Mecha, and our father, Achai Taa'ah, are at.
>
> The stars represent the cardinal directions, east, west, north and south.
>
> The moon represents our mother, Maala Mecha, the mother of all creation.

The sun represents our father, Achai Taa'ah, the father of all creation.

The black cross represents the memory of all our ancestors who have died in the many wars to protect our people, our land, our customs and our religion. (Pascua Yaqui Tribe, *The Significance of the Yaqui Flag*, undated pamphlet)

The flag is so well designed that one can find many interpretations of its graphical attempt to define the Pascua Yaquis. For example, the white stripe bears a black cross, alluding to both the Catholic faith of the Yaqui people and the Easter celebrations so important in modern Yaqui life. Above the cross and close to the red stripe, the new crescent moon (actually representing Maala Mecha) in yellow could denote Easter, which follows the first new moon of spring. Directly below the cross is a yellow sun (of Achai Taa'ah) that might also recall the rising sun of Easter Sunday, which revealed the miracle that is the center of the Christian faith—Christ's rising from the dead.

The sun has been depicted in various ways. The actual flag flying outside the Tribal Administration building bore a sun with thirty-two rays of varying width. Tribal documents show a flag with eight even rays similar to designs found in southwestern petroglyphs. A pamphlet entitled *The Significance of the Yaqui Flag* shows a sun with twelve triangular points. It is the sun that is significant, not its exact representation.

Each corner of the flag normally bears a five-pointed yellow star. The explanation has been given that these stars represent the prime directions, but they could just as easily represent the four Yaqui settlements in the Tucson area. These stars are not always represented on Pascua Yaqui flags. One photo, showing only a portion of a tribal flag, shows no stars at all. No definitive reason for the disappearing stars has been found, but one might hypothesize that the starred version represents all the Yaquis in central Arizona. The flag without stars may represent only the reservation itself.

Whatever the symbolism for the varying design elements of the Pascua Yaqui flag, they combine to represent an ancient people with a complex history and an evolving culture that continues to thrive in the twenty-first century.

Passamaquoddy Tribe of Maine

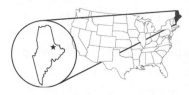

The Passamaquoddy Tribe of Maine was once part of the Abenaki Confederacy, an alliance of Algonquin-speaking tribes in the northeastern part of what is now the United States and the nearby regions of Canada (*ENAT*, 178). "Abenaki" means "People Who Dwell at the Sunrise" or "People of the Dawn." "Passamaquoddy" means "Those Who Pursue the Pollack," an important Atlantic food fish. The confederacy has been reawakened since the relighting of its fires in Restigouche, Québec, home of the Micmac people (Margaret Dana, letter dated 15 May 1997). The members of the confederacy are the Abenaki, Micmac, Passamaquoddy, and Penobscot Nations. The current flag of the Passamaquoddy people was adopted on a ninety-day trial basis in June 1995 (Passamaquoddy Tribal Council resolution, 8 June 1995). Because that trial period was never followed by other tribal legislation, the flag is considered official.

That new design (called the "scroll") is a white flag bearing the new seal of the Passamaquoddy Tribe. Around a central red circle, doubly edged in black, are four groups of five black stick figures, holding hands. Between these figures are the letters "N," "W," and "S" in black, representing compass points, and a black star edged in white and black, representing the eastern location of Passamaquoddy lands. These denote the unity of the Passamaquoddy "with all Native Americans from the North, South, East, and West" ("Interpretation of the Pleasant Point Passamaquoddy's Tribal Logo," unsigned, undated letter, Pleasant Point Reservation, Maine).

The red "Circle of Life" recalls the "Red Race" (ibid.). Within it are four plants depicted in yellows and greens, representing the eastern woodlands.

Black dots form an inner ring with the plants. Curving above the ring of dots in black is "PASSAMAQUODDY TRIBE" and below the ring "PEOPLE OF THE DAWN." Centered on the circle is a scroll and a "dripping feather," representing the 1980 settlement of land claims with the federal government. The scroll depicts a sunrise over the land at Passamaquoddy Bay and the sun's reflection on its waters, in natural colors. These images affirm the aboriginal rights of the people and a recognition that this bounty was given to the Passamaquoddy Tribe by the Great Spirit.

A previous, unofficial flag predated the settlement of land claims with the federal government. This dark-blue flag had many elements carried over to the current flag, including a large central yellow disk signifying the sun, the compass points and star, and the same words. Its central image, however, was a white pollack skewered by a pair of upward-pointing fishing spears, usually in black and forming a rough "X."

The Passamaquoddy delegate to the Maine legislature uses special automobile license plates bearing the tribal seal. The flag of the Passamaquoddy Tribe also flies at sea. Fishing boats belonging to members of the tribe frequently bear the tribal flag when plying the waters off Maine, in the sole known use of a tribal banner as a maritime ensign.

Pawnee Nation of Oklahoma

The Pawnee people were among the first United States Indians to encounter Europeans, starting with Francisco de Coronado in 1541. More recently, the Pawnees have migrated from their original homeland in what is now Texas to the Great Plains, ranging from Oklahoma through Nebraska. Today the Pawnees live in Oklahoma.

The name "Pawnee" is derived from the Caddoan *pariki* ("horn"), describing their unique hairstyle, an upright curved scalplock (*ENAT*, 179–81). The Indians of the Plains referred to the Pawnees as "Wolves" for their cunning and courage. This term translated into Pawnee as "Men of Men."

The current flag of the Pawnee Nation of Oklahoma, dating from 1977, reflects a long association with the United States ("The Flag of the Pawnee Indians—Pawnee Nation," Pawnee Nation of Oklahoma, unsigned, undated letter). It is blue and bears a small stylized representation of a U.S. flag in the upper left. The U.S. flag has a ring of thirteen six-pointed white stars.

The central symbol, a wolf's head, appears above a crossed tomahawk and sacred pipe, all in red. The wolf recalls the tribe's Plains name, while the other images represent peace and war. The wolf, tomahawk, and pipe all have narrow white borders. Below are seven white arrowheads for the wars in which Pawnees have fought in the service of the United States: the Indian Wars, the Spanish-American War, both world wars, the Korean War, the Vietnam War, and Desert Storm. At the top of the flag are blue, white, and red stripes; at the bottom, red, white, and blue stripes.

As a whole, the flag means "Pawnee Indians, in peace and war, always courageous and always loyal to America." Unique to the Pawnee flag are the specifics of the pole and finial atop the pole. The main Pawnee flag flown at tribal headquarters in Pawnee, Oklahoma, is mounted on an old-style Pawnee lance with a genuine flint spearhead. The shaft of the lance has a special strip of buckskin with intricate beadwork designs along the length of the staff. Attached to the spearhead at the top are four real eagle feathers, representing the four bands of the Pawnees.

(The bald eagle is a protected species in the United States; hunting it is illegal. Out of respect for the beliefs and customs of Native Americans, however, the Interior Department and the National Parks Service collect all bald eagles that die from natural causes, disease, or poaching and give the feathers to the various tribes for use in their ceremonies and customs.)

On Homecoming Days, Armistice Day, Christmas, and occasions of state, the Pawnees attach a sprig of cedar to the staff. Cedar, used in sacred ceremonies, is a token of peace and the prayers of the Pawnee people. The Pawnees consider their flag a sacred symbol—under Pawnee law it must never be desecrated or allowed to touch the ground.

Penobscot Tribe
of Maine

The Penobscots of eastern Maine are one of the two easternmost Native American peoples. "Penobscot," an Algonquin word meaning "the rocky place" (*ENAT*, 183–84), refers to the rocky falls of the Penobscot River—the home of the Penobscot people for centuries.

The flag of the Penobscot tribal government is white with the tribal seal in black (Brenda Fields, tribal administrator, letter dated 16 February 1995). The circular seal shows the bust of a Penobscot warrior—possibly Sockalexis—in profile, surrounded by an ornate border that resembles three tombstones, each forming a cross. On the arm of each cross is the name of one of the three virtues constituting the tribal motto—"PURITY," "FAITH," and "VALOR." In a ring around the bust is the name of the tribe in English and in Penobscot: "PENOBSCOT INDIAN NATION" and "BUR-NUR-WURB-SKEK" in black. Behind the warrior is a pine forest.

The three crosses symbolize the Holy Trinity (interview by Dave Martucci with Wayne Mitchell, Penobscot tribal land use officer). Each cross also carries a year: under "PURITY" is "1605," the year the Englishman Captain Weymouth kidnapped five Penobscots and took them to England; under "FAITH" is "1687," the year the first Catholic mission was established on Indian Island; under "VALOR" is "1612," the year of the war with the Eastern Abenakis. At the base of each of the three crosses, outside the circle, are tree branches representing tribal growth.

Two dates appear in a ring surrounding the portrait. At the top is "1669," commemorating the war with the Iroquois; at the bottom is "1749," marking the treaty of peace with Massachusetts that ended King George's War. The twelve flint fire starters in the ring symbolize the unity of the tribe. The entire seal has a serrated edge—a whole circle to represent the sun.

In addition to the tribal government flag, the Penobscot people have a "tribal flag" that hangs in the Tribal Council Chambers (ibid.) and has been described as multicolored, bearing a wikiyup and other symbols.

Peoria Tribe of Oklahoma

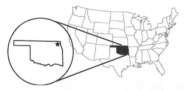

The Peoria Tribe of Oklahoma has a long and complicated history. The Peorias are a band of the Illinois Tribe, which was considered one of the westernmost groups of the Algonquin people. By 1833 continued encroachment by European-Americans had forced the Peorias, along with their fellow band of Illinois, the Kaskaskias, to move west to present-day Nebraska and Kansas. There they joined with two Miami bands, the Weas and the Piankashaws. These four bands, later relocated to what is now northeastern Oklahoma, are now known as the Peoria Tribe of Oklahoma (Peoria Tribe of Oklahoma, *Official Emblem of the Peoria Tribe of Indians of Oklahoma,* flyer, n.d.).

The flag of the Peorias of Oklahoma reflects this history. The seal of the Peoria Nation appears on a white background. On a red disk, which recalls the trials of the ancestors of the Peorias, is a large arrowhead, white on the flag but depicted in natural colors when used as a seal (copy of seal provided by Annin & Co., Roseland, N.J.). The large arrowhead, pointing downward as a sign of peace, represents the present generation of the Peoria people and their promise to work as individuals and as a tribe to cherish, honor, and preserve the heritage and customs left to them by preceding generations. The combination of the two emblems—the disk and the arrowhead—means that the Peorias will live in peace but will be suppressed by no one.

Four arrows cross the large arrowhead to form two overlapping "X"s: turquoise for the Piankashaws and the native soil; red for the Peorias and the sun; blue for the Weas and the waters; and green for the Kaskaskias and the grass and trees. The colors act as a reminder that the soil, sun, waters, and plants are gifts of the Great Spirit and should not be taken for granted. The arrows promise future generations that the spirit of a united Peoria people cannot be broken and that its heritage and customs will never be forgotten.

From the red disk hang five white-and-black eagle feathers, one for each elected member of the Peoria Tribal Business Committee: the chief, second chief, secretary-treasurer, and the first and second council members. The emblem was designed by tribal member Alice Giles Burgess and approved by the committee on 29 January 1983. It was presented to the tribal membership at the annual meeting the following March.

Apache Tribe of Oklahoma

Bay Mills Indian Community of the Sault Ste. Marie Band of Chippewa (Ojibwe) Indians

Cabazon Band of Cahuilla Mission Indians

Alabama-Quassarte Tribal Town (Creek)

Assiniboine and Sioux Tribes of the Fort Peck Indian Reservation

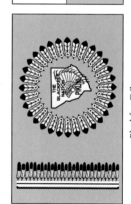

Bois Forte Band (Nett Lake) of Chippewas (Ojibwes)

Ak-Chin Indian Community (Tohono O'odham and Pima)

Aroostook Band of Micmac Indians of Maine

Blackfeet Tribe

Absentee-Shawnee Tribe of Indians of Oklahoma

Arapahoe Tribe of the Wind River Reservation

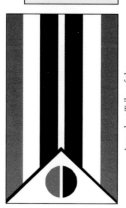

Big Pine Band of Owens Valley Paiute Shoshone Indians

Caddo Indian Tribe of Oklahoma

Catawba Indian Nation

Cherokee Nation

Cherokee Braves (historic)

Cheyenne and Arapaho Tribes of Oklahoma

Cheyenne River Sioux Tribe

Chickasaw Nation

Choctaw Nation of Oklahoma

Citizen Potawatomi Nation

Cocopah Tribe of Arizona

Coeur d'Alene Tribe

Colorado River Indian Tribes (CRIT)

Confederated Tribes of the Colville Reservation

Coquille Tribe of Oregon

Crow Tribe of Montana

Confederated Tribes and Bands of the Yakama Indian Nation

Confederated Tribes of the Warm Springs Reservation of Oregon

Cow Creek Sioux Tribe

Confederated Salish and Kootenai Tribes of the Flathead Reservation

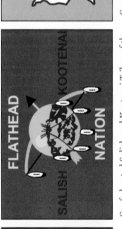

Confederated Tribes of the Umatilla Reservation

Cow Creek Band of Umpqua Indians of Oregon

Comanche Indian Tribe

Confederated Tribes of the Siletz Reservation

Coushatta Tribe of Louisiana

Eastern Band of Cherokee Indians of North Carolina

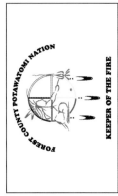

Forest County Potawatomi Community of Wisconsin Potawatomi Indians

Gila River Indian Community (Pima and Maricopa)

Delaware Tribe of Indians

Flandreau Santee Sioux Tribe of South Dakota

Fort Sill Apache Tribe of Oklahoma

Delaware Nation (formerly Delaware Tribe of Western Oklahoma)

Eastern Shoshone Tribe

Fort Mojave Indian Tribe (Mohave)— Arizona, California, and Nevada

Flag of Plenty Coups

Eastern Shawnee Tribe of Oklahoma

Fort Belknap Indian Community (Assiniboine and Gros Ventre)

Hopi Tribe of Arizona

Hoopa Valley Tribe

Ho-Chunk (Winnebago) Nation of Wisconsin

Hannahville Indian Community of Wisconsin
Potawatomi Indians of Michigan

Jamestown S'Klallam Tribe of Washington

Iroquois League

Iowa Tribe of Oklahoma

Hualapai Indian Tribe

Karuk Tribe of California

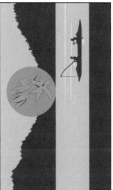

Kalispel (Pend d'Oreille) Indian Community

Kaibab Band of Paiute Indians

Jatibonicu Taino Tribal Nation of Borikén

Kiowa Indian Tribe of Oklahoma

Lower Elwha Tribal Community (Klallam)

Mashantucket Pequot Tribe of Connecticut

Kickapoo Tribe of Oklahoma

Lower Brulé Sioux Tribe

Makah Indian Tribe

Kialegee Tribal Town (Creek)

Leech Lake Band of Chippewas (Ojibwes)

Lummi Tribe

Kaw (Kanza) Nation

Lac du Flambeau Band of Lake Superior
Chippewa (Ojibwe) Indians

Loyal Shawnee Tribe

Mille Lacs Band of Chippewas (Ojibwes)

Miccosukee Tribe of Indians of Florida

Menominee Indian Tribe of Wisconsin

Muckleshoot Indian Tribe

Mohegan Indian Tribe of Connecticut

Modoc Tribe of Oklahoma

Miami Tribe of Oklahoma

Mississippi Band of Choctaw Indians

Navajo Nation

Muscogee (Creek) Nation (historic)

Muscogee (Creek) Nation

Minnesota Chippewa (Ojibwe) Tribe

Northern Cheyenne Tribe

Flag of Smohalla

Nez Percé Tribe of Idaho

Navajo Seal

Oneida Tribe of Wisconsin

Oneida Nation of New York

Omaha Tribe of Nebraska and Iowa

Oglala Sioux Tribe

Paiute Indian Tribe of Utah

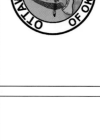

Ottawa Tribe of Oklahoma

Otoe-Missouria Tribe of Indians

Osage Tribe

Paiute-Shoshone Indians of the Bishop
Community of the Bishop Colony

Pascua Yaqui Tribe of Arizona

Passamaquoddy Tribe of Maine

Pawnee Nation of Oklahoma

Peoria Tribe of Oklahoma

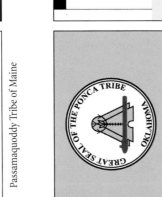

Poarch Band of Creek Indians of Alabama

Ponca Tribe of Indians of Oklahoma

Ponca Tribe of Nebraska

Pueblo de Cochiti

Pueblo of Cochiti

Pueblo of Nambé

Pueblo of Picuris

Pueblo of San Ildefonso

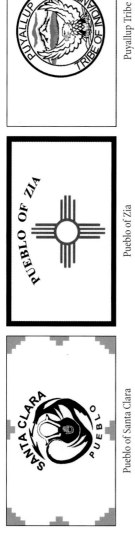

Pueblo of Santa Clara

Pueblo of Zia

Puyallup Tribe

Quapaw Tribe of Indians

Quileute Tribe

Quinault Tribe

Red Lake Band of Chippewa (Ojibwe) Indians

Reno-Sparks Indian Colony

Flag of Winnemucca

Rosebud Sioux Tribe

Sac and Fox Nation

Sac and Fox Tribe of the Mississippi in Iowa

Salt River Pima-Maricopa
Indian Community (de jure)

Sault Ste. Marie Tribe of Chippewa
(Ojibwe) Indians of Michigan

Seminole Tribe of Florida, Inc.

St. Regis Band of Mohawk
Indians of New York

Santee Sioux Tribe

Seminole Tribe of Florida

St. Croix Chippewa (Ojibwe)
Indians of Wisconsin

San Carlos Apache Tribe of the
San Carlos Reservation

Seminole Nation of Oklahoma (historic)

Saginaw Chippewa (Ojibwe)
Indian Tribe of Michigan

Salt River Pima-Maricopa Indian
Community (de facto)

Seminole Nation of Oklahoma

Sisseton and Wahpeton Sioux Tribe

Squaxin Island Tribe

Swinomish Indians

Seneca Nation of New York

Spokane Tribe

Suquamish Indian Tribe

Seneca-Cayuga Tribe of Oklahoma

Southern Ute Tribe

Stockbridge-Munsee Community
of Mohican Indians of Wisconsin

Seminole Tribe of Florida
(earlier flag)

Skull Valley Band of Goshute Indians of Utah

Standing Rock Sioux Tribe of
North and South Dakota

Tohono O'odham Nation of Arizona

Tulalip Tribes

Ute Indian Tribe of the Uintah and Ouray Reservation

Tlingit and Haida Tribes

Torres-Martinez Band of Cahuilla Mission Indians of California

Upper Skagit Indian Tribe of Washington

Three Affiliated Tribes of the Fort Berthold Reservation (Mandan, Hidatsa, and Arikara)

Tonto Apache Tribe of Arizona

United Keetoowah Band of Cherokee Indians of Oklahoma

Thlopthlocco Tribal Town (Creek)

Tonkawa Tribe of Oklahoma

Tunica-Biloxi Indian Tribe of Louisiana

Wichita and Affiliated Tribes

Yavapai-Prescott Tribe

Affiliated Tribes of Northwest Indians (ATNI)

White Mountain Apache Tribe

Yavapai-Apache Nation

Zuñi Tribe

White Earth Band of Chippewas (Ojibwes)

Yankton Sioux Tribe of South Dakota

YOSEMITE

MIWOK

Yosemite Miwoks (Jackson, Shingle Springs, and Tuolumne Rancherías)

Washoe Tribe of Nevada and California

Wyandotte Tribe of Oklahoma

Yavapai Tribe of the Fort McDowell Indian Community

United Sioux Tribes (UST)

Inter-Tribal Council of New England (ICONE)

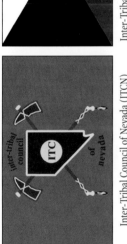

Inter-Tribal Council of Nevada (ITCN)

Inter-Tribal Council of California (ITCC)

Hawaiians

Chickamauga Cherokee Nation

Cherokee Tribe of Georgia

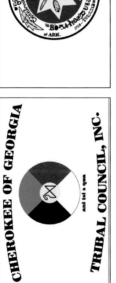

United South and Eastern Tribes (USET)

Metis Nation in New England (MNNE)

Jatibonicú Taíno Tribal Band of New Jersey

Ka Lahui Hawai'i

Independent Hawaiians

Piqua Sept of Ohio Shawnee Tribe

Southern Cherokee Nation

Wyandot Nation of Kansas

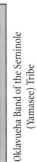

Oklavueha Band of the Seminole (Yamasee) Tribe

Southern Band of the Tuscarora Indian Tribe

Thunder Mountain Lenapé Nation

Micmac Nation

St. Francis Sokoki Band of Abenakis

Texas Cherokee Nation

Miami Nation of Indiana

Powhatan Renape Nation

Taino Turabo Aymaco Tribe of Borikén

Poarch Band
of Creek Indians
# of Alabama

The Poarch Creek Indians, who live in southern Alabama, number over 2,000. Their flag was created by the collaborative effort of John Kemp, Buford Rolin, Katherine Sells, and Creek chairman Eddie L. Tullis and may well be the only tribal flag with a "Registered Trademark" ® symbol on it.

In the poem "Tribal Symbol," tribal member Larry Jackson describes the flag:

> Red stands for the red sticks a fighting man
> He would fight to the death for his land
> The white in the feather meant a friendly clan
> They lived near the rivers and played in the sand
> The circle of gold stands for the place we live
> With lovely sunset and the land has so much to give
> Green is for the color of the corn and the trees
> Corn for life and trees for seed
> Direction of travel is shown by the logs
> No matter which you take
> It must come from the heart
> The line of red is blood in the vein,
> Throughout all the nations, all is not the same
> The feathers are the nations, nations of two
> Lifestyles are different but the words are true.

The tribe's seal appears on the medium-green background of the flag. The seal consists of a white cross with pointed ends in the four cardinal directions. The Poarch Creeks call the bars of this cross "logs." A yellow ring edged in black is superimposed on the cross with the words "POARCH" above and "INDIANS" below, separated by small red circles. Within the ring, on the center of the horizontal log, is the word "CREEK." All the lettering is in a red typeface trade-named "Southern." A small black ® appears slightly to the right of the lower end of the vertical "log."

The cross and the ring fit exactly inside an imaginary square set on its corner, with each side roughly one-third the length of the flag. Red stripes, forming the middle third of the logs, recall the red saltire (diagonal cross) of Alabama. The vertical stripes start near the center of the disk, while the horizontal stripes start outside the yellow outer ring.

At the ends of the horizontal log hang two feathers. The left feather is black with a red central element and white accents and has a jagged red trim at the top; it is attached to the horizontal log with three beads of red, white, and red. To the left side of the feather are two black-bordered colored beads (the top one yellow, the bottom one red) attached with thin black ties to the left end of the log. At the bottom of the feather are two more black-bordered beads attached with ties to the lower tip of the feather (the upper one red, the lower one yellow).

The right feather is also black with white accents but has a white central element and a white jagged trim at the top; it is attached to the horizontal log with three beads of yellow, red, and yellow. To the right and at the bottom of the feather is the same arrangement of beads as on the left feather, but with reversed colors.

According to the Poarch Creeks, "The circle symbolizes the Circle of Life; the green background stands for the forest and the green corn from which the Creek gathered their subsistence; the four logs mark the four directions. The white feather represents the white or friendly Creek town and clans, while the red feather denotes the red warrior towns and clans. The red strips symbolize the blood of the Creeks spent in their efforts to maintain their homelands. The red and yellow beads stand for trading with neighbors."

Thanks to Daniel McGhee and Lori Findley from the Community Relations Department of the Poarch Creeks for the explanation of the symbolism of their tribal flag and the poem.

Ponca Tribe of Indians of Oklahoma

Those Poncas who remained in the Indian Territory (today Oklahoma) when Chief Standing Bear and his clan returned to what is now Nebraska (see Ponca Tribe of Nebraska) form the basis of the Ponca Tribe of Oklahoma. The name "Ponca" means "Sacred Head." The modern Poncas, descendants of those forcibly exiled by the federal government in 1877, now number more than 2,500.

The flag of the Ponca Tribe of Oklahoma is a golden buff-yellow field with the tribal seal in the center. The seal is a white disk with an image of three clustered tipis. When the Poncas went on their two annual buffalo hunts, they lived in tipis. The remainder of the year they resided in fortified towns in lodges made of earth or covered with buffalo hides. At the top point where the three tipis meet is a circle representing the sun. These elements are the same golden yellow as the flag's field.

In front of the tipis is a red pipe. In years past, the Ponca people lived in the area of Pipestone National Monument in southwestern Minnesota (*ENAT*, 196). Pipestone is a major source of the fiery red stone catlinite used to make the pipes employed by many tribes.

Circling the tipis and pipe is the legend "GREAT SEAL OF THE PONCA TRIBE" in the upper portion of the seal in black, with the word "OKLA-HOMA" at the bottom. The tribal seal is widely used by the Poncas. For example, the Ponca Tribal Police use a shoulder patch on their uniforms bearing the tipis and pipe emblem from the seal.

Ponca Tribe of Nebraska

In 1877 the Poncas, a tribe whose historical roots lay along the banks of the Niobrara River in what is now north-central Nebraska along the border with South Dakota, were forcibly relocated to the Indian Territory (modern Oklahoma). Due to the harsh conditions, the lack of arable land, and the terrible winter of their first year in their new home, nearly a quarter of the Ponca Tribe died. Among the dead was the son of the Ponca chief, Standing Bear. The chief had promised his son that he would be buried in his old homeland along the Niobrara.

To keep his promise, Chief Standing Bear and more than sixty members of his clan began a long funeral procession back to northern Nebraska. Shortly after they reached their traditional home, they were arrested by a detachment of the U.S. Cavalry and were imprisoned in Omaha.

In 1879 a judge ruled that the Poncas of Chief Standing Bear had the same right as any people to return to their home. Shortly after the trial the federal government granted the Ponca Tribe a reservation along the Niobrara (*ENAT*, 196–97). Today the descendants of Chief Standing Bear's clan still live in Nebraska and South Dakota in the area of the Niobrara, where their flag now flies.

The Ponca flag has a white field bearing the tribal seal in black and white in the center. Bordering the flag are four bars of different colors. Along the left edge is a white stripe, stopping just short of the base of the flag. Along that base, ending close to the right edge, is a yellow stripe. The right edge bears a red stripe that terminates just shy of the top. And the top edge bears a black stripe that almost reaches the left edge of the flag. These are the traditional four sacred colors of many Native Americans, standing for the four prime directions and the four human races. Four, which many tribes consider a sacred number, can also represent the seasons and other natural elements that come in fours. A Ponca named Jerri Cross designed the flag. (*Indian Center Museum—The Gallery of Nations* [Wichita, Kansas: Indian Center Museum, 1996], 9).

The seal has as its basis a spirit hoop, sometimes referred to as a dreamcatcher. From the hoop dangle four black-and-white eagle feathers, reiterating the sacred number four. At the center of the spirit hoop is a tipi. On its right are a sacred pipe and two crossed arrows, symbolizing both peace and friendship. On the left of the tipi are the sun and what appears to be a staff bearing a Ponca headdress. This may be a representation of the "Sacred Head" (which is the meaning of the name "Ponca"). Arcing over the spirit hoop is the name "Ponca Tribe of Nebraska" in black.

Pueblo of Cochiti—
New Mexico

The Rio Grande in New Mexico has served as the life's blood for the Pueblo Indians for centuries. The deserts of New Mexico make water a precious resource, which led the Keres-speaking people of the Pueblo of Cochiti to settle along the western banks of the river long before the coming of the Europeans and names like "New Mexico" or "Rio Grande."

The approximately 1,000 members of the Pueblo of Cochiti now hold 28,000 acres out of a land that was once vast and free (*REAI*, 17). They are one of seven pueblos that speak the Keres language, the others being Acoma, Laguna, San Felipe, Santa Ana, Santo Domingo, and Zia (*ENAT*, 209).

The flag of the Pueblo of Cochiti is light yellow or buff, bearing the tribal seal in the center and "PUEBLO DE COCHITI" (the pueblo's name in Spanish) arching above it in black.

The pueblo's seal is a golden circle edged in black and then blue. Within the seal appears a ceremonial drum used for dances and other rites. The beating surface and the lacing are black. The lower triangles formed by the lacings are blue, while the upper triangles are red. Along the top and bottom of the sides of the drum are white bands separated from the triangles by narrow black stripes. On the golden disk the words "PUEBLO DE COCHITI" appear in red above the central drum and "NEW MEXICO" below it.

Pueblo of Nambé— New Mexico

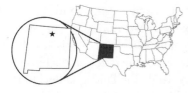

The 19,000-acre Pueblo of Nambé (*NAA,* 281) is home to about 400 members (*REAI,* 30) of the Tiwa Nation, one of four tribes of Pueblo Indians along the Rio Grande (*ENAT,* 206–09). The others are the Keres, Tewas, and Towas.

The Pueblo of Nambé flag is the tribal seal on a white background. In the center of the seal is a light-brown outline drawing of a kiva, the ceremonial center of pueblo life. Two uprights of a ladder extend from the entrance hole in the roof. This is an image of the actual kiva found in the Pueblo of Nambé. It is surrounded by an ornamental ring representing the "circle of life," composed of light-brown triangles on the exterior and dark-brown triangles on the interior, separated by a narrow white border.

On either side of the seal appear stylized corn plants, a major source of sustenance for the pueblo, whose pollen is frequently used in religious rites. The plants are green, with yellow pollen-bearing tips. Beneath each of these two corn stalks are three light-brown triangles of earth pointing apex-downward, edged in white and dark brown. The legend "NAMBÉ O-WEEN-GÉ," meaning "village of Nambé," arches in black over the entire design. The design was proposed by a member of the tribe.

Thanks to Michelle Mirabel of the Nambé governor's office for information about the flag.

Pueblo of Picuris— New Mexico

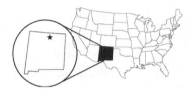

Located about twenty miles south of the city of Taos, New Mexico, is the 1,500-acre reservation of the Pueblo of Picuris. It is the second-smallest of the nineteen pueblos in New Mexico (only the Pojoaque Pueblo is smaller). Approximately 200 people reside within the boundaries of the reservation. Picuris is one of four pueblos that are home to the Tiwa-speaking people of the Rio Grande area, the others being Isleta, Sandia, and Taos. The remaining fifteen pueblos belong to the Keres, Tewa, or Zuñi people.

The flag of the Picuris Pueblo is probably white and bears the seal of the pueblo in the center. The colors of the seal are reminiscent of the pottery of the pueblos of the Southwest, brownish-red and black with a little blue. The seal is essentially a circle, with the name "PICURIS" on top and "PUEBLO" on the bottom in black. One the left side of the seal is a small antelope (a major source of meat) and an example of local pottery, while the right side has a feather and two stalks of corn, the main source of food for centuries.

In the center is a representation of a reddish-brown pueblo, complete with a ladder to access the roof entrance. The red-brown color recalls the adobe brick of the pueblo. All New Mexico pueblos except for those of the Zuñis are made of adobe. On top of the pueblo is a fire (shown in blue), with its smoke rising into a stylized raincloud. The building lies upon an arch that may represent a hilltop or a rainbow; the exact meaning is unknown. This hill/rainbow is composed of a red-brown structure over a blue stripe. The reddish-brown raincloud is a stepped pyramid like those found in Mexico, Guatemala, and Belize. At the base of the cloud is a blue stripe with three white elements above it (the largest one in the center): the upper parts of these are semicircles, which taper downward into a pair of concave arches terminating in a point. From the blue stripe descend vertical blue lines representing rain, a precious gift to the arid lands of New Mexico. The central device is bracketed by two blue lightning bolts, which barely touch the roof of the pueblo.

Pueblo of San Ildefonso— New Mexico

Silver and turquoise jewelry and pottery of reds and black and other natural shades come to mind when one thinks of the artwork of the Southwest. These are also the things that inspire the symbols of the Pueblo of San Ildefonso.

Located approximately twenty miles northwest of Santa Fe, New Mexico, the Pueblo of San Ildefonso is home to about 600 members of the Tewa-speaking Pueblo Indians, making it one of the smaller pueblos in population. San Ildefonso has a rich artistic heritage: some of the finest Native American pottery comes from the region. Several noted modern potters have emerged for San Ildefonso.

The seal of the pueblo depicts a bird in the distinctive artistic style of the Tewas, using the four main colors found in the arts of New Mexico. The legs and lower body of the figure are turquoise. The head and wings are the deep reddish rust color of the clays found in the area. The tail feathers, the end of the wing, and the eye are black and white. The artistic style of the bird recalls the designs found on the pottery and jewelry produced by the people of San Ildefonso.

The bird rests on a white disk that bears the name "San Ildefonso Pueblo" in turquoise arcing across the top and "TEWA" in black below it. The white disk is enclosed by a silver-gray ring with the phrase "Where the water cuts through" in English at the bottom and in Tewa at the top: "Po-Woh-Ge-Oweenge." This lettering is in the same reddish rust color as the bird's head.

When used on the pueblo's flag, the seal rests on a field of silver-gray. The overall look of the flag suggests silver jewelry bedecked with pieces of turquoise, black onyx, white quartz, and red coral. It is a graphic tribute to hundreds of years of artistic talent found in a small pueblo just up the road from Santa Fe.

Pueblo of Santa Clara— New Mexico

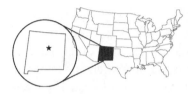

Four tribes constitute the eastern Pueblo Indians along the Rio Grande in central New Mexico: the Keres, Tiwas (see Pueblo of Nambé), Tewas, and Towas (*ENAT*, 206–9). (The western Pueblo Indians are the Hopis and the Zuñis [see Hopi Tribe of Arizona and Zuñi Tribe].) The 2,500 residents of the nearly 50,000 acres of the Santa Clara Pueblo belong to the Tano-Tewa or Tewa Tribe.

Flying over the Pueblo of Santa Clara is a flag designed by a former governor of the pueblo, Edwin Tafoya. He presented the design as a gift to his tribe. Light-blue "step" designs appear in each corner of a white background and centered on each edge. The corner designs have four steps; the edge designs have two. These patterns recall the pueblo architecture and adobe structures of the Indian nations of New Mexico.

Santa Clara is famous for pottery with distinctive black and white coloring. At the flag's center is a wedding vase in black with a white outline of a bear claw, symbolizing strength and protection. A "water serpent" image, common in Santa Clara pottery, surrounds the wedding vase in black. Curving around the central image are the words "SANTA CLARA" above and "PUEBLO" in smaller letters below.

As manufactured locally, the flag is nearly square (approximate ratio of 1.2 long by 1 tall), rather than having the rectangular proportions common in commercially manufactured flags.

Pueblo of Zia— New Mexico

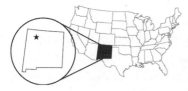

Pueblo means "village" in Spanish, but for Native Americans it describes villages with a specific type of architecture: the multifamily, multistory structures built by certain tribes in the southwestern United States. Six main nations are considered "Pueblo Indians": the Hopis of Arizona, the Zuñis of the New Mexico–Arizona border regions, and the four tribes along the Rio Grande in New Mexico—the Tiwas, Tewas, Towas, and Keres (*ENAT,* 206–9).

The Pueblo of Zia is part of the Keres Nation. This pueblo has been occupied continuously since about A.D. 1250 (Pueblo of Zia, *Welcome to the Pueblo of Zia,* undated pamphlet). The current Zia Pueblo Reservation includes about 118,000 acres (*AIDD,* 42) approximately thirty-five miles northwest of Albuquerque, New Mexico. From this pueblo came New Mexico's very recognizable state emblem, the Zia sun symbol.

Dr. Harry Mera, designer of New Mexico's flag, was a physician and an anthropologist at the Museum of Anthropology in Santa Fe. His design was inspired by a pot on display in the museum (Leslie Linthicum, "Native Sun," article from an unidentified magazine, n.d.). That pot, made by an anonymous Zia potter in the late 1800s, featured a circle of white ringed in red with three rays emanating from each of the four cardinal directions. In the center were two triangular eyes and a rectangular mouth in black. Mera simplified the design into the red ring with four rays that forms the striking symbol of New Mexico today. In 1925 New Mexico adopted Mera's burgundy sun on a field of gold as its state flag.

To the Zia people, the sun design is an ancient symbol. It reflects tribal philosophy with its wealth of pantheistic spiritualism, teaching the basic harmony of all things in the universe (State of New Mexico, *The Zia Sun*

Symbol, undated pamphlet). Four is a sacred number to the Zias, as it is to many other Native American peoples. It recalls the four directions, the four seasons, the phases of the day (sunrise, noon, evening, and night), and the four stages of life (childhood, youth, adulthood, and old age). Four also signifies the number most often used by the "Giver of All Good Gifts." The Zias believe that humans have four sacred obligations—to develop a strong body, a clear mind, a pure spirit, and a devotion to the well-being of their people.

To celebrate their link with the prime symbol of the state in which they live, the Zias have adopted a white flag featuring the red Zia sun symbol exactly as it appears on the state flag (Stanley Pino, governor, Pueblo of Zia, letter dated 21 March 1995). Above the Zia sun arches the inscription "PUEBLO OF ZIA" in black, and a black border surrounds the flag (drawing provided by the Office of the Governor, Pueblo of Zia). The combination of red, white, and black recalls the work of that anonymous potter of over a century ago.

Puyallup Tribe— Washington

The original Puyallup Reservation was established by the Medicine Creek Treaty of 1854 and consisted of 1,280 acres. On 20 January 1856 the reservation was enlarged to 18,062 acres. The people raised wheat, oats, and hay on natural meadows near tidal flats. The Puyallups had a trade school for Indians of all tribes in 1906. The allotment of the reservation ended in 1886.

The growing population of Tacoma caused its citizens to seek removal of restrictions on allotted reservation lands. The first result was that on 19 August 1890 Congress authorized the sale of Puyallup Reservation tracts. Then an act on 3 March 3 1893 provided a commission to select and appraise portions of allotments that were not required for Indian homes and part of an agency tract that was not needed for school purposes. The land selected and appraised was set for sale by public auction.

The 1893 statute provided that the reservation land not sold would remain in Indian hands and not be sold for ten years. After that period non-Indians could deal directly with the Indians. Half of the reservation was sold during this time.

The Puyallup Tribe's constitution was approved by the secretary of the interior on 13 May 1936. The governing body is the Puyallup Tribal Council. In a suit on 20 February 1984 the United States Supreme Court upheld a U.S. Circuit Court of Appeals ruling that twelve acres taken over by the Port of Tacoma in 1950 belonged to the Puyallups. In February President George H. Bush signed a bill settling Puyallup tribal claims against federal government. The tribe was paid $77.25 million.

To show its sovereignty, the Puyallup Tribe uses a white flag bearing the tribal seal in the center. The main element of that seal is the eagle, a recurring theme in the flags and seals of tribes in the Northwest. The Puyallup seal depicts a white eagle with yellow beak and talons whose outspread wings point upward. The talons rest on a white branch or rock. Behind the eagle can be seen a mountain of the Cascade Range, towering above a landscape of conifer forests and a blue river. Surrounding the central device is a white ring bearing the name "PUYALLUP TRIBE OF INDIANS" in black. In addition to being used on flags, the seal has been reproduced in many other forms, including blanket-like "throws," one of which was displayed at a conference of the Associated Tribes of Northwest Indians in Portland, Oregon (*A Guide to the Indian Tribes of the Pacific Northwest*, 166–69; copyright © 1986, 1992 by the University of Oklahoma Press).

Quapaw Tribe of Indians— Oklahoma

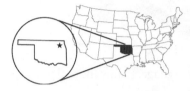

The Quapaw or Ogahpah or Ugakhpa people are so called because they formerly lived along the west banks of the Mississippi River, south of most other Siouan-speaking tribes. "Ogahpah" means "Downstream People." The Algonquins and the French gave them another name: "Arkansas," which meant "Bow People of the South Wind." It is from this nation that both the river and the state derive their names.

In the original homeland of the Quapaws grew a bush called the Osage Orange whose wood was excellent for making bows. The French dubbed this land "aux arcs" or "at the place of the bows." This term has since been corrupted into Ozarks, the name of the mountain chain running through Arkansas and southern Missouri (*ENAT*, 209–10).

During the colonial era the Quapaws avoided war with the Europeans, living in a region visited by few white explorers of any colonial power. By the early 1800s, however, the Quapaws were force to cede much of their homeland to the ever-increasing white settlers. By 1824 they had agreed to move to what is now Texas along the Red River. Because the Red River frequently flooded their new home, the Quapaws returned to the Arkansas area. By 1833, with complaints from the white population, the federal government forced the Quapaws to move to the Indian Territory. In 1867 they were again forced to sign over the bulk of their lands. Today the Quapaws retain only a small parcel of Historic Trust Lands—less than 13,000 acres.

Fortunately, both lead and zinc deposits were found on the territory remaining in the hands of the Quapaw people in 1905. This mineral wealth has provided a source of income for the Quapaw Nation.

Until recently, the flag of the Quapaw Nation was dark blue and bore the tribal seal in the center. Above the seal was the word "O-GAH-PAH,"

the name of the Quapaws in their Siouan language. Below the seal was the legend "Quapaw Tribe." All lettering was in white.

The seal of the Quapaws (copy of seal provided by Annin & Co., Roseland, N.J.) represents an Indian shield depicting a bison standing upon a green base before a light-blue sky (sometimes with clouds). The Quapaws followed the lifestyle of the Plains Indians in the past, so the bison was the essential creature in their world. Ringing the central image is a dark-red and white rough edging, representing the rawhide material from which the shield was originally made. Hanging from the top, bottom, and sides of the shield are four eagle feathers. As with many other Native American peoples, the feathers recall the four directions: east, south, west, and north.

Recently, the original flag was altered by dropping the designation "Quapaw Tribe," leaving only the tribe's name in its native language: "O-GAH-PAH." The field of the flag was also changed. Now only the left side is dark blue. The right side is red. The change must have occurred sometime after 1995, when the Quapaw Tribal Headquarters confirmed that the flag was blue only. The symbolism of the added red is not known. The official flag also bears a vertical yellow bar (which runs behind the shield) dividing the red and blue halves. On the blue side an extremely narrow yellow line borders a wider red stripe, then a narrow yellow strip, followed by a wider red stripe and finally the main yellow bar that divides the flag. The same pattern appears on the red side of the flag, except that the base color is blue accented by yellow lines. A simpler version of the flag also exists, which omits the entire central division, allowing the blue half to touch the red.

Quileute Tribe— Washington

The Quileutes belong to the Northwest Coast peoples whose diverse cultural groups predate by several millennia the European exploration of North America. Their tribal lands on the Olympic Peninsula near La Push, Washington, overlook the Pacific Ocean about forty miles south of Cape Flattery, the state's northwestern tip. A principal aspect of their culture was the killer whale (orca) hunt—an ordeal that lasted many days, using mussel-shell-tipped harpoons, spruce-root ropes, and an ocean-going canoe of red cedar.

The Quileute Tribal Council adopted the flag after a contest in the late 1980s, nearly a century after federal recognition in 1889. Its background is light gold or beige. The name "Quileute Tribe" in heavy black cursive script appears on a black-bordered red banner across the top of the central design, which is contained in an irregular semicircle with the light-gold (or beige) sky above and the blue ocean below.

A large black canoe dominates the lower part of the ocean. Two angled red stripes mark each end, with the words "Since 1889" in thin white cursive script between them. At either end of the canoe a stylized white killer whale is outlined and highlighted with heavy black borders. In the background are two light-brown islands, with dark-brown highlights and green fir trees and grassy moss. Between and above the islands float three black eagles under billowing white clouds. Below the central image is "La Push, Washington" in heavy black cursive script.

Each design element is important to the identity of the Quileute people. The ocean provided not only food but clothing, tools, and spiritual cleansing as well. The strongest of the five men's societies was dedicated to the

whale. The canoe—the essential means of transportation for all Northwest Coast peoples—represents the Quileutes' past way of life and brings
them together as a people in the present. The islands, A-KA-Lat or James
Island and Little James Island, lie just offshore from the mouth of the
Quileute River. A-KA-Lat, site of the oldest Quileute villages, was also used
as a fortress and as a burial site for chiefs. Eagles often fly over this island
and nest there.

Thanks to Barbara Bocek from the Quileute Historic Preservation Office for the picture and description of the flag and to Allen Black for important details.

Quinault Tribe— Washington

The Quinaults, members of the Coastal Salish peoples, have lived along the Pacific coast of Washington for perhaps thousands of years, enjoying rich hunting, abundant fishing, and a mild climate (*NAA*, 285).

As with most Coastal Salish peoples, fishing was the Quinalts' primary occupation, using enormous canoes. Explorers Lewis and Clark described the canoes: "upward of fifty feet long, and will carry 8,000 to 10,000 pounds' weight, of from 20 to 30 persons" (*NAA*, 415). The seal of the Quinault Nation celebrates and commemorates these great canoes. The seal, which appears on the plain white field of the flag, is enclosed by a light-blue ring with "QUINAULT" at the top, "INDIAN" across the center on a light-blue bar, and "NATION" at the bottom, all in white.

The upper section of the seal shows a Pacific coastal island scene, with green trees and black-and-white landscape elements. In the lower section a brown eagle with outstretched wings—a symbol of fishing prowess to many Pacific Northwest tribes—flies above a large brown Quinault canoe. The eagle and canoe contrast with an orange setting sun in the background, which signifies the home of the Quinault people in the westernmost reaches of the continent. The seal has a very light blue background.

Red Lake Band
of Chippewa
(Ojibwe) Indians—
Minnesota

One of the northernmost bands and reservations of the Chippewa or Anishinabe people found in the United States, the 565,000-acre reservation belonging to the Red Lake Band, is found in north-central Minnesota (*NAA*, 280). The centerpiece is the large Red Lake for which the reservation is named. That lake (which is actually two lakes—Upper Red Lake and Lower Red Lake—connected by a very narrow mouth) is also the focus of the seal of the Red Lake Band, which appears on a white flag.

The seal of the Red Lake Band bears the image of both Upper and Lower Red Lake as well as several of the rivers that feed the lakes. Below the lakes is a grove of coniferous trees recalling the pine forests of northern Minnesota.

These central images are surrounded by a ring edged in red. Across the top of the ring in black appear seven totem animals of the Ojibwe people, which also reflect the wildlife of the area. The Bear, Turtle, Bullhead, Otter, Eagle, Marten (the largest of the weasels), and Kingfisher totems represent the various Ojibwe clans. In the lower part of the ring is the legend "RED LAKE NATION" in red. Hanging from this circular seal are two eagle feathers, recalling the warrior shields of the past.

Reno-Sparks Indian Colony—Nevada

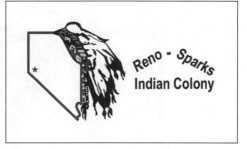

The Reno-Sparks Colony is located, appropriately, in the area around the cities of Reno and Sparks in the westernmost corner of Nevada. It is home to some 650 members of two tribes whose historic areas span much of the central Far West (*REAI*, 29). The Washoes are mostly found in central California and Nevada, while the Paiutes stretch from Oregon through California, Nevada, Utah, and northern Arizona. Both tribes are known for the small numbers of tribal members found in any one location. Altogether there are twenty-three reservations, colonies, and rancherías across the West that are home to the Paiutes, while the Washoes have five separate sites.

The Reno-Sparks Colony has a straightforward white flag with the legend "Reno-Sparks Indian Colony" in black letters on the right. On the left half is a map of Nevada in blue outline, with a blue star to show the location of the colony. Hanging from the northeastern corner of the map is an impressive headdress with a mass of white-and-black feathers. The band of the headdress is depicted in ornate detail. The quills of the feathers are red. The band is medium blue, like the map and star, but features beadwork designs in black, blue, yellow, and red. Draping from the headdress are more beadwork designs: the one closest to the map is composed of blue, yellow, and red beads, while the farther one is shown in yellow and black. The date of adoption of this flag is unknown.

Another flag associated with the Paiute Tribe in Nevada is that of Chief Winnemucca or Truckee (which means "all right"). Chief Winnemucca was actually associated with the Pyramid Lake Paiutes, but his memory deserves to be included with the only Nevada Paiutes listed in this text. Chief Winnemucca served as Captain John C. Fremont's guide into California in the 1840s and always remained on  good terms with the white hordes moving into and through the lands of the Paiutes. For his service to the government of the United States, he was awarded a personal flag, one of only two known to have been granted to Indian chiefs (the other is the flag of Chief Plenty Coups [see Crow Tribe of Montana]). Winnemucca's flag was essentially a United States flag with a special blue corner (called the canton), showing an upright tomahawk with its blade facing the pole. On the tomahawk was a crossed pair of arrows, forming an "X." Chief Winnemucca is known from some old photos to have carried his personal flag in parades in Carson City in the 1880s.

Rosebud Sioux Tribe— South Dakota

Along South Dakota's southern border lies the Rosebud Reservation, the sixth most populous reservation in the United States, home to more than 9,600 members of various bands of the Lakota people (*AIA,* 43). It takes its name from Rosebud Creek.

The reservation claims one of the oldest tribal flags of any United States Indian nation, designed in a contest in the early 1960s (James R. Abér, "Symbols of the Rosebud Sioux Tribe," *Flag Bulletin* 36:2 [March/April 1997]: 64–71). For a long time after the adoption of the design, the flag existed solely on paper because its complex graphics made it too expensive to manufacture.

Eventually, tribal elders approached Julie Peneaux, secretary of the Rosebud Tribal Office, who sewed as a hobby and agreed to make a flag from the design. Until 2002 she was the sole manufacturer of Rosebud Sioux flags, having sewn six (Julie Peneaux, letter dated 11 May 1995).

In the flag's elaborate design, twenty red "roses" in an oval ring (wider than it is tall) represent the twenty Rosebud Sioux communities. Each rose bears a white Sioux tipi in its center, oriented outward (*Explanation of the Design of the Rosebud Sioux Flag,* undated pamphlet). The ring of roses encircles a three-layered rainbow-colored diamond or "god's eye," which stands for the reservation itself. The innermost layer is yellow, the middle blue, and the outer layer red. A blue cross on white in the center of the diamond recalls the pipe of peace and the extension of friendship to all who come to the reservation (flag provided by the Rosebud Sioux Tribal Headquarters). The cross is actually a bule, two crossed lines representing the number four.

Arching over the diamond in blue is "ROSEBUD SIOUX TRIBE," flanked by a pair of white-and-black eagle feathers above a pair of orange sacred pipe heads; below it is "ROSEBUD, SOUTH DAKOTA," also in blue. The feathers signify achievement of goals—an eagle feather was once only worn as a symbol of a great deed; the sacred pipes allude to the peaceful relations between the tribe and the United States. Around the outer edge of the flag is a red border of small triangles, echoing the traditional tipi with red triangles around the bottom, which welcomed visitors seeking food and shelter.

The white field—for purity—represents the north, from which the snows come. Red—a ceremonial color for thunder, lightning, and forms of plant and animal life—refers to the sunrise and the east. Yellow—for the land of sunshine, a nickname for South Dakota—signifies the south. Blue—recalling water, wind, the sky, clouds, the moon, and the day—symbolizes the west. Black stands for the night and the mysteries of life. Although orange is without specific significance, it joins the colors red and yellow, thus bringing together the land and the plants and animals that dwell upon it.

Sac and Fox Nation— Oklahoma

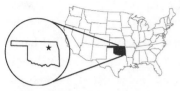

The seal of the largest of the three Sac and Fox bands (see Sac and Fox Tribe of the Mississippi in Iowa) honors two noted members: the athlete Jim Thorpe and the great chief Black Sparrow Hawk (or Black Hawk). The circular seal (provided by the Sac and Fox Tribal Library) bears a black and white depiction of a sparrow hawk with a shield on its chest. The colors black and white refer to the two social classes of the tribe, the Oskacla and the Kiskoa (Juanita Goodreau, library assistant, letter dated 6 January 1995). The shield contains symbols of the four countries with which the Sac and Fox people had alliances: Spain, France, Britain, and the United States.

Above the hawk emblem, five Olympic rings recall the great Sac champion Jim Thorpe, one of the finest athletes of all time. A black ribbon arches overhead between the tips of the hawk's wings, with the legend "MA-KA-TAI-ME-SHE-KIA-KIAK" ("Black Sparrow Hawk") in white (*The Sac & Fox Emblem,* undated pamphlet). A red band encircling the seal reads "SAC & FOX" above and "NATION" below in white. On the flag the seal is centered on a light-gray field.

Chief Black Sparrow Hawk or simply Black Hawk opposed the forced eviction of his Sac people from their lands straddling the Mississippi River at the village of Saukenuk, now Rock Island. In 1832, aided by the shaman Winnebago Prophet, Black Hawk rallied various tribes to his cause. He led this alliance in a desperate but ultimately losing war against the white settlers; he is now honored as a man of principle and honesty who knew what was right for his people. Jim Thorpe in his own life had to overcome adversity to achieve greatness, had his Olympic medals taken away from him, yet continued—never giving up. The seal and flag pay tribute to two men who represent great ideals for the Sac and Fox people.

Sac and Fox Tribe of the Mississippi in Iowa

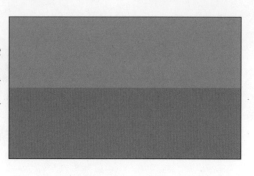

The Sacs or Sauks, an Algonquin word meaning "Yellow Earth People," and the Fox or Meskwakis, meaning "Red Earth People," originated in what is now Illinois and Wisconsin (*ENAT*, 210–12). Today the two tribes, which have been close allies and friends since joining in 1734 to repulse attacks by an alliance of the Ojibwes and the French (*ENAT*, 86–87), occupy three distinct reservations in Iowa, Kansas, and Oklahoma.

The Sac and Fox Tribe of the Mississippi in Iowa has a parcel of land in central Iowa known as the Meskwaki Indian Settlement. This Iowa band possesses a flag of simple design but complex meaning. The bicolor flag of green over red signifies that the two nations have come together as one people (sketch and explanation provided by the Sac and Fox Tribal Headquarters).

Green symbolizes life, peace, and spring and represents the "peace chief," one of the three members of the tribal authority. Red stands for death, war, autumn (a time when much of life fades away), and the "war chief." (The third member, the shaman or "ceremonial chief," is not represented.) When war was imminent, the traditional white feathers of tribal sacred pipes would be replaced by red feathers.

Saginaw Chippewa (Ojibwe) Indian Tribe of Michigan

The state motto of Michigan is *Si Quaeris Peninsulam Amoenam Circumspice* (If You Seek a Pleasant Peninsula, Look about You). No people can attest to the truth of that motto better than the Saginaw Chippewas. Located on the Isabella Reservation in Mt. Pleasant, Michigan, the Saginaw Chippewas are almost at the center of the Lower Peninsula, about sixty miles north of the capital, Lansing. The reservation of more than 1,100 acres is home to nearly 1,000 members of the tribe. The entrance to the reservation is dominated by the immense Soaring Eagle Casino and Resort.

Inside the casino is a showcase displaying the emblem of the Saginaw Chippewas and a photo of the designer, Julius Peters, a tribal member. The logo of the Saginaw Chippewas was designed in the early 1970s as part of a contest. It was first displayed publicly on a float in a 1973 parade. That logo has appeared on both versions of the flag of the Saginaw Chippewa Nation.

In the words of Julius Peters, the designer:

This logo not only represents the Saginaw Chippewa Tribe, but it symbolizes two very important people that had a major impact on my life. At the age of seven, I lost my mother. I then went on to live with my Grandfather and my Grandmother. The middle of the logo symbolizes the headdress worn by my Grandfather, Simon Peters. Simon Peters was a traditional man with old Indian values. My grandfather's headdress was made of Eagle and Pheasant feathers. The Eagle is a sacred bird of the Indians. He chose the Pheasant feathers for the reason that it was a beautiful bird to him. The top of the logo symbolizes the yoke my grandmother, Annie Peters, wore upon her chest. She had once told me the floral design meant beauty and love.

The acorns upon the logo were worn by both my Grandfather and Grandmother. They considered the acorns to be a symbol of Indian people. My grandparents had once stated to me, "The acorns are like the Indian people. Once small and new to the world, but with time, love, and care, they will stand tall, beautiful, and mighty." In a sense, the words they spoke to me are coming to be true. The once small Tribe that I grew up to know, is growing and prospering. May the Grandfathers in the sky look upon us and bless us. Therefore, the logo of the Tribe will always be a symbol of two very missed and loved people in my life. (Saginaw Chippewa *Tribal Observer* [Mt. Pleasant, Michigan], 1 August 2001, 3B)

On the original tribal flag, the logo of the Saginaw Chippewas appeared by itself in the middle of a white flag. In 1999 the flag design was modified slightly by adding the words "SAGINAW CHIPPEWA" arcing over the top of the logo and "INDIAN TRIBE" below the logo. In both versions all elements on the flag are brown.

Thanks to Chief Phil Peters and the Saginaw Chippewa Tribal Council for donating a flag so that the design could be reproduced with accuracy and to the staff at the tribal headquarters for supplying information on the symbolism and history of the emblems of the Saginaw Chippewas.

St. Croix Chippewa (Ojibwe) Indians of Wisconsin

Located in northwestern Wisconsin, the St. Croix Chippewas (Ojibwes or Anishinabes) have been residents of the area since the mid-1600s. While most of the Ojibwes depended upon fishing for their main source of sustenance, the St. Croix people became traders, exchanging furs and foodstuffs with both English and French explorers, and eventually came under the control of the United States.

The St. Croix Ojibwes lost recognition by the federal government in 1854. This happened frequently to tribes that had adapted to coexistence with the Eurocentric population that overpowered the Native American populations. To continue to retain their identity, the St. Croix people had to merge with other nearby Ojibwes; but in 1934 the federal government relented and once again recognized the existence of a distinct St. Croix Ojibwe people. They were officially recognized as the St. Croix Chippewa Indians of Wisconsin. With this recognition came the right to a reservation, which has continued into the twenty-first century.

The ancient heritage of the Ojibwes is celebrated on their flag. The Ojibwes' main crop was wild rice (not corn, like that of many other tribes), which grew in the lakes of present-day Minnesota, Wisconsin, and surrounding areas. The centuries-old tie between the Ojibwes and the wild rice is the central focus of their flag.

The light-green flag has the tribal seal in black in the center. It depicts a wild rice plant growing from the waters (represented by dark-green squiggly lines) of the upper Midwest. Behind the plant, the sun rises above a distant shoreline. Surrounding this logo is the tribe's name in black letters: "ST. CROIX CHIPPEWA INDIANS OF WISCONSIN." The name is bordered by a thin line separating it from the central logo and a ring of tiny diamond-like shapes separating it from the field of the flag.

St. Regis Band of Mohawk Indians of New York

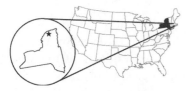

The Mohawks called themselves the "People of the Place of the Flint." Within the Iroquois League, they were the "Keepers of the Eastern Door" because of their geographic location (see Iroquois League). Today's Mohawk Nation spans the border between the United States and Canada. In the United States, the Mohawks are mostly on the St. Regis Reservation, just south of the Québec–New York border; these St. Regis Mohawks are part of the Akwesasne Band.

In 1974 about 200 St. Regis Mohawks seized a 612-acre parcel of land at Eagle Bay on Moss Lake in the Adirondack Mountains, claiming original title to it. They called this land Kanienkah, which means "Land of the Flint." The dispute was settled in 1977, when the State of New York awarded the Mohawks land along Schuyler and Altoona Lakes in Clinton County.

From the Kanienkah uprising came a flag used by Mohawks in Canada and the United States and on all Mohawk lands. It was originally described by its designer, Karoniaktajeh (Louis Hall), secretary of the Ganienkeh Council Fire:

> The field of the flag is red, a warm color and one highly favored by Native Americans. The yellow disk in the center symbolizes the sun with its rays reaching the edge. The Indian head [Mohawk warrior] in the center wears

a single feather, indicating oneness or unity of purpose in our drive to national and racial survival. The face is represented in brown and orange, the hair and feather in black with highlights of blue. The flag is a symbol of the unity of purpose toward economic, political, and spiritual sovereignty by Native Indians, such as are enjoyed by all the peoples of the world. (Karoniaktajeh, "Ganienkeh," *Flag Bulletin* 16:4 [July/August 1977]: cover and 108–11)

The Kanienkah flag has become common at protests throughout the lands of the entire Iroquois League. The ideals of the flag have been exemplified by other actions taken by the Mohawks. The Mohawk Nation issues its members passports, which, somewhat surprisingly, have been accepted by many border officials. This level of international acceptance of nationhood is unparalleled in other tribes and may reflect heightened awareness stemming from wide use of the Mohawk flag.

Salt River Pima-Maricopa Indian Community— Arizona

On the northern border of the city of Scottsdale, Arizona, the Salt River Reservation is home to 5,000 members of the Pima and Maricopa Tribes (*AIDD*, 41). The Salt River Community and its larger companion to the south of Phoenix, the Gila River Community, were once administered as a single unit. The two communities split in 1961 and now function as separate entities.

The Salt River Pimas and Maricopas have two flags—one de jure, with the true seal of the community; and one de facto, with a simplified version. The true community seal can be seen throughout the reservation; the tribal headquarters displays a large replica of the seal at its main entrance. On a white ring are the words "GREAT SEAL" at the top and "SALT RIVER PIMA MARICOPA INDIAN COMMUNITY" along the bottom in black. Black upward-pointing arrows separate these phrases (seal provided by the Salt River Tribal Headquarters).

Within the ring is a depiction of the "Man in the Maze," a recurring symbol in Pima art of the human journey through life. The man's life begins at the center of the maze and ends when he reaches the top. As he overcomes obstacles represented by the maze, he becomes stronger and wiser. The man and the maze walls are black on a yellow background. This image also appears on the flag of the counterpart reservation (see Gila River Indian Community [Pima and Maricopa]).

The flag of the Salt River Community is royal-blue with a variant of the seal in the center. In this simplified seal, the words "SALT RIVER" and "ARIZONA" appear in black on a yellow disk, surrounding a stylized symmetrical maze image in black, without the "Man in the Maze." This simplification was probably done for economic reasons, since the actual seal would be very expensive to reproduce accurately.

Thanks to NAVA member Harry Oswald for the photograph of the flag.

San Carlos Apache Tribe of the San Carlos Reservation— Arizona

The largest of the Apache reservations, covering some 1,900,000 acres, is the San Carlos Reservation east of Phoenix, Arizona. The great chief Cochise was taken there along with his followers after his surrender in 1873 (*GAI*, 122–23). Geronimo led his followers away from this reservation when they broke for freedom from the oppression of the U.S. military in 1881 and 1884 (see Fort Sill Apache Tribe of Oklahoma).

The Apaches on the reservation include the Aravaipa, Chiricahua, Coyotero, Mimbreño, Mogollon, Piñaleno, San Carlos, and Tonto Bands (ibid., 123). Their reservation was created in 1871 and reduced five separate times to accommodate white miners seeking copper and silver and Mormons, whose need for water led to the reduction around the Gila Valley.

The San Carlos Apache flag features their tribal seal on a white background. The seal celebrates the natural beauty of the lands of the San Carlos Apaches and their major economic resources. The circular seal is surrounded by a serrated black edge and a red ring. On an inner white ring with an orange border are the words "APACHE TRIBE" and "SAN CARLOS ARIZONA," separated by five-pointed stars, all in black. The center of the seal is a geographic tableau of the reservation, showing the mountains, a lake, and two plants of the reservation—the piñon pine and the saguaro cactus—in natural colors. Below this scene is a Hereford steer's head, signifying the importance of cattle ranching to the Apaches. Next to it are mining symbols: a pick and shovel on the left and a piece of peridotite ore on the right.

A second version of this flag hangs in the "Gallery of Nations" at the Indian Center Museum, part of the Mid-America All-Indian Center in Wichita, Kansas. This version, supplied to the museum by the San Carlos Apache Tribe, bears a red outline map of the reservation behind the seal, as on another Apache flag (see White Mountain Apache Tribe). A red border around the flag separates four colored bars on the edges of the flag from the white field—the left bar is yellow, the top is white, the bottom is dark green, and the right is black.

Santee Sioux Tribe—Nebraska

The Santee Sioux people provided the Dakotas with their names. While other Sioux refer to themselves as "Lakotas" or "Nakotas," the Santees call themselves "Dakotas." All three terms mean "allies" (*ENAT*, 222–28). The Santees in Nebraska are part of a group located in several reservations in Minnesota, Nebraska, and South Dakota (see Flandreau Santee Sioux Tribe of South Dakota).

The flag of the Santee Sioux of Nebraska is dark blue, with the seal in full color. The seal features a brown and white bald eagle with outspread wings, facing left in a position reminiscent of the arms of the United States (Smithsonian Museum of the Native American, Resource Room, New York). The eagle clasps a black arrow in its talons, with a red sacred pipe below. On the chest of the eagle is a yellow shield in the shape of a downward-pointing arrowhead with the bust of a Sioux chief in full headdress, facing left. Arching above the eagle in blue lettering is "SANTEE SIOUX TRIBE" and below it "OF NEBRASKA." All elements appear on a white disk recalling the shields of the warriors of the Sioux Nation.

Sault Ste. Marie Tribe of Chippewa (Ojibwe) Indians of Michigan

In northeastern Michigan, based on 293 acres of reservation land, is the Sault Ste. Marie Tribe of Chippewa (Ojibwe) Indians, the largest of the Michigan tribes, with a tribal enrollment of over 24,000.

The Sault Ste. Marie Chippewa flag has a black background, which is unusual for any flag. It bears a colorful seal replete with symbolism. The seal is divided into quarters of different colors, each representing a compass direction and bearing the image of an animal that symbolizes a particular clan. A teal-blue body of a turtle, completely circular and edged in aquamarine, forms the center of the seal. The tribe describes its flag's symbolism (*Wabun-Anong*, pamphlet, June 1982) in this way:

> TURTLE represents to our people the Mother Earth we stand upon, sustaining us with constancy and generosity, and is the central part of the symbol. . . . We are cared for by our Earth Mother with her blessings of food, clothing, shelter, and medicine. . . . We give thanks to Earth Mother, the direction below us. . . . Turtle emerged from the water with Earth on its back, providing a living place for human beings and all creatures between sky and water. Turtle is the medium of communication, the emissary of beings of this world and time and beings of another world and dimension of time. Turtle symbolizes thought given and thought received and represents clarity of communication between beings. Aqua-green symbolizes plant life and growing things.

On the back of the turtle a black crane with white body and wing accents prepares to take flight toward the west, and to its left is a mountain-ash branch in black.

CRANE represents our people's eloquence of leadership and direction. The voice of the Crane is unique and infrequent. When Crane speaks, all listen. Crane is the spokesperson for the clans. MOUNTAIN ASH TREE is the sacred tree of the Anishnabek ["Our People"] . . . able to survive in places where other trees cannot. Its leaves, berries, and bark are used for medicines. The Mountain Ash is used as an example for strength, durability, and strong character.

Radiating from the central turtle are four arc sections separated by aquamarine lines. The yellow quarter to the right (east) depicts a black rabbit with white highlights, bordered in red.

EAST, the direction of the rising sun, is thought of as a Grandfather personifying the winds and natural phenomena of that direction. East is the direction of the physical body. It symbolizes all that is new in the creation, like all newborn creatures, including man. Like the rising sun, a new day is brought to light. So it is with all things. Knowledge is brought to consciousness and like the circling of the sun, the seasons change. East is the time of change. It is the spring, the time of change from blackness to beauty. It is the sun breaking over the horizon.

RABBIT represents Manabozho, a messenger of Kitche Manitou [Great Spirit], an intermediary on earth among different species of beings; and an advocate for the Anishnabek, to whom he imparted the gift of knowledge. From the east leading to the west is a YELLOW PATH. It is said by our elders that this is the path of life, the path of the Great Warrior, the Sun. We give thanks to our eastern Grandfather.

The lower quarter representing the south is red, with an image of a black eagle with white accents.

SOUTH, a continuation of our circle of life, is the direction of maturing life, like young men and women. It is the time of year we call summer, the time we call mid-day, and the time of day the eagle soars. South is the direction of full understanding.

EAGLE receives from Kitche Manitou the gifts of strong wings, keen sight, and proud bearing. Eagle symbolizes courage and preknowledge. His sphere is the mountains and the heights. RED symbolizes earth and fire. We give thanks to our southern Grandfather.

The black quarter to the left (west) depicts a black deer with white highlights, edged in yellow.

WEST, the direction of the setting sun, is the time of gradual change as from daylight to darkness, from life to death. It is evening, the change of life in midagedness. It is change like the leaves or the hair on our heads from natural colors to the likes of natural frost. West is the time of full maturity. It is the time of insight. West is the direction of the emotional part of ourselves.

DEER receives from Kitche Manitou the gift of grace. Deer symbolizes to our people love. BLACK symbolizes change from this life. We give thanks to our western Grandfather.

The white quarter at the top (north) shows a black bear with white highlights, standing upright and edged in red.

NORTH is the time of our elders, our old people. It is a time of wisdom, so much like the answers found in our dreams. It represents the night, as a time called midnight, and a time called winter when things are as unpredictable as our dreams. North is representative of those things that are positive, a time of snow and purity.

BEAR received from Kitche Manitou the gifts of courage and strength. Bear is representative of all medicine powers in creation. Claws dig medicine roots. Bear passes knowledge on through dreams, visions. WHITE symbolizes spirituality. We give thanks to our northern Grandfather.

Enclosing the seal are three thin rings—the inner ring green, the middle one yellow, and the outer one red.

RAINBOW is the beautiful bridge to the spirit world and the colors of the universe. Red is symbolic of earth and fire. Yellow is the path the sun crosses through the day. Blue is symbolic of sky and waters. From wherever we stand upon our Earth Mother we have companionship of these four directions.... The direction above recognizes the daytime and nighttime skies of our creation. This is where we look to acknowledge the Great Spirit, the Creator. The Creator gives us everything we know.... Therefore, our greatest acknowledgment is to the Creator of all the universe. We give a grateful thanks.

A new logo recently adopted by the tribe features the crane taking flight toward the east, carrying a mountain-ash branch in its beak. The image is surrounded by a ring, outside of which the words "Sault Ste. Marie Tribe" curve to the upper left and "of Chippewa Indians" to the lower right, separated by two turtles. The entire logo is usually represented in black or gold.

Thanks to Jessica Jeffreys at the tribal headquarters in Sault Ste. Marie, Michigan, for the pamphlet with the flag's description.

Seminole Nation of Oklahoma

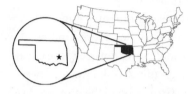

The majority of the Seminoles were removed from Florida in the 1830s and resettled in Indian Territory (see Seminole Tribe of Florida). The Seminoles of Oklahoma retain their traditional ties to the lands of their ancestors, however, and their symbols recall those homelands. The flag of the Seminole Nation of Oklahoma is white with the tribal seal in the center (Dena Brady, acting executive secretary, letter dated 15 February 1995). The seal (copy provided by Annin & Co., Roseland, N.J.) has a braided border in yellow and black around a white ring with "THE GREAT SEMINOLE NATION" above and "OF OKLAHOMA" below in black.

Inside a narrow yellow ring is a typical scene from the life of the Seminoles in Florida's Everglades: a man in a dugout canoe paddles toward a village and the lush green forest. All elements appear in natural colors ("Official Seals of the Five Civilized Tribes," *Oklahoma Chronicles* 17:4 [December 1940]: 357–59). The seal echoes the old seal of the Seminoles of Florida (see Seminole Tribe of Florida).

The flag may have been inspired by the design created for the Seminole Nation by the Alabama Department of History in 1940 when the Seminole people, as former residents of Alabama, were included in the opening of the Alabama Hall of Flags.

This was not the first flag of the Seminole Nation. During the U.S. Civil War, the Confederacy presented flags to members of the "Five Civilized Tribes" allied against the Union. Miss Alice Leeper, daughter of the Confederate agent to the Indian Territory, presented a flag to the Seminoles (*True Democrat* [Little Rock, Arkansas], 29 August 1861; *Looking Glass* [March 1991]). The flag was "a crescent and red star in a green union" with diagonal "bars of red and white" (compared to the vertical bars of the flag presented to the Creek Nation) (see Muscogee [Creek] Nation).

The seal is currently being updated with slight enhancements (D. Brady, 1997 letter). The new seal has not yet been received by the Executive Directorate of the Seminole Nation, but it will probably result in a modification of the flag.

Seminole Tribe of Florida

The Seminole Nation consists of three bands based in Florida (*NAA*, 251) and one large group forcibly removed to Indian Territory (Oklahoma) during the early 1800s (see Seminole Nation of Oklahoma). The Seminoles, whose name means "Runaways," are actually a composite tribe made up of members of many nations that fled the onslaught of white settlers from their lands in what is now Georgia and surrounding states. These Indians were joined by escaped black slaves granted sanctuary by the Seminoles, a practice that brought about the Seminole Wars.

Those Seminoles who remained in present-day Florida continued to fight the government of the United States from their strongholds in the

Everglades. An infamous episode of the 1830s involved a flag of truce carried by their leader Osceola. General Thomas Jessup tricked Osceola with an offer of peace talks and imprisoned him instead. A peace treaty between the United States and the Seminoles of Florida was not signed until 1934. The three bands of Seminoles located in Florida today are the Seminole Tribe of Florida, the Seminole Nation of Florida, and the Oklavueha Band of Seminole Indians.

The Seminole Tribe of Florida adopted a flag after a contest in August 1966 to symbolize their sovereignty over the lands they have occupied for almost 300 years. The tribal seal was centered on a dark-blue field, backed by a cross of small red, white, and blue chevrons forming an "X," which recalls the state flag of Florida, a red "X" on a white background (*FBUS*, 261–63). This seal was similar to the seal employed by the Seminole Nation of Oklahoma. It depicted a Seminole standing in a canoe, poling through the swamplands. In the background were a palm tree and a chickee—the traditional dwelling of the Seminoles—with a campfire below it (the main element of the current tribal seal). All elements were shown in natural colors. Surrounding this scene was a white ring with the words "SEMINOLE TRIBE OF FLORIDA" in black arcing over the top and "IN GOD WE TRUST below, separated by small black dots.

The 1966 flag has been replaced by the current flag, designed by Chief Jim Billie (*NAVA News* [September/October 1993]: 3). The flag is similar in design to the flag of the Miccosukees, neighbors of the Seminoles' Big Cypress Reservation in south-central Florida. Both flags have four horizontal stripes of white, black, red, and yellow (see Miccosukee Tribe of Indians of Florida). The Seminoles of Florida add their tribal seal, which is very similar to the Miccosukee seal, to those stripes.

The tribe is ruled by two bodies, the Tribal Council and a corporate board representing the Seminole Tribe of Florida, Inc. Centered on the seal of the Tribal Council in black and red is a chickee built on palmetto stilts, with a campfire below it. Above the chickee in black are the words "TRIBAL COUNCIL." The seal of the corporate board depicts a Seminole paddling a canoe. In a white band surrounding the central image (outlined by black rings) in black is the legend "SEMINOLE TRIBE OF FLORIDA" above on the Tribal Council seal and "SEMINOLE TRIBE OF FLORIDA, INC." on the corporate seal, with "IN GOD WE TRUST" below, separated by small black dots. Both versions of the seal and flag are used.

The new flag flies prominently outside the Seminole bingo parlor and casino in the Okalee Indian Village (the smaller of the two main Seminole reservations) along U.S. Route 441 near Fort Lauderdale. A row of at least two dozen flags —alternating United States and Seminole—runs the length of the parking lot. In front of the capitol of the Semi-nole Tribe (an eight-story office tower) three poles fly the United States flag in the place of honor, the flag of the Seminoles, and the flag of Florida. It is unusual for a sovereign Indian nation to display the local state flag; most tribes simply ignore the flag of the surrounding state.

With the new flag of the Seminole Tribe of Florida, the Indians of southeastern Florida have one unified design to confirm their sovereignty on lands they have occupied for almost 300 years.

Seneca-Cayuga
Tribe of Oklahoma

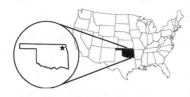

The Seneca-Cayugas are descendants of those members of the two westernmost nations of the Iroquois League that were removed to Oklahoma. The Senecas are still an important tribe in New York (see Seneca Nation of New York). The Cayugas originally lived in the Finger Lakes region of western New York; while still present in New York, they no longer hold any tribal lands there.

Of the five original members of the Iroquois League, the Cayuga Nation controlled the smallest territory (*ENAT,* 40–41). During the American Revolution, most Cayugas sided with the British, their longtime ally. After the American victory, many Cayugas migrated to Ontario, where today they live on the Oshweken reserve (see Iroquois League).

The Seneca-Cayuga Tribe of Oklahoma uses a light-blue flag. At the center is a large white disk with "SENECA-CAYUGA TRIBE" in black arching across the top and "OF OKLAHOMA" in smaller letters below. In the middle of the disk is the "great tree," a symbol sacred to all Iroquois (copy of seal provided by Annin & Co., Roseland, N.J.). Surrounding this is a bear-claw necklace, symbolizing strength and power. Around the necklace are thirteen animal shapes in black outline, yellow, or tan. These totems, exemplifying certain admirable traits, symbolize thirteen tribal clans. Counterclockwise from the upper left are the Wolf, Squirrel, Hawk, Eel, Heron, Beaver, Bear, Hare, Porcupine, Snake, Snipe, Turtle, and Deer. These represent all eight New York Seneca clans and five Cayuga clans.

Seneca Nation of New York

The Senecas were originally called "Sen Uh Kuh" ("Great Hill People"). The name "Seneca" derived from the similarity in sound to the Roman name familiar to European ears. The Senecas, the most powerful of the tribes in the Iroquois League, served as the "Keepers of the Western Door" (see Iroquois League). The Iroquois viewed their confederacy as one huge long house, their traditional dwelling (*ENAT*, 215–16). It fell to the Senecas to protect the western gateway to the heart of Iroquois land.

The three state-recognized Seneca reservations in western New York (Cattaraugus, Oil Springs, and Allegany) all fly the same white flag with the seal of the tribe in blue, white, and red (flag provided by Advertising Flag Co.). The seal contains maps of the three reservations in blue across the center. Above and below the maps are blue silhouettes of eight totemic animals—Deer, Heron, Hawk, Snipe, Bear, Wolf, Beaver, and Turtle—associated with particular Seneca clans (*ENAT*, 216). Around the outer white ring (which is outlined by thin blue lines) in red are the words "SENECA NATION OF INDIANS" at the top and "Keepers of the Western Door" along the bottom.

Sisseton and Wahpeton Sioux Tribe— North Dakota and South Dakota

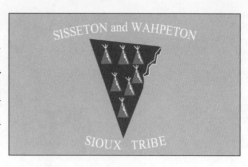

The Lake Traverse Reservation, a distinctive triangle in the northeastern part of South Dakota and southeastern part of North Dakota, is home to the Sisseton and Wahpeton Bands of the Santee Sioux.

Like nearly all flags of Dakota branches, the Sisseton and Wahpeton flag features the tipi as a significant design element. As the rulers of the northern Plains, the Sioux constantly traveled, following the vast buffalo herds and using the tipi as a nomadic shelter. While the tipi is a unifying symbol among the various Sioux groups, the Sisseton Band did not begin to use the tipi until it was forced westward, and members of the Wahpeton Band never used the tipi at all. They relied instead on a bark-covered *tipi tonka* as a summer house and a domed earthen lodge for their winter dwelling (http://swcc.cc.sd.us/culture2.html, 1998).

The tribe's light-blue flag bears the triangular map of the reservation in dark blue. On it seven red tipis accented in white represent the seven districts of the reservation. On the official flags displayed in the tribal offices, each district is named. Arching over the reservation map in white are the words "SISSETON and WAHPETON" and below the map "SIOUX TRIBE."

Skull Valley Band of Goshute Indians of Utah

Possibly the most foreboding landscape in the United States is the area called the Great Basin, the remains of a long-gone seabed that now covers the states of Nevada and Utah plus areas of surrounding states. The cactus- and creosote-covered deserts of Arizona are lush in comparison. Even plants struggle for their existence in the Great Basin. Its largest water source is the saline Great Salt Lake.

Before the advent of white settlers, the Great Basin was home to several tribes of peaceful Indians. The harsh conditions there in some ways enforced a peaceful coexistence, since the search for food so preoccupied the people: intertribal warfare would have been an unprofitable luxury they could not afford. When the white settlers arrived in the area, they saw the indigenous population digging in the soil for root crops and thus called them "Digger Indians." Among those lumped together under this derisive term were the Goshutes of Nevada and Utah.

The Skull Valley Band of Goshutes, numbering under 100 residents on its small reservation, is the easternmost representative of the Goshute Nation. It is located in western Utah, west of the Great Salt Lake.

Over this parched land of the Skull Valley Band flies a white flag bearing an adapted version of the tribal seal. Across the white field stretch the brown mountains that form Skull Valley. Rising behind them is a large yellow sun with thirteen yellow rays emanating from it. Below the mountains is the tribal name in red: "SKULL VALLEY BAND" appears on the first line in stretched-out letters, a smaller "OF" centered below, and a slightly bowed "GOSHUTE" on a third line. No information is available as to the designer of the flag or date of adoption.

On the blue background of the round tribal seal is a sun with twenty-three rays. The name of the tribe is placed in a black band surrounding the graphic in pale yellow letters rather than in the central graphic.

Southern Ute Tribe—Colorado

The Ute Nation, for whom Utah is named, today occupies three reservations spreading across Utah, Colorado, and New Mexico (*ENAT*, 244–45). The Southern Ute Reservation in Colorado is home mainly to two bands, the Mouaches and the Capotes.

The flag of the Southern Ute Tribe is light blue with "SOUTHERN UTE TRIBE" in white across the top (photo provided by the Southern Ute Executive Office). Centered below is the tribal seal, which represents the "circle of life"; several elements within it symbolize facets of Southern Ute life. The seal's edge is a ropelike braid of light blue and white. Immediately within the circle in red is "GREAT SEAL OF THE SOUTHERN UTE INDIAN TRIBE" above and "IGNACIO, COLO." below.

Centered in the seal is the profile of a Ute chief (representing the entire tribe) facing left, in red, orange, black, blue, and white—the colors of the rainbow and of nature. Surrounding the chief's profile are the natural resources of the reservation and cultural icons of the Ute people in natural colors. Directly below the profile is a sacred pipe, from which hang two feathers. The pipe indicates that the Utes are a peace-loving people, while the two feathers represent the Great Spirit and the healing power that comes from a single peaceful people. Below the pipe are two leafed branches that recall the green things of the earth and the harmony that people share with nature.

Below the pipe and branches is a small Colorado state flag. The inclusion of the Colorado emblem is unique—no other Native American flag

or seal depicts a state flag, and only a few include any state symbols. (Many tribes purposely exclude the state flag in parades and similar events.)

To the left of the profile are a gas well and two grazing sheep; to the right are a tractor and a grazing steer. Together these symbolize the main pursuits of the Ute tribe—agriculture, ranching, and mining. Above the profile a mountain range recalls the Ute homeland, with an elk and bear—animals that share the land with the Utes. The sun at the top watches over the tribe, while the river stands for the six rivers that cross the reservation. All the symbols appear in natural colors.

The Executive Office of the tribe believes that the flag and seal were adopted in 1970 or 1971 when a contest was held to choose a name for the Piño Nuche Lodge and Restaurant, one of the major businesses on the reservation.

Information concerning the flag and seal of the Southern Ute Tribe (Eugene Naranjo, letter dated 2 February 1995) comes from two Ute tribal artists, Ben Watts and Russell Box, Sr.

Spokane Tribe—Washington

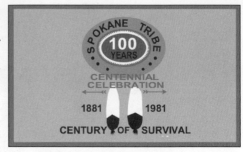

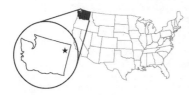

The Spokane Reservation in eastern Washington is home to the Spokane Tribe, an inland Salish-speaking people related to the Flathead, Coeur d'Alene, and similar tribes (*ENAT*, 252).

The Spokane flag is the banner from the tribe's 1981 centennial (photos supplied by Jim White). The flag has a yellow-orange field bordered in red. In the upper center is a multicolored oval shield with two white-and-black eagle feathers hanging from it. The phrase "100 YEARS" appears on a blue background in the center of the shield (the number in yellow and the word in black). This inner oval is ringed by white, red, and tan bands. The white band is serrated; the outermost tan band bears the legend "SPOKANE TRIBE" in black above and six black dots below.

The words "CENTENNIAL CELEBRATION" in red overlap the bottom of the tan border, underlined by red arrows pointing outward. To the left and right of the feathers are "1881" and "1981" in black. Across the bottom of the flag, overlapping the tips of the feathers, is "CENTURY OF SURVIVAL" in green. Although the banner dates from the 1981 celebration, the Spokanes continue flying it as their official tribal flag. This appears to be the sole instance among tribal flags where a celebration banner evolved into a flag.

Thanks to NAVA member Jim White, who examined the flag outside the tribal headquarters in Wellpinit, Washington, in 1996.

Squaxin Island Tribe— Washington

Squaxin Island (located in the southern-most part of Puget Sound, directly north of Washington State's capital, Olympia) is the site of the Squaxin Island Reservation. This small reservation of less than 1,000 acres is home to several tribes, including the Nisqually, Steeli-acoom, and Squaxin Island Tribes. The resident population of the reserve is about 1,000 people. All resident tribes belong to the Coastal Salish group of Native American peoples, like many other Washington Indians.

These tribes have resided in the greater Puget Sound area for over a thousand years and have relied upon the resources of the sound and the surrounding forests for sustenance. The area around Squaxin Island and its bounty are celebrated on the flag and seal of the Squaxin Island Tribe. Like the flags of many other tribes throughout the United States, the Squaxin flag is white, with the tribal seal in the center. That seal is a light-blue circle containing an outline of Squaxin Island, a mountain repre-senting the Cascades, two sea birds in flight, a salmon, and an Indian paddling a distinctive Northwest-style canoe. Upon the island is its name in black letters. Both the salmon and the canoe symbolize the fishing skill of the tribes, especially the importance of salmon to the existence of the people of Squaxin Island.

Surrounding the seal is a ring outlined in black bearing the names of the resident tribes in their own languages in black, including "Squawskin" (Squaxin Island Tribe) and "Nuschtsatl" (Nisqually).

Thanks to Harry Oswald of Portland, Oregon, for obtaining a photograph of the flag during a meeting of the Associated Tribes of Northwest Indians.

Standing Rock
Sioux Tribe
of North and
South Dakota

The Standing Rock Sioux Reservation is one of nine Sioux reservations spreading from northern Nebraska to North Dakota. The reservation centers on the town of Fort Yates, North Dakota, and straddles the border between the two Dakotas. It was created in 1873 out of land set aside under the treaty of 1868 as the "Great Sioux Reservation" and is home to the Yanktonai and Hunkpapa Bands of the Teton Sioux.

According to legend, the Standing Rock was the Arikara wife of a Dakota warrior and her child, who had been turned to stone. The stone was considered *wakan* or holy by the Sioux people. They transported it whenever they moved, carrying it on a lavishly decorated travois pulled by a specially adorned horse. When the Sioux settled on the current reservation, they placed the Standing Rock on a brick pedestal outside the reservation agency's office, where it remains to this day ("Symbols of the Standing Rock Sioux Nation," *NAVA News* [May/June 1989]: 6).

The flag of the Standing Rock Sioux is medium blue with the tribal seal in the center (provided by Standing Rock Sioux Tribal Headquarters). The seal's outer ring is white edged by two narrow red bands and bears the words "STANDING ROCK SIOUX TRIBE" in red above and "JULY 1873" below.

The seal contains a circle of eight white tipis reminiscent of the Oglala Sioux flag (see Oglala Sioux Tribe), representing the eight districts of the reservation, on a red background. The ring of outward-pointing tipis encloses a yellow disk depicting the Standing Rock in white on its red pedestal. Around the disk are the names of the eight districts in red, starting with the Fort Yates district at the top, followed by Cannonball, Wakpala, Kernel, Rockcreek, Bear Soldier, Little Eagle, and Porcupine. (According to chairman Charles Murphy, only one copy of the flag exists. It cost over US$500 and is kept in the tribal headquarters in Fort Yates.)

Stockbridge-Munsee Community of Mohican Indians of Wisconsin

MOHICAN NATION

STOCKBRIDGE - MUNSEE BAND

The Mohicans (also spelled Mahicans) were a northeastern tribe whose lands spanned what is now Massachusetts, Connecticut, Vermont, and eastern New York. As with most eastern tribes, many were forced to move west as the European settlements turned into the United States. Some Mohicans remain to this day in their original homelands, but the largest concentration of Mohicans can be found in Wisconsin—the Stockbridge-Munsee Band.

The Stockbridge-Munsee Community of Mohicans might be considered the closest existing people to generic "Algonquins." Algonquin is a language group composed of languages spoken by several tribes that stretched from eastern Canada throughout the Middle Atlantic colonies (later states).

The "Stockbridge" part of the tribe's name originated back in the Housatonic Valley of Massachusetts, where an English settlement and mission to the local Indians was established and named "Stockbridge" (*NAA*, 119–20).

As the Mohicans were forced ever farther to the west, many were absorbed into the tribes of their Algonquin cousins, the Delawares or Lenni Lenapés. One of the Delaware bands eventually wound up sharing a Wisconsin reservation with the Stockbridge Mohicans: the Munsee Band. Thus the current name reflects the union of Stockbridge Mohicans and Munsee Delawares—bringing two separate parts of the Algonquin-speaking peoples together. Since 1856 the Stockbridge Munsee Mohicans have controlled about 16,000 acres with a tribal capital in Bowler, Wisconsin. The modern Stockbridge-Munsees number around 1,600, with about half living on the reservation (*REAI*, 24).

The Stockbridge-Munsee Community employs a white flag bordered on the three exterior sides by a narrow red band of fringe. Centered on the flag is the tribal seal.

The seal is round and is divided into four quadrants, each of which has a narrow outer stripe in one of the four sacred colors and incorporates one of the tribal totems. The upper-left quarter is edged in red and bears a gray wolf. The upper-right quarter is edged in black and shows a golden turkey. The lower-left part has a white band and a black bear. The lower-right is edged in gold and depicts a dark-gray turtle. The four quarters are separated by narrow gray lines. Centered in the seal is a complex red emblem that was created by a Mohican artist, Edwin Martin. Widely used by the Stockbridge-Munsees as a logo, this emblem is called "Many Trails." It symbolizes "endurance, strength, and hope for a long-suffering, proud, and determined people" (Indian Center Museum, Topeka, Kansas, *Indian Center Museum—Gallery of Flags,* undated, 7). Below the sides of the circle are two black-and-white eagle feathers, standing for the two original tribes.

Arching over the seal in large black letters is the name "MOHICAN NATION." Underneath the seal in black is the legend "STOCKBRIDGE-MUNSEE BAND."

Suquamish Indian Tribe— Washington

Seattle, the largest city in the Pacific Northwest, is named for Chief Seattle of the Suquamish Indian Nation. Born about 1790 (*DAI,* 370), Chief Seattle remained on good terms with the white settlers during the Indian Wars of 1855 and 1858. In 1890, the centennial of his birth, the city erected a monument over his grave.

Seattle's own Suquamish people also remember their great chief. Residents of the Port Madison Reservation (*NAA,* 285) on the western shores of Puget Sound across from Seattle, they display his image on their flag, which is made on the reservation. The flag is divided in half vertically: the left half is black, the right half is red. A large yellow oval (oriented lengthwise) bears a portrait of Chief Seattle in black. A white band surrounds the oval, with "TREATY OF POINT ELLIOT—1855" (which Chief Seattle signed) across the top in black and "CHIEF SEATTLE" below. Across the bottom of the flag is "SUQUAMISH TRIBE" in white.

The colors of the field and seal constitute the four primary colors of Native American art and belief: red, white, yellow, and black. As with many other tribes, the colors recall several aspects of life—the four directions, the four human races, the four seasons, the four natural elements, and the four ages of a human life. The Suquamish people combine these four colors (which unite them with other Native Americans) with imagery unique to them (which shows their distinct place in history) to create meaning in their flag.

Thanks to Scott Crowell of the Suquamish Tribe for information about the flag.

Swinomish
Indians—
Washington

SWINOMISH TRIBAL COMMUNITY

The Coast Salish Swinomish Tribal Community is located on the eastern shore of Puget Sound in northwestern Washington. Members of the community descended from the Swinomish, Kikiallus, Samish, and Lower Skagit Tribes who lived in the Skagit River valley and on the coastline and islands around the river's mouth. All spoke the Coast Salish language. Tribal chairperson Brian Cladoosby says that, according to tradition, the Swinomish Tribe originated "when a chief's son wandered from camp with his dog and suffered many hardships. Through purification of the spirit, he obtained great powers that enabled him to convert his dog into a beautiful princess, who became the wife and mother of the people whom he created by sowing rocks on the earth."

During the 1840s and 1850s the smallpox, measles, and tuberculosis brought by whites killed most of the Indian population. Armed conflict led to the 1855 Treaty of Point Elliot, known by the Coast Salish as the Mukilteo Treaty. Implemented over the twenty years it took for U.S. Senate ratification, it led to the scattering of many Indians around Puget Sound in search of employment.

The flag of the Swinomish Tribal Community reflects two central cultural themes that members have retained across generations—fishing and ceremonial traditions. Fishing remains a central tribal activity and provides an important focus of cultural association. Salmon barbecues, races, and games are held on holidays and other major cultural events. The

Swinomish people often caught sockeye salmon with a distinctive fishing spear. Spiritual meaning permeates all aspects of Swinomish culture, forming a central element of everyday life. The Swinomish celebrate the Seowyn religious and ceremonial traditions, which frequently use drums.

The Swinomish flag features a drum, a spear, and the community name on a yellow background. An eight-sided white drum edged in black in the upper left bears the image of a leaping salmon. Depicted in the distinctive Pacific Northwest Coast style, the salmon is white and black with red elements in the tail, eye, and body. Eight red decorative symbols surround the salmon around the drum's edge. Behind the drum, pointing to the right, a horizontal black-and-white fishing spear is attached to a red rope with white accents. To the right of the drum and under the spear are the words "SWINOMISH TRIBAL COMMUNITY" in black, in three lines.

The combination of ceremonial and animate symbols (the drum and the fish) alludes to the mythology passed through generations of Swinomish people, according to which the Indians and all living things had a common language and helped one another in their struggle through life. The flag uses the four traditional colors of American Indian design (red, white, black, and yellow, which carry multiple meanings (see Miccosukee Tribe of Indians of Florida).

Thanks to Brian Cladoosby, Swinomish tribal chairman, for providing the creation story along with most of the information in this section from the tribal publication *Portrait of a Homeland.*

Thlopthlocco Tribal Town (Creek)— Oklahoma

OKEMAH, OK   EST. 1834

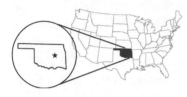

One of the four members of the Oklahoma Creek Confederacy is the Thlopthlocco Tribal Town based in Okemah, Oklahoma, along with one of the other two tribal towns, the Kialegees. Like the Kialegees, the Thlopthloccos are headed by a tribal town king, the only two instances of a monarchical title being applied to the head of a Native American nation in the United States (*REAI*, 31–32).

In many ways the flag of the Thlopthlocco Creeks is similar to the flag of their cousins the Kialegees. The dark-red flag of the Thlopthloccos has a white circle in the center that contains the seal of the tribal town. Like the Kialegee seal, the Thlopthlocco seal's central element is a crossed pair of Creek stickball sticks with the basket ends pointing upward. Between the two sticks is a black circle representing the Creek stickball ball. Both items allude to the Creeks' creation of the sport hundreds of years ago.

Below the crossed sticks is a campfire, which signifies the Sacred Fire from which villagers would take coals back to their homes so they could rekindle their own hearth fires. This ritual occurred at the end of the Green Corn Ceremony or Busk, from the Creek word *boskita* meaning "to fast" (*ENAT*, 74–76). The Green Corn Ceremony was the most important of all the rituals among the Creek people. During this ceremony, women cleaned their homes and tools and men repaired the communal buildings like the Ceremonial House shown on the flag of the Kialegees. As part of

the ceremony, the hearth fires in each home were put out. The Creek people would drink the "Black Drink" to induce vomiting, thus purifying their bodies, and some would dance the Green Corn Dance.

The Sacred Fire pictured on the flag was then lit, and a great feast would commence. The ceremony concluded with a communal bath, again for purification. Thus the entire village was ready to begin anew, facing the coming year with all past wrongdoings except murder forgiven (ibid.). Therefore, the inclusion of the Sacred Fire in the Thlopthlocco seal can be seen as representing the beginnings of a new life for the Creeks in Oklahoma after being evicted from their traditional homelands in present-day Georgia and Alabama.

The name "THLOPTHLOCCO" appears at the top of the seal in black and "CREEK TRIBAL TOWN" in the bottom portion. Hanging from the seal, turning it into a warrior's shield, are four feathers in black and white, symbolizing the sacred number four (the four directions, the natural elements, the human races etc.).

Below the shield in white is the name of the town in which the Thlopthloccos are presently located, "OKEMAH, OK" and the date of the Thlopthloccos' reorganization in Indian Territory: "EST. 1834."

Three Affiliated Tribes of the Fort Berthold Reservation (Mandan, Hidatsa, and Arikara)— North Dakota

Located in northwestern North Dakota is the Fort Berthold Indian Reservation, which is home to the Three Affiliated Tribes of the Mandan, the Hidatsa, and the Arikara Nations.

The Mandans were among the earliest residents of the Great Plains, having migrated there during the 1400s (*ENAT*, 123–25). They were firmly rooted into the land around the Missouri River when Lewis and Clark spent the winter with them in 1804. The Mandans lived in permanent villages composed of earthen lodges and engaged in a wide variety of agricultural practices. Like most tribes of the Plains, they also took part in annual buffalo hunts to supplement their diet. The Mandans were friendly to white visitors to their lands and paid a terrible price for that friendliness. In 1837 they were affected with smallpox, a totally alien disease. In that year the Mandan Nation of over 1,600 was reduced to a mere 125 survivors! In 1845 the few remaining Mandans moved voluntarily to the Fort Berthold Reservation.

The Hidatsas were the northern neighbors of the Mandans, also living along the banks of the Missouri River in what is now North Dakota. The Hidatsas, like the Mandans, were essentially farmers and lived in permanent villages (*ENAT*, 92–93). Their lifestyle was similar to that of the Mandans; but their language more closely resembled Sioux, and their religious ceremonies differed in certain aspects.

Like the Mandans, the Hidatsas were visited by the Lewis and Clark expedition, remained friendly with white travelers, and suffered the same ghastly fate. Prior to 1837 the Hidatsas numbered over 3,000, divided into 10 villages. In 1845 the 50 souls who escaped the smallpox plague moved to the Fort Berthold Reservation.

The third tribe, the Arikaras (pronounced A-rick-a-ras) or Rees, got their name from their ancient custom of wearing two upright bones in their hair. The word *arikara* means "horns" (*ENAT,* 23–29). The Arikaras were the southern neighbors of the Mandans, while the Hidatsas lived to their north. The three tribes shared lifestyles and customs and lived quite peacefully with one another, though they did face raids from the much larger Sioux Nation. These raids were usually in search of more horses, a commodity of great import on the Plains, especially when hunting buffalo. Unlike the Mandans and Hidatsas, the Arikaras did fight with white settlers, attacking a band of European-Americans in 1823.

By 1851 the Arikaras had settled in many villages throughout their range. They suffered through the great smallpox epidemic of 1837 but survived in greater numbers than their neighbors. A second epidemic killed even more Arikaras, and in 1862 they joined their former neighbors on the Fort Berthold Reservation. In 1871 the federal government designated the Fort Berthold Reservation as the permanent home for these three nations. Since that time, due to the small numbers of survivors, these three peoples have acted as one, though keeping their identities and customs alive.

The Three Affiliated Tribes of the Fort Berthold Reservation first used a white flag bearing the seal of the Mandan, Hidatsa, and Arikara Nation in the center. That seal was oval, wider horizontally than vertically (sample seal provided by the Tribal Headquarters of the Three Affiliated Tribes). On a light-blue background was a map of the Fort Berthold Reservation, including the bright blue of Lake Sakakawea, which runs through the reservation. Over the reservation map was a bald eagle in natural coloring, holding a ceremonial tribal lance bedecked with eagle feathers. A white band circling the seal bore the three tribal names, the combined designation as the "Three Affiliated Tribes," and "May 15, 1936," the date when the three tribes began governing themselves. All lettering was in black.

In 1997 the three tribes adopted a new seal, which has been added to the new flag. This circular seal features a landscape in which a hill is the most prominent feature. Smoke signals rise into the sky above the hill. On a red band surrounding the landscape are the names "MANDAN, HIDATSA & ARIKARA" in black letters edged in white. From the base of the seal come four ears of maize (corn): one red, one black, one yellow, one white. These are the four sacred colors to Native American tribes across the continent (see Miccosukee Tribe of Indians of Florida). Below these are three eagle feathers, one for each of the three tribes. The new seal brings to the forefront the tribal names, which had been all but ignored in the old seal. Now the sad connotations of the name "Fort Berthold" are subsumed, and the reemergence of the three great nations of North Dakota is celebrated in the new tribal seal.

Tlingit and Haida Tribes—Alaska

Two of the best-known nations in Alaska are the Tlingits and the Haidas. Their traditional lands span the international boundaries that separate Alaska from the Canadian province of British Columbia. On the United States side of their lands, these tribes inhabit the Alaskan panhandle and the coastal islands off that strip of land.

Like their kin farther south, the Tlingit and Haida people are among the greatest Native American woodcarvers. The ultimate example of the artwork of the Tlingit and Haida people may be found just outside many traditional wooden plank homes—the totem pole. The distinctive style of carving exemplified by the totem pole can be seen in the design of the flag of the Tlingit and Haida Central Council.

The flag is white, with their unusually shaped seal in the center. The edge of the seal is almost rectangular, with the two upper corners rounded off. The black line used to form the outer edge varies in width, becoming heavier as it rises from a very narrow baseline.

Within this border is a central map of Alaska shown in dark blue, the color of the state flag. Flanking the map and overlapping it with their beaks are two "supporters," the eagle and the raven. These birds, shown in a reddish-brown and in the style of the Tlingit and Haida carving, represent the two clans of the Tlingit lands. Such birds also figure heavily in the mythology and tribal lore of most tribes in the Northwest. Arcing over the central device are the tribes' names, "TLINGIT and HAIDA," in a distinctive black typeface, with the words "CENTRAL COUNCIL" underneath the emblem. On each side of the seal are rows of five details that look like deer prints, in the same reddish-brown as the two totem birds.

Tohono O'odham Nation of Arizona

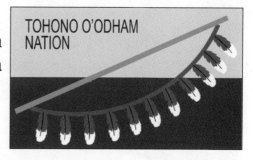

The Tohono O'odham Nation occupies a vast 2.75 million acres in southern Arizona (*NAA*, 275), the second largest reservation in area in the United States. The Tohono O'odhams or "Desert People" were formerly known as the Papagos, a term derived from the Pima-language phrase "Papahvio-otam" or "Bean People."

The land of the Tohono O'odham Nation is the Sonora Desert, where life has always been hard. In the thousand years that the Tohono O'odham people have lived in the region they have become experts at survival in a climate alien to most human beings. They have found a wealth of food in the form of cacti, gourds, beans, squash, and other hardy plants (*ENAT*, 176–78).

Today the Tohono O'odham people continue to engage in agriculture, subsistence ranching, and mining, especially the sale and lease of mineral rights to copper mining concerns to support their living (*GAI*, 120–21).

The flag of the Tohono O'odham Nation reflects the reservation's topography and flora in a simple but effective way. The bicolored flag is yellow over purple (sample flag provided by the Turquoise Turtle, Sells, Arizona). These colors suggest the sun breaking over a distant mesa (made purple by the shadows of the mesa walls) and the brilliant flowers of the saguaro cactus, a major food source for the ancient Hohokam people— the ancestors of the Tohono O'odhams. Crossing this field on the obverse only is a red staff from which hang eleven feathers representing the eleven districts into which the huge reservation is divided.

Flags for the Tohono O'odham Nation were previously made on the reservation and came in a full range of sizes. The small desktop flags made

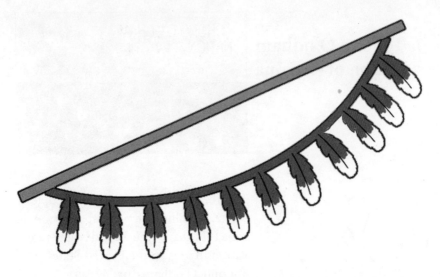

by a local shop (Turquoise Turtle, Sells, Arizona) have become so popular that a backlog of orders keeps the shop's employees busy. This is one instance of local pride expressed through the tribal flag that has brought improvement (if only on a small scale) to a severely underemployed people. Recently, the popularity of the flag has outgrown the small local enterprise's capabilities, and a commercially manufactured supply of three- by five-foot flags has arrived in the capital city, Sells, Arizona.

With this new order a change has occurred in the flag. The name "TOHONO O'ODHAM NATION" has been added to the canton in red letters, emphasizing the identity of the flag. The popularity of the flag is quite evident as one drives through the heart of Sells. It can be seen at the tribal schoolhouse, the tribal headquarters, the tribal courthouse, and several other buildings. This new design appeared only in 2000. Prior to that time, a streamer bearing the tribe's name flew above the flag, keeping one of the simplest and most dramatic Native American flags in the United States uncluttered with writing.

Thanks to the kind and generous staff at the Tohono O'odham Tribal Headquarters in Sells, Arizona, for their assistance and appreciation of our efforts to show their flag to the world.

Tonkawa Tribe of Oklahoma

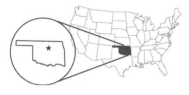

The members of the modern Tonkawa Nation are descendants of at least twenty scattered bands from today's eastern and central Texas. They called themselves "Titska Waticsh," "Most Human of People." The neighboring Wacos called one of the principal bands "Tonkawas" (*AIA*, 87–88). The Tonkawas have lived in what is now northern Oklahoma near the Poncas since 1884 (*ENAT*, 239–40) and today number around 1,300 (*REAI*, 32).

The Tonkawa flag is royal blue, with the tribal seal in the center. The words "TONKAWA TRIBE" are written in white across the top and "OKLAHOMA" across the bottom (flag provided by Homer Miller Co., Oklahoma City, Oklahoma).

The seal recalls the "circle of life" and is divided in half, white above and red below. A stylized Peyote Spirit Bird, which has served in several formats as the logo of the Tonkawas, points upward in the center. The bird is divided in half vertically, pink on the left and blue on the right. Behind it lies a sacred pipe with a brown mouthpiece, black pipe head, brown stem, and blue, yellow, and red beadwork adorning the length of the stem. A yellow sun with ten rays rises above the head of the bird. Above this is a thin red crescent moon with points facing downward. (The old seal from before the 1990s consisted of just this moon and the divided bird.)

A red hill looms behind the bird. The red earth refers to Oklahoma's name, which is Muscogee for "Land of the Red People." Surrounding the seal is a narrow white band edged in black. Across the top in black are the words "SEAL OF THE TONKAWA TRIBE" and at the bottom "APRIL 21, 1938." The date is separated from the tribe's name by six black stars on either side.

Tonto Apache Tribe of Arizona

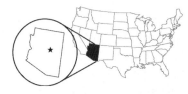

The Apaches are made up of groups distinguished by their slightly differing dialects (*ENAT*, 13–16). The Tontos are actually two of these groups, the Northern Tontos and the Southern Tontos. *Tonto* is Spanish for "fool," a derisive term applied by Europeans not only to some Apaches but also to Mojaves, Yavapais, and Yumas (*DAI*, 420). The Tonto Apaches live on their traditional lands near the White Mountains of Arizona, based in the town of Payson.

The Tonto Apaches use a white flag with the tribal seal in the center: a white cross edged in black on a light-blue disk. The cross is a representation of a star. (The star is represented with four squared points in the art of many Native American peoples.) A white ring (edged in black inside and light blue outside) surrounds the central disk, with the words "TONTO APACHE TRIBE" arching over the top in red and "of Payson, Arizona" curving below.

The star bears four feathers—one in the center, one in the uppermost arm, and one in each of the two side arms. The lower arm is empty. Next to each feather appears a streak of stylized lightning as depicted in Apache art, in black (center), yellow (top), white (left), and blue (right). These

four colors recur in the art of southwestern tribes, reflecting not only the nearby mountains but also the four "clouds" or worlds through which humans passed to get to this world (see Navajo Nation for a more detailed explanation). From each feather hang four colored streamers, of blue, red, green, and yellow (center); yellow, green, blue, and red (top); red, green, yellow, and blue (left); and green, yellow, blue, and red (right).

The colors of the seal of the Tonto Apaches have additional, sacred meanings: black for death and the west; white for life, snow, and the north; blue for the sky and the south; yellow for the sun and the east; green for the earth; and red for fire and heat.

Thanks to NAVA member Harry Oswald for providing information gathered at the tribal headquarters of the Tonto Apaches in Payson, Arizona.

Torres-Martinez Band of Cahuilla Mission Indians of California

With some 25,000 acres in Riverside County, California, the Cahuillas of the Torres-Martinez Band, generally referred to as Mission Indians, continue to live in the arid California desert that has been home to them for more than a thousand years. Long before white explorers arrived in the Americas, the Cahuillas had adopted a lifestyle that accommodated the strict requirements of desert living. They adapted to the foods available in the dry land and dug wells to retrieve water when none could be found on the surface.

The modern Torres-Martinez Band get its name from the reservation, which is in turn named for an early village named Toro and the Martinez Indian Agency located in the Coachella Valley area of southern California. Today the Torres-Martinez Band numbers some ninety members.

The band employs a white flag with a design created by Ruby Modesto and executed by an artist known only as Gruffum. The central element of the design is a deer, probably a mule deer, which for centuries was a common sight on the lands of the Cahuillas. Behind the deer is a full moon, recalling the deer that came to the rare lakes and streams to drink nightly by the light of the moon. The water sources quenched the thirst of the Cahuilla people and the deer and were indispensable for the survival of plants. These thriving plants are represented by a pair of palm trees seen in the distance. Both the moon and the deer are depicted "counter-charged," a heraldic term meaning that the image is split in half, with light-colored elements in one half being mirrored as dark elements in the other.

The emblem of the Torres-Martinez Band is reddish brown, recalling the deer's pelt. Other items in the logo are the mountains that form the Coachella Valley and the rolling sand of the desert. Surrounding the central design is the official name of the band—"TORRES MARTINEZ DESERT CAHUILLA INDIANS"—and below the design a phrase in the native language of the Cahuillas: "MAU-WAL-MAH SU-KUTT MENVIL," meaning "Among the palms, deer moon." The phrase encapsulates the tribal symbol, which represents the history of the land so long home to the Cahuilla people.

Tulalip Tribes—
Washington

With about 3,373 members owning about 22,000 acres (*NAA*, 286) north of Seattle, Washington, the Tulalip Tribes constitute one of the many small tribes that are part of the coastal Salish-speaking peoples of the Pacific Northwest. The tribes are composed of both Tulalip and Sno-homish people.

The Coastal Salish people are one of several nations in the Northwest whose artwork defines the image of northwestern tribes in the minds around the world. These are the people of totem poles, elaborate masks, carvings, and decorated boats and canoes. They are the fishers and hunters who live on the salmon, the orca, and the bounty of Puget Sound.

The close association between the people and the life of the sound is dramatically exhibited in the flag of the Tulalip Tribes. On a simple white field is displayed an orca or killer whale, both a symbol of strength and power and a major source of food in the traditional life of the Tulalip people and many of their neighbors in the Washington State area. The representation of the killer whale is in the traditional art style of the Northwest Tribes (see Makah Indian Tribe for another example), depicted in black and white. In keeping with European heraldic rules (though probably just by coincidence), the whale faces the hoist or pole end of the flag.

Arcing over the killer whale's back in red sans-serif letters is the name "TULALIP TRIBES." The two words are separated by the large dorsal fin of the killer whale, which identifies it as a male of the species. This flag, with its red, white, and black elements combined with gold fringe, incorporates the four traditional colors of Native Americans from all corners of the United States.

In 1998 the logo of the Tulalip Tribes underwent some small alterations. The flag of the Tulalips will also probably be changed, although this was not specifically stated.

Thanks to the Tulalip tribal members attending the meeting of the Affiliated Tribes of Northwest Indians for allowing NAVA member Harry Oswald to photograph their beautiful flag.

Tunica-Biloxi Indian Tribe of Louisiana

TUNICA BILOXI TRIBE
OF
LOUISIANA

Cherishing Our Past
Building For Our Future

The Tunica and Biloxi Indians have lived on their reservation near present-day Marksville, Louisiana, for over two centuries, during which the tribes, though speaking completely different languages, have intermarried extensively.

Traders and entrepreneurs of the first order, the Tunicas once exercised influence over a wide territory encompassing what is now Arkansas, Oklahoma, Missouri, Tennessee, Louisiana, Alabama, and even Florida, where the Spanish under De Soto encountered them in 1541. But under severe pressure from diseases, famine, and warfare, the Tunicas steadily moved southward, following the Mississippi River.

The Biloxis were a tribe on the Mississippi Gulf Coast at present-day Biloxi, Mississippi. They were the first people the French colonizers encountered in 1669. The Biloxis, like the Tunicas, formed a strong alliance with the French, which brought them important economic and political benefits.

Through their commercial skills and adaptability the Tunicas accumulated unprecedented quantities of European artifacts, primarily from the French, with whom they established close political and military ties, but also from the Spanish. The discovery in the mid-1960s of the "Tunica Treasure," called the greatest archeological find in the Lower Mississippi Valley, led to a struggle that not only triggered the largest return of American Indian grave goods ever but laid the foundation for a new federal law, the Native American Graves Protection and Repatriation Act. (This act declares that grave goods and other objects held by museums or federal and state agencies that are identifiable as pertaining to a particular tribe must be returned to that tribe.)

The motto on the Tunica-Biloxi flag, "Cherishing Our Past, Building For Our Future," summarizes four and a half centuries of tribal history and highlights their lasting contributions to a key Native American belief: the reverence for and preservation of ancestral remains (Jefferson Hennessy, "The Tunica Triumph," *Acadiana Profile: The Magazine of the Cajun Country* 17:1 [September/October 1995]: 10ff.).

The flag was developed by the tribe in 1992. Its background is white. At the center-left are the words "TUNICA BILOXI TRIBE OF LOUISIANA" above in black and the motto below. On the right is the head of an eagle in white, with black detail and a yellow beak. The forked-eye eagle design reproduces a well-known artistic motif from the Mississippian Period (A.D. 700–1800), widely used on conch shells, copper, and pottery. The eagle is superimposed on a white-bordered red disk symbolizing the sun and a black-rayed design around the disk (separated by a white ring) that alludes to the known but unseen power behind the sun. Three white eagle feathers with black trim and red dots edged in black hang below the disk.

The feathers recall an ancient Tunica-Biloxi myth in which a tribal priest wished to send a prayer to the sun but did not know how to get it there. He called upon his friend the bear, who said—for in those days people and animals could understand one another plainly—that he could carry it only to the top of the tallest tree. Fortunately, the bear knew someone able to deliver the prayer all the way to the sun: Brother Eagle. And the eagle, according to the legend, circled ever higher and higher until he reached the sun—a beautiful woman. She said to the eagle, "Wait, give me one of your feathers; I will kiss it with my hot breath, and then you carry it back to the Tunica-Biloxis as a sign that I have chosen them as my people." And that is why, to this day, the tip of an eagle's feather is still scorched black from the kiss of the sun. That is also why the sun is symbolized by the red dots included on the feathers that are depicted on the Tunica-Biloxi flag. The flag is displayed in front of the Tunica-Biloxi Museum, at the tribal headquarters, and in the tribal council chambers.

Thanks to Dr. William Day, director of the Tunica-Biloxi Museum that houses the Tunica Treasure and serves as a shrine to tribal ancestors, and to Earl Barbry, Jr., assistant director of the museum and son of the famed Earl J. Barbry, Sr., chairman of the Tunica-Biloxi Tribe since 1978.

United Keetoowah Band of Cherokee Indians of Oklahoma

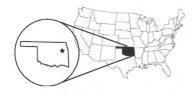

The Keetoowah Cherokees are a political entity separate from the Cherokee Nation, although both are based in Tahlequah, Oklahoma. The Keetoowahs are recognized federally as a separate tribe, as is common among tribes that have geographically separated branches, but it is unique to have separate recognition for bands of the same tribe in the same location. The tribal seal was originally adopted in 1968 and modified in 1991. The tribal flag features the seal on a white background, signifying that the Keetoowah people are at peace. The current chief, John Ross, explains the seal of the Keetoowah as three circles surrounding a central blue disk (seal provided by the United Keetoowah Band). The green outer circle contains nineteen black seven-pointed stars. The orange middle circle has "UNITED KEETOOWAH BAND" above and the same name in Cherokee script below in black. The yellow inner circle contains eleven black seven-pointed stars. The central light-blue disk features a seven-pointed star (with its points divided into red and yellow halves and a tiny black dot in the center), surrounded by a green oak-branch wreath. Around the central seal in the field are four black seven-pointed stars. These four stars recall the cardinal directions, a recurring theme in Native American flags and seals, although these stars are oriented to the northeast, southeast, southwest, and northwest.

Chief Ross explained that the thirty black stars within the rings stand for the extinguished campfires of the original Keetoowah villages in their homelands of present-day North Carolina and Georgia. They act as a reminder of the Keetoowahs' ties to their original lands. The three circles stand for the colorful history of the Keetoowahs. The seven-pointed central star (as used by many Cherokee bands) stands for the seven original clans of the Cherokees, while the oak branches symbolize strength (see Cherokee Nation and Chickamauga Cherokee Nation).

Upper Skagit
Indian Tribe
of Washington

 The small reservation of the Upper Skagit people is located on the upper reaches of the eastern shore of Puget Sound in Washington. They are one of several Coastal Salish tribes (*ENAT*, 37–38) who have lived for thousands of years by fishing and hunting. They supplemented the salmon, essential to their traditional lifestyle, with deer and other animals of the dense forests.

Pacific Northwest cultures developed a distinctive style seen on totem poles, on masks, in embroidery, and in various other art forms. Their totem poles celebrated family history and honored family members with many animal figures. The eagle symbolizes the Upper Skagit people, since both are skilled in fishing and support their families through their prowess.

The flag of the Upper Skagit people depicts a highly stylized eagle in the dramatic style of the totem-pole artists. This use of Pacific Northwest artwork appears to be unique to Native American tribal flags and uses a motif dating back thousands of years. The black eagle fills most of the red background. Two very large eyes dominate its upper third. Below them its black triangular beak pokes down between two rows of teeth. Underneath this level, in the widest part of the drawing, is the eagle's body with its wings aimed downward. At the center of the lowest level three small rectangular shapes form the tail, and on the sides are the eagle's sharp talons.

Ute Indian Tribe of the Uintah and Ouray Reservation—Utah

The Uintah and Ouray Reservation, originally established by President Abraham Lincoln in 1861, stretches over a land trust of over 1 million acres in the northeastern corner of Utah. Bordered to the north by the Uintah Mountains, which reach as high as 13,000 feet, the land is home to about 3,200 Northern Utes.

In what the Utes call *weetus* ("long-ago Ute history"), twelve different bands roamed throughout present-day Utah and Colorado as well as in northern Wyoming and New Mexico. The Spanish, who arrived around 1600 in search of gold, named them "Yutah," from which derive both "Ute" and "Utah." By 1867 the six Utah Ute bands had been forced onto the Uintah Reservation. They became known as the Uintah Utes or Uintah Noochew, "Noochew" ("the People") being their name for themselves (*Uintah & Ouray Ute Indian Tribe,* a special information handout compiled by the *Ute Bulletin* 30:14 [26 March 1996]). In 1881–82 three of the six Colorado Ute bands were also relocated to the Uintah Reservation (the other three bands are now known as the Southern Utes and the Ute Mountain Utes).

The flag representing these Northern Ute bands is faithful to their history and their creation story. Ferdanan Manning, Jr., designed it in 1980; it was formally adopted by tribal council resolution. Northern Ute graphic artist Robert Colorow updated it in 1991 and defined its colors: yellow as "Spanish yellow," orange as "international orange," blue as "blue-bird," and red as "brick red" (all other color references are his).

On a white background, the flag features a centered seal enclosed by a red band with thin black partitions or rays. A dark-brown eagle with gold-brown highlights on its outstretched wings dominates the seal. The powerful eagle is the messenger of the Creator in Ute mythology, protectively enclosing within its wingspan the Northern Utes. The three main Ute bands are represented by the upper bodies of three figures silhouetted in white against the chest of the eagle. The center figure wears a neckerchief, faintly outlined in black; each of the others wears a feather on the back of the head.

The eagle's wings span a blue sky and a yellow sun edged in black shining over the Ute lands below, just as Sinawaf, the Creator, placed the Utes high in the mountains to be closer to him. The yellow legs of the eagle (tipped by black talons with white accents) grasp a sacred pipe with a red bowl and stem and an amber midsection with spice-brown oval end-sections. From a black arc that connects the end-sections hang twelve feathers, symbolizing the twelve original Ute bands. At the top, the feathers are separated by a five-sided design composed of an upper rectangular orange section and an irregular yellow pentagonal lower section. The top half of each feather is white and is separated from the black bottom half by two bands: the top orange, the bottom red. Every feather is split down the middle by a black-edged white rachis (shaft).

Above the pipe is a typical Ute decorative design: two black triangles with a black-edged yellow border enclose a blue middle portion; in the center is a black diamond with a black-edged yellow border. On either side of the central diamond are two slightly elongated diamonds; the upper portion is orange, and the bottom is rust brown.

The lower half of the seal is white. A dark-brown elk-skin tipi (just inside the eagle's wing on the left) has a black framework pole and dark-brown ventilation and entrance flaps. Dominating the white background on each side of the central silhouettes stand two mountain peaks outlined in brown, symbolizing the "Peak to Peak to Peak" definition of the original Uintah Valley reservation boundaries.

Thanks to Larry Cesspooch, director of public relations for the Northern Utes at the Fort Duchesne tribal headquarters, for supplying documentation on the history, legends, and flag of his nation.

Washoe Tribe of Nevada and California

The Washoes probably originated among the coastal tribes of present-day California and either migrated or were forced to move east to areas surrounding Lake Tahoe on the Nevada-California border. Today the Washoes of California and Nevada occupy a series of small "colonies" in Nevada and reside off these reservations in both states. A Tribal Council based in Gardnersville, Nevada, governs the colonies under a single flag.

The flag is dark blue, with the tribal seal in gold and blue in the center (seal provided by the Washoe Tribe of Nevada and California). The seal depicts the geography, flora, and fauna of the lands of the Washoes. With a backdrop of mountains, the foreground contains images of three main sources of sustenance for the ancient Washoes—the piñon pine (*dagum*), the trout (*atabei*), and the deer (*mumdaywe*). Surrounding the central emblem is a ring filled with a geometric pattern of triangles and diamonds. Around the upper rim of the outer ring of the seal is the legend "SEAL OF THE WASHOE TRIBE OF NEVADA AND CALIFORNIA" in blue. On the lower rim are two crossed eagle feathers for the two states the Washoe Nation today calls home.

White Earth Band of Chippewas (Ojibwes)— Minnesota

The reservation of the White Earth Band of Chippewas (Ojibwes) in northern Minnesota was established by treaty in 1867.

The elaborate White Earth flag flies proudly outside their casino and their tribal center (Barb Nelson, public relations officer, letter dated 17 January 1995). The flag has many elements on a white field (photo provided by the White Earth Band of Chippewas). At the top and bottom are narrow stripes in blue, the traditional color for the sky and water. The red borders on the left and right sides, serrated on the inner edge, stand for the people themselves. In the center a yellow disk represents the sun. Overlying the sun is a white bust of the bald eagle, Migizi, the most revered animal in the Ojibwe culture. Arching above the sun and eagle is the name "WHITE EARTH" in red, and below the central image is "TREATY OF 1867."

Beneath the disk is a red sacred pipe, a symbol of spirituality. For the Ojibwes, smoking tobacco signifies respect and honor for Mother Earth; the pipe carrier is a very important member of the traditional community. A stylized floral design in green and pink flanks the central disk on either side. This design (perhaps a morning glory or a similar vined plant) recalls the traditional beadwork with which the Ojibwes decorate their clothing and other articles.

White Mountain Apache Tribe— Arizona

The White Mountain Reservation— sometimes still referred to as the Fort Apache Reservation—is the second-largest Apache reservation in the country. Located east of Phoenix, Arizona, it encompasses 1,665,000 acres and includes vast pine forests, mountains, and high desert. These environments are honored in the seal of the White Mountain Apaches.

The flag is white, showing the tribal seal superimposed on a red outline map of the reservation (photo provided by All the King's Flags, the Phoenix, Arizona, manufacturer of the flag sometime after 1990). Within the seal a rainbow rises against a pale blue sky over a landscape with an elk standing by a river near a wikiyup. In the distance are snow-capped mountains; at the base of the seal is a pine forest. An earthen Apache vase in the foreground is flanked by two feathers of red and yellow and a pair of lightning bolts in yellow near the outer edges of the seal.

Surrounding this very elaborate central area is a black ring with "* WHITE MOUNTAIN * APACHE TRIBE *" below in white and "GREAT * SEAL" above in yellow. Four eight-pointed stars separate the parts of the legend: a white star at the top, black on the right, yellow on the left, and purple (sometimes shown as red) at the base. As on many tribal flags (see Miccosukee Tribe of Indians of Florida), the colors red, white, yellow, and black play a major symbolic role, and the stars refer to the cardinal directions.

Wichita and Affili-
ated Tribes—
Oklahoma

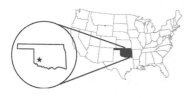

Located in west-central Oklahoma is the Historic Trust Area of the Wichita Nation. This land of some 68,000 acres is shared with the Western Delaware and Caddo Nations (*NAA*, 284). The Wichita people themselves really represent several tribes: the Keechis, the Tawakonis, and the Wacos united or merged with the Wichita Tribe in the late 1800s (*ENAT*, 249–50). Their official title is the Wichita and Affiliated Tribes.

The flag of the Wichita and Affiliated Tribes is royal blue and bears their tribal seal in white in the center. At the base of that seal (sample seal provided by the Wichita and Affiliated Tribes) is a depiction (in white with brown accents) of the traditional-style house of the Wichitas from their days as Indians of the Plains: the Wichita grass house. These homes, which formed permanent villages, were constructed of long poles arranged in a circular pattern that were bent to meet in the center of the circle (*ENAT*, 249). The framework was tied together with slender branches or reeds called "wattles." This shell was then covered with dried buffalo grass. A fire can be seen burning inside the grass house shown on the flag.

Above the grass house is a white disk recalling both the circle of life, so important to Native Americans, and the moon, a powerful celestial body in traditional Native American lore. The disk of the white "moon" contains a line drawing of a warrior holding an ear of corn in his left hand and a warrior's staff in his right hand. Corn was a staple food of the Wichitas in their days as a tribe of the Great Plains. Above the disk is a

six-pointed white star. To the left of the grass house is a white antelope, and to the right is a white bison. The house, antelope, and bison all rest upon a narrow black baseline.

Above the logo is the word "WICHITA" and below it "TRIBE" on the bottom of the flag. In a smaller font are the names of the three affiliated tribes: "KEECHI" to the left of the seal, "WACO" to the right, and "TAWAKONI" between the seal and the word "TRIBE" below. All the lettering is in orange.

The new seal shows the grass house with the fire inside centered on a navy-blue field; arching around the house are seven four-pointed stars. Below the house is a sacred pipe bearing four feathers, one for each of the four tribes composing the modern Wichita Nation. The seal is now surrounded by a dark-blue ring (edged with narrow gold bands) bearing the inscription "Seal of the Wichita and Affiliated Tribes" in gold.

Thanks to Harry Oswald for providing photographs of the Wichita flag.

Wyandotte Tribe of Oklahoma

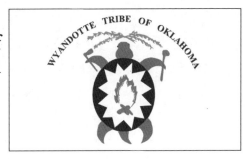

"Wyandotte" (sometimes appearing as "Wyandot," "Wendot," or "Guyandot") is thought to mean "Islanders" or "Peninsula Dwellers." The Wyandottes call themselves the "Keepers of the Council Fire." They originally lived in what is now Ontario, between Lakes Huron and Ontario. In Canada the Wyandottes are known as Hurons (*ENAT*, 99–101). Those Wyandottes who moved south into the present United States settled in the Great Lakes and upper New York regions. By 1842, however, they had sold their lands east of the Mississippi River and settled in what is now Wyandotte County, Kansas (see Wyandot Nation of Kansas). Most were later relocated to northeastern Oklahoma as today's Wyandotte Tribe.

The tribal flag is white, with "WYANDOTTE TRIBE OF OKLAHOMA" arching across the top in black. In the center is a turtle, an earth symbol alluding to the creation story. Above it are four green sprigs of willow to represent lasting life. The turtle holds a sacred pipe and a war club in red, for peace and war, respectively. The oval shell is black, while its flippers, tail, and head are brown. Centered on the shell is a white jagged-edged oval with twelve points, for the twelve clans of Wyandottes (copy of seal provided by Annin & Co., Roseland, N.J.).

In red and white on the turtle's back is a "sacred meeting fire," the traditional method of tribal governance, which involves sitting around the meeting fire and discussing tribal matters. These fires were known as the "Council Fires" and burned constantly in the old villages of the Hurons. One ancient Huron ceremony was the Dance of Fire (Wyandotte Business Committee, unsigned, undated letter), which for the dancers entailed carrying smoldering coals or heated rocks in their mouths and plunging their arms into boiling water. The aim of the Dance of Fire was to call upon the Oki (Spirit) to cure the sick.

Yankton Sioux Tribe of South Dakota

The Yankton Sioux reservation is in South Dakota, near Nebraska on the Missouri River. While in their native dialect they are "Nakotas," other Sioux groups call themselves "Lakotas" or "Dakotas." All three terms mean "allies." Officially, the Yankton Sioux Tribe is called "Ihanktonowan Dakota Kyate."

The Yankton Sioux or Nakota people adopted a unique tribal symbol on 24 September 1975. With minor alterations, this symbol serves as a seal, logo, and flag. The flag is red and bears various designs in yellow (photo provided by the Flag Research Center). It was designed by Gladys L. Moore, a Yankton Sioux. On the left side, reaching from the bottom to top, is a stylized sacred pipe. Its tip just touches the top center of the flag at an angle, forming an angular section that recalls a Nakota tipi (*Yankton Sioux Official Tribal Insignia—The Design*, undated flyer). On the right side of the flag are two yellow stripes ending in curved tips: the upper one comes in from the right; the lower one starts at the center of the flag and goes toward the right. These elements form stylized letters, "Y" on the left in yellow and "S" on the right in red, standing for "Yankton Sioux."

Crossing the yellow portions of the flag approximately one-third from the bottom is an undulating red line. This symbolizes a prayer to bind the home in love and safety. Red is the symbol of life. It was traditionally painted around the lower parts of tipis to indicate that visitors would be welcomed or to identify a tipi as one of several in which a feast would be held. Red thus projects an image of life and friendliness. To many Sioux, yellow signifies happiness in the home and suggests a friendly tipi in the sun.

When this design is printed as a logo or seal, three legends are added to the flag design. Above the top yellow bar on the right is added a yellow stripe with the name "YANKTON SIOUX TRIBE"; underneath the top bar is a second yellow stripe with the words "Land of the Friendly People of the Seven Council Fires"; beneath the lower bar a short yellow stripe reads "1858." All these inscriptions are in black. On the flag, the writing appears directly on the red background without the extra yellow stripes.

Yavapai-Apache Nation—Arizona

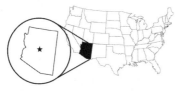

In the battle to save their ancient homelands from the ever-encroaching white society, two tribes—each with a distinctive culture, history, and way of life—became allies. The Yavapais, based in central and western Arizona, were a Yuman-speaking tribe related to the Mojaves and the Yumas that practiced a nomadic lifestyle following the cyclical maturation of food crops (*ENAT*, 256–57). The Apaches were a wide-ranging tribe that stretched from present-day Kansas and Oklahoma across the Southwest and into Mexico. They were an Athapascan-speaking people related to the Navajos and many of the subarctic tribes still living in northern Canada (ibid., 13–16). The smaller Yavapai Tribe did have ongoing relations with the Tonto Apaches—so much so that they were sometimes called the Yuma Apaches.

As the U.S. Cavalry captured the Yavapais and Apaches, it concentrated them on several reservations associated with the cavalry outposts, forts, and camps. Yavapais were initially forced onto the San Carlos, Camp McDowell, and Camp Verde Reservations. By 1900 the Yavapais had left the San Carlos, but Camp Verde and Camp McDowell continued to serve as a home for both tribes (and for the Mojaves as well at Camp McDowell).

After over 125 years of living together, the Apaches and the Yavapais have now become a single entity—the Yavapai-Apaches. Their tribal seal recognizes their origin as two distinct tribes. The circular seal is ringed by a white band with the legend "THE GREAT SEAL OF THE" in black across the top and "YAVAPAI-APACHE NATION" on the bottom.

The central device features Bell Rock, shown in realistic shades of red, pink, gold, orange, and brown. The sky behind the rock is deep pink, topped by a rainbow with five stripes—red, orange, yellow, green, and light blue. Bell Rock is framed by two white eagle feathers with brown shafts and tips. The seal's background is golden yellow to the left of the feather on the left and brilliant red to the right of the other feather. At the base of the seal, arcing up to about a third of its height, is a white Apache "crown." Its weaving is indicated by black accents. The crown is topped by ten black points ending in small white circles. Design elements on the crown include two spiraling orange suns and two small orange crosses.

David W. Sine, a local artist and the creator of the seal, explains its symbolism:

> In our culture the circle symbolizes the cycle of life—one must face the world going away from home and, when life has been completed, returning back to one's land. [The feathers recall that] . . . [i]n the beginning we were two distinct tribes, warring against people coming into our valley; intermarriages made our relations very strong, as shown in the seal, as being together to the very end, as our forefathers were all herded to San Carlos.
>
> [The crown] . . . [s]ymbolizes the Apache in our people, pride in being what we are. Bell Rock symbolizes the Yavapai in our people, for it is they who have their roots in the canyon and the surrounding area, and their legends are tied to the land around all of us from the beginning of time.
>
> [The] . . . [r]ainbow symbolizes our religion—we are taught to believe in something, and walk in the beauty of life, and not to deviate from our beliefs.

According to Mr. Sine, each color employed has specific meanings as well:

> Yellow—symbolizes the power of pollen, divinity, and perfect ceremonial control;
> Blue—symbolizes the fruitfulness of Mother Earth;
> White—symbolizes the purity of nature's gifts and beauty;
> Red—symbolizes the power we have within ourselves to lay down our lives for others, as our forefathers shed their blood for us to be free;
> Orange—symbolizes the power of the sun to create and recreate with its radiation.

The flag of the Yavapai-Apache is white. Slightly inside the edge of the flag a narrow stripe runs around all four sides. This stripe is a different color on each side: red on top, yellow on the bottom, black on the left, and green on the right. Centered on the flag is a full-color representation of the seal.

Thanks to Karla Reimer of the Yavapai-Apache Nation in Camp Verde, Arizona, for providing this description as well as an actual copy of the flag.

Yavapai-Prescott Tribe—Arizona

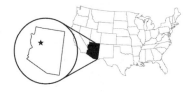

The Yavapais are the "People of the Sun," an appropriate name for a nation that has lived in today's Arizona for nearly a millennium. With the coming of the United States to the Southwest, the Yavapais joined their Apache neighbors in resisting the encroachment of the white settlers. This resulted in the Yavapais being shipped to the San Carlos and Camp Verde Reservations with their Apache allies (*ENAT*, 256–57). By the start of the twentieth century, many of the Yavapais had left the San Carlos and joined their fellow Yavapais at Camp Verde and Camp McDowell (now Fort McDowell). In 1935 a small reservation was created solely for the Yavapais north of the city of Prescott: this is the home of the modern Yavapai-Prescott Indian Tribe. With only about 1,400 acres and a membership of around 175 (*REAI*, 9) the Yavapai-Prescott Tribe and its reservation are among the smallest in Arizona.

As with many smaller tribes, the Yavapai-Prescott Tribe has only recently adopted a tribal flag. The flag was approved on 2 April 2002 after several years of review by tribal elders and the Board of Directors. The years of discussion were the result of veterans' groups and school organizations within the tribe asking for the creation of a flag.

One argument in favor of a flag was that it "would instill pride, reverence, honor, and understanding of the Yavapai-Prescott Indian Tribe. The colors and symbols of the proposed Yavapai-Prescott Indian Tribal Flag represent the history, religion, and culture of the tribe. When officially adopted and displayed, the flag will publicly represent the tribal government and tribal members" (Nancy Lee Hayden, letter dated 10 October 2002).

The flag adopted by the tribe is dark blue, bearing the tribal seal and name in golden yellow. At each of the cardinal points of the compass around the central image is a small diamond: north, black; east, light blue; south, red; and west, white. On either side of the seal are plain golden crosses just above the mid-point of the flag. The tribe's name appears directly under the seal in two lines: "YAVAPAI-PRESCOTT" and "INDIAN TRIBE."

According to Yavapai-Prescott tribal member Nancy Lee Hayden (letter dated 10 October 2002):

> The blue color of the . . . flag represents what some Elders of the Yavapai-Prescott Indian Tribe, such as Florence Jones, related to Patricia McGee about the Yavapai being "from the sky." It also represents water and "Komwidapokwia," the mother of this generation of Yavapai, who was the only survivor of the world flood.
>
> The Tribal Seal represents the four worlds of the Yavapai and is illustrated using the color yellow for the petals of the sun, and the yellow color of the sun also represents the story of "Skatakaamcha," the culture hero of the Yavapai, whose father was the sun.
>
> The crosses represent the most important symbol of the Yavapai, the equilateral cross which was used by Komwidapokwia and Skatakaamcha for healing. The Spaniards gave the name *Cruzados* to the Yavapai because they wore crosses in their hair. It also represents the star where they now are residing, Venus, which appears both as the Morning Star and as the Evening Star. Many Yavapai women are given a name with "star" (hamsi) included.
>
> "When Morning Star rises high, Skatakaamcha plays in sky."
>
> Komwidapokwia gave the Yavapai four stones for medicine and directions. These stones were white, turquoise, red and black. These stones are illustrated near the edges of the basket in the four directions.

The seal itself, which resembles a basket, is composed of three concentric rings, each containing six golden petals. The innermost petals are a solid weavelike pattern reminiscent of the basketry of the Yavapai people. In the middle ring each petal bears a blue cross with a gold dot at the intersecting point. The petals of the outer ring each have a blue stick figure similar to the Man in the Maze appearing on the seals of the Pima-Maricopa tribes (see Salt River Pima-Maricopa Indian Community and Gila River Indian Community [Pima and Maricopa]).

Between the petals within each ring are blue backgrounds. The inner-most ring is solid blue. The middle ring contains golden dogs represented in an artistic style like that of the Man in the Maze. The blue areas of the outer ring all bear a golden Man in the Maze flanked at shoulder level by gold crosses with blue dots. The seal is frequently seen in other media simply in black and white.

Thanks to Nancy Lee Hayden, who provided this information as well as a bitmap version of the flag.

Yavapai Tribe of the Fort McDowell Indian Community— Arizona

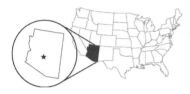

Located just north of Phoenix, Arizona, is the Fort McDowell Reservation, home to three different tribes: the Apaches, the Mojaves, and the Yavapais (*REAI*, 1). The Yavapais, known as the "People of the Sun" (*DAI*, 455), originally inhabited an area of present-day central Arizona stretching east from the Colorado River and north of the Gila River (*ENAT*, 256). The Yavapais also have two smaller reservations: the Yavapai-Prescott Reservation (*REAI*, 3) and the Camp Verde Reservation, both to the north (*REAI*, 1) (see Yavapai-Prescott Tribe and Yavapai-Apache Nation).

Although Apache and Mojave people share the reservation with them, only the Yavapais of Fort McDowell have a flag. That flag is light blue, with the tribal seal in the center. Only one copy of the flag is known, stored at the local veterans' hall. It is made of silk, beautifully embroidered, and obviously intended for use in parades or ceremonies. Unlike many Native American nations engaging in the gaming industry, the Yavapais do not fly their tribal flag outside their casino.

The seal on the flag, however, is quite visible throughout the reservation (for example, on the sides of the reservation's police cars). The seal depicts the Arizona landscape in shades of blue and green, with the Rio Verde shown in blue crossing the land. Rising out of the mountains in the background are five yellow rays of the sun. The foreground is dominated by a saguaro cactus on the right and four arrowheads at the base of the seal. These arrowheads, possibly evoking the sacred number four, appear in white, blue, gold, and red. The entire landscape serves as a backdrop

for the head of a bald eagle (in natural colors), a bird sacred to many Native American peoples and the national symbol of the United States.

A gold band surrounds the seal, separated from the landscape of the seal by a wavy black line and from the light-blue background of the flag by a narrow black ring. On the gold band in black arc the words "FORT McDOWELL YAVAPAI RESERVATION" across the top and "ARIZONA" below.

Thanks to NAVA member Harry Oswald for his photograph of the flag of the Fort McDowell Yavapais.

Yosemite Miwoks (Jackson, Shingle Springs, and Tuolumne Rancherías)— California

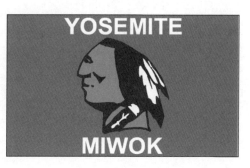

No official flag is known for the most inland bands of the Miwok people, the residents of three small rancherías near Yosemite National Park in central California: Jackson (pop. 21), Shingle Springs (pop. 18), and Tuolumne (pop. 135) (*AIDD*, 39–41). Yosemite Miwoks also live beyond the three rancherías. A member of their tribe, Frank Jordan, an itinerant repairman of antique bathtubs, has designed and proposed a flag.

That flag is red and bears the head of a Miwok man in profile (facing left) in shades of brown, white, and black, wearing white-and-black feathers. Above his head in white edged in black is the word "YOSEMITE" and below it "MIWOK."

Thanks to NAVA member Jim Ferrigan for a sample Yosemite Miwok flag.

Zuñi Tribe— New Mexico

Today the Zuñis of New Mexico occupy a reservation of 410,000 acres (*NAA*, 36–43) bordering Arizona. Traditionally they lived in seven pueblos along the banks of the Zuñi River. As with other Pueblo Indians, the people built multistory houses accessed by a series of interconnecting roof/patios and ladders. The Zuñis differed from other Pueblo Indians in that their pueblos were made of stone and covered with plaster (*ENAT*, 261–63) rather than made of adobe (sun-dried brick).

Although agriculture remains the primary occupation of the Zuñis, an increasing number devote themselves to the arts of silversmithing and stone-cutting. The Zuñis, who number more than 7,000 (*AIDD*, 42), are one of the leading southwestern tribes in the production of silver and turquoise jewelry (*GAI*, 114–15). They also craft fetishes, small carvings of animals that offer protection and knowledge. The Zuñis celebrate this art on their tribal seal, which is also found on the tribal flag (unsigned letter dated 15 February 1995).

The seal (provided by the Zuñi Tribal Headquarters) is a gray circle whose top border is formed by an elongated Kachina dancer with a rainbow arching between his chest and waist. Such dancers are involved in the rituals of the Indians of the Southwest, especially the Navajos, Hopis, and Zuñis. Kachinas come with many visages, each bringing special meaning and powers. These dancers perform several different ceremonies, including those to bless a family's home, to seek a good harvest or to give thanks for one, to implore the Great Spirit for rain, and to heal the sick. While Kachina dancing is a very popular tourist attraction for many tribes, it retains its importance as a religious ritual.

The center of the seal shows a bowl bearing several fetishes and a necklace of fine Zuñi silverwork and turquoise. Above them are two flat-topped mesas, characteristic of the lands of the Zuñis. At the base of the seal are six dark-blue four-pointed stars for the six members of the tribal council. The bottom border is a common stepped-design motif of southwestern Indians in red, recalling the shape of the traditional pueblo (see Pueblo of Santa Clara). The words "GREAT SEAL OF THE ZUÑI TRIBE" appear above the central disk. The phrase is repeated in Zuñi on an orange band outlining the central emblem.

~ *Intertribal* ~
Organizations

Affiliated Tribes of Northwest Indians (ATNI)—Idaho, Montana, Oregon, and Washington

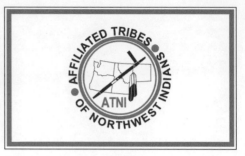

The Affiliated Tribes of Northwest Indians (ATNI) speaks as one voice for the many different nations in the four-state region it covers. Tribes such as the Flatheads, the Yakamas, the Nez Percés, and the Umatillas belong to the association, which brings together peoples from Idaho, Montana, Oregon, and Washington. Such associations coordinate economic development, governmental relations, and health and education issues. A prime concern of ATNI is fishing rights.

The ATNI flag (sample flag provided by Elmer's Flag & Banner, Portland, Oregon) is white, with a red border along the outer edges on all four sides. In the center is ATNI's circular emblem, surrounded by two red rings. The emblem bears an outline map in black showing the four states covered by the association. Superimposed on the map is a sacred pipe symbolizing the cooperation among member tribes, with two white-and-black feathers attached. Below the map is the acronym "ATNI" in red. Surrounding the emblem in black are the words "AFFILIATED TRIBES" in the upper left and "OF NORTHWEST INDIANS" below, with red circles between them.

Inter-Tribal Council of California (ITCC)

INTER-TRIBAL COUNCIL of CALIFORNIA, INC.

UNITY for all California INDIANS

With 107 federally recognized tribes either totally or partly within its borders, California has three times as many tribal entities as any other state (*AIDD*, 39–41). Most of these tribes are extremely small, however, and the area they control is limited. The largest of the tribes totally within California are the Hoopa Valley and the Karuk Nations, with just over 2,000 enrolled members each (ibid.). The Hoopa Valley Reservation is the largest in area, with 93,000 acres.

Because of their small size and their broad distribution across the state's vast area, California's Native American peoples coordinate their interests, concerns, and needs through the Inter-Tribal Council of California. Based in the state capital, Sacramento (*REAI,* 88), it acts as a voice for all California tribes in their relationship with the state's government.

The Inter-Tribal Council's flag is gold, recalling California's nickname, the Golden State. Across the top of the flag in red letters is "INTER-TRIBAL COUNCIL OF CALIFORNIA, INC." Below this, centered on the remaining portion of the flag, the corporate logo appears in full color.

The logo is a complex image. Facing a barely visible rising yellow sun is an Indian with upraised arms superimposed on (or transforming into) a stylized bird. He has black hair, brown skin, and an ochre breechcloth and sandals. His wrists bear white bands, possibly affixed to the bird. The bird's wings and tail are black, white, and ochre. Its beak, rising above the Indian's head, is ochre with a black tip. The sun appears to be rising over a brown hill against a white circle. The white circle is framed by a rainbow with arcs of red (outermost), orange, yellow, green, blue, and purple. Underneath the logo is the legend "UNITY for all California INDIANS" in red.

Thanks to NAVA member Jim Ferrigan for obtaining information about this flag.

Inter-Tribal Council of Nevada (ITCN)

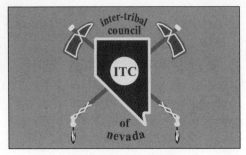

Nevada is home to four major nations, the Goshutes, Paiutes, Shoshones, and Washoes (*NAA*, 257–59). They are dispersed throughout the state in eighteen reservations and colonies (*AIDD*, 41–42) that range in area from 20 to 477,000 acres and in population from 6 to 1,000 residents (ibid., 41).

Based in the town of Sparks, the Inter-Tribal Council of Nevada (ITCN) is an organization of these tribes and colonies. It was formed under Nevada law as a nonprofit corporation in February 1966 to provide administrative economies of scale and to give the small Nevada tribes a single large community voice. The ITCN's Executive Board is made up of the chairpersons of the eighteen tribal units within the state.

The ITCN flag is orange with the organization's emblem in the center: a blue map of Nevada, edged in white with a yellow circle in its center. On the circle in black is "ITC" for Inter-Tribal Council. Behind the state map is a pair of crossed tomahawks in natural colors; from each hangs a single feather. Arching over the top of the emblem in lowercase blue letters is the phrase "inter-tribal council" and below it "of nevada."

Inter-Tribal Council of New England (ICONE)

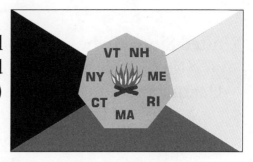

According to Chief Jim "Standing Otter" Hooker of ICONE, "a Gathering of people of Native American heritage was first organized in June 1997 by those seeking to learn about the heritage and ways of their ancestors. The Council was, for the most part, Cherokee. It did not take long, due to an honest wish to pay Honor and Respects to our Ancestors, before others of various Native American heritages sought to become part of this unity of knowledge and desire to learn came full circle. Thus ICONE was established in January 2002." The Council of Elders began the project of developing a flag in early January and accomplished this some six weeks later, by mid-February. "The design was chosen to Honor all our Brothers and Sisters. It is a sign of Unity, Honor and Respect for All," according to Chief Hooker.

The four basic colors of the ICONE flag—white, black, red, and yellow triangles meeting at the center—represent the four colors of humankind. The turquoise hue of the central heptagon is symbolic of the Sacred Circle and Father Sky. The green in the abbreviations for the states (New Hampshire, Maine, Rhode Island, Massachusetts, Connecticut, New York, and Vermont) honors Mother Earth. The four brown logs represent the four directions, and the color brown symbolizes the Center of All Things. The seven flames represent the Seven Sacred Ceremonies or the Seven Directions of Life; these are just two examples of the many beliefs represented by the number seven.

Thanks to Chief Hooker for providing information on the flag.

United Sioux Tribes (UST)—North Dakota and South Dakota

UNITED SIOUX TRIBES

The United Sioux Tribes (UST), based in Pierre, South Dakota, is a development corporation with eleven member tribes. Formed in May 1970 to "promote the general welfare, health, economic development, educational opportunities, and provide assistance" to its members (UST Mission Statement), it can speak as a single voice when there is agreement on a subject.

The current members, most of whom are from South Dakota, are the Cheyenne River Sioux, Crow Creek Sioux, Devil's Lake Sioux (North Dakota), Flandreau Santee Sioux, Lower Brulé Sioux, Oglala Sioux of the Pine Ridge Reservation, Rosebud Sioux, Santee Sioux (Nebraska), Sisseton and Wahpeton Sioux, Standing Rock Sioux, and Yankton Sioux (*Presenting the United Sioux Tribes,* pamphlet [Pierre, South Dakota, n.d.]).

The flag of the United Sioux Tribes is white, with the corporate logo in the center and "UNITED SIOUX TRIBES" in black beneath it (photo provided by the United Sioux Tribes). The logo is a ring of eleven stylized white tipis with red tops. It resembles the well-known Oglala Sioux flag (see Oglala Sioux Tribe). The tipis point outward, with their bases resting on an inner black ring surrounding a white disk. This central disk contains a black circle with four red triangles (representing arrowheads) pointing outward from it. The four arrowheads refer to the four compass directions, the four seasons, the four natural elements, and the four human races. When the logo is used on stationery, the black ring on the flag is usually altered to light blue. The use of black on the flag is a cost-saving device.

Thanks to Kandace Kritz, executive assistant of the United Sioux Tribes, for information on the United Sioux Tribes and on other Sioux tribal flags. Her assistance facilitated the complete documentation of the flags of every Sioux tribe in South Dakota.

United South and Eastern Tribes (USET)—Southern and Eastern United States

"BECAUSE THERE IS STRENGTH IN UNITY"

The United South and Eastern Tribes, Inc. (USET) was founded in 1969 as "The United Southeastern Tribes" in Cherokee, North Carolina, by four southeastern tribes—the Eastern Band of Cherokees, Mississippi Band of Choctaw Indians, and Miccosukee and Seminole Tribes of Florida. These leaders believed that by uniting as an intertribal council they could more effectively deal with a variety of common tribal issues as well as with the federal government.

That belief—reflected in the motto "BECAUSE THERE IS STRENGTH IN UNITY" in black in the lower part of the flag—was borne out over the next decade as membership steadily increased. The group's name was changed in 1978 to "United South and Eastern Tribes, Inc." to reflect the geographical expansion of its membership from Maine to southern Florida to eastern Texas. Based in Nashville, Tennessee, USET includes twenty-three federally recognized tribes, representing a population of more than 50,000. USET provides a forum for exchanging ideas and information among member tribes as well as a vehicle for obtaining grants from federal, state, and private-sector sources.

The USET flag, adopted in 1997 primarily for use during processionals at USET meetings, incorporates the original "Strength in Unity" idea in several ways, including the red border of the flag, the motto, the two red concentric rings enclosing the seal, the circular array of twenty-three black sacred pipes with bowls pointed outward, and the central red dot. Unity has been the primary tenet of the organization.

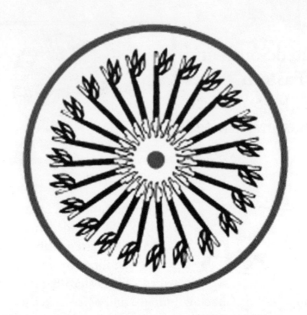

The seal was created in the earliest days of the association. It was much like its present-day version, consisting of a two-ringed circle. In the outer circle was the original name "UNITED SOUTHEASTERN TRIBES, INC." above and "Established 1969" below. Within the inner circle were four sacred pipes, standing for the four founding tribes. This early logo appears to have been printed entirely in gold. In 1978, along with the name change, the colors of the seal were modified to show the two encircling rings in red and almost everything else in black. The first letter of each word in the organizational name appears in red to highlight the acronym by which it has become best known (USET).

⁓ *Tribes* ⁓
without Federal Recognition

Cherokee Tribe of Georgia

The Cherokee Tribe of Georgia is a state-recognized Indian tribe, but it is not federally recognized. It is located in St. George, Georgia, about twenty-five miles west of Jacksonville, Florida, and has offices in Columbus, Georgia.

Like many of the Cherokee tribes that do not have federal recognition, the Cherokees of Georgia are the descendants of those Cherokees who eluded the "round-up" and forced eviction of the Cherokee people known as the "Trail of Tears." This removal from all their lands east of the Mississippi was by order of President Andrew Jackson. Many of these individuals and families managed to survive in the East by integrating themselves into the new society and lifestyle developing around them.

It is this ability of their ancestors to survive in the changed world that now denies the Cherokees of Georgia the tribal recognition that in recent decades has finally seen the beginnings of a rebirth across America. Like others without that recognition, the Cherokees of Georgia struggle to maintain and develop the many aspects of their heritage.

One symbol employed by the Cherokees of Georgia to reassert their identity is their tribal flag. The flag is white, with the emblem of the tribe in the center. The circular emblem is divided into four equal quarters, forming an "X." The four segments (clockwise, starting from the top) are blue (sometimes shown as turquoise), red, white, and black.

In the center is a smaller circle of yellow bearing a glyph in the script of the Cherokee language. Below the emblem appears the Cherokee phrase "ani-tsi-s-qua" in black, which may be a representation of the actual Cherokee name, "Ani Yun Wiya" or "Real People."

Arcing over the emblem across the full length of the flag is the name "CHEROKEE OF GEORGIA" in black and below it "TRIBAL COUNCIL, INC."

Chickamauga Cherokee Nation— Arkansas and Missouri

In 1991 the Chickamauga Cherokees of the Sac River and White River Bands ended their union with the Northern Cherokee Band and took their traditional name, "Chickamauga Nation" (see Cherokee Nation). Arkansas and Missouri have recognized them; federal recognition is pending.

These two southern bands formerly used a seal that bore a seven-pointed star, the unifying symbol of the Cherokee people, with a single feather used as a prayer fan (*Sac River & White River Bands of the Chickamauga Cherokee Nation of Arkansas and Missouri,* undated pamphlet). The new seal, which appears on a white field on the tribal flag, adds many elements to the old seal. The circles formed by the seal represent the enclosed, dependent moon, a symbol of the life of all creatures of heaven and earth.

Most of the writing is in the Cherokee script devised by the great chief Sequoyah. At the top is the phrase pronounced "Hunetlanuhi Tohewa," meaning "Great Spirits" (sample seal provided by the Chickamauga Cherokee Tribal Headquarters). These are the names of the Supreme Being of the Native Cherokee and Christian faiths in the Cherokee language. The location of the phrase symbolizes God's position over all things. The tribal name appears in red on the seal (but not on the flag), for the "blood of life given by our mothers and shed for us by our warrior fathers" (explanation attached to the seal)

At the base of the outer circle are two dates: "1755," when the Chickamaugas came into existence and began their migration to the Ozark

Mountains; and "1983," when the tribe achieved state recognition. The names of the two bands in the Cherokee script ring the bottom of the outer circle. Near the top on either side sacred symbols appear within two yellow lightning bolts. The left bolt contains living sourwood, a plant used in the eternal fire, in Eagle Dancer wands, and in traditional tribal medicine. On the right bolt is the Uktena, a serpent with red and blue antlers, which symbolize the balanced duality of the sexes, of war and peace, and of animals and plants among living things.

The inner red circle represents the sun, source of all energy. It also signifies the heat of the "Grandfather Fires" and the red flesh of all animal life. The seven-pointed gold star inside it represents the seven original clans of the Cherokee people and symbolizes the Morning Star, the beacon to guide the scattered Chickamaugas back to their rich origins.

Above the red circle appears "Chickamauga-Cherokee Nation," with "of Ark." and "& Mo." at either side. The crossed blow-gun dart and Cherokee sacred pipe in the central star emphasize the Chickamaugas' cultural heritage in both war and peace. The large golden eagle feather in the center is the feather of the Chickamauga Nation. It is placed upright in supplication to the supreme being and further symbolizes the tribe's "right dealings, honesty to all creation, and the duty they have to God" (explanation attached to the seal). This feather actually serves as a prayer fan, and its seven spots recall the seven sacred rites and the seven holidays of the Cherokee life cycle.

Below the prayer fan is the council fire, evoking the tribe's central focus and expressing the traditional religion. Below the star is the "Pure Rock," a crystal that serves as a traditional tribal holy object. The crystal is associated with Ushikah, the election and balancing of the head chief once every seven years. According to the Chickamauga designer Richard Craken, also known as Star Buck, "seeing this seal and knowing its meanings completes the whole in the mind which is the Spiritual realm of our Creator, God." Craken designed the seal and flag based upon an 1895 seal. The current flag and seal were adopted and reaffirmed at the tribe's general council meeting in Eureka Springs, Arkansas, in 1990.

Thanks for Richard Craken for information on the seal and flag.

Hawaiians

Although the Hawaiians, being of Polynesian ancestry, are not "Native Americans" in the traditional sense, they are a people native to lands within the current borders of the United States. Furthermore, they are struggling for many of the same rights as are mainland indigenous peoples and have endured similar indignities and fates.

In fact, of all Native peoples within the United States, the Hawaiians have the longest tradition of using flags. In 1793 Captain George Vancouver presented a British Union Jack to Kamehameha I, the great king who united the Hawaiian Islands under his rule (*FBUS*, 130–34). (Because the British Union then consisted solely of England and Scotland, the flag was without the red "X" or cross of St. Patrick, which was added in 1801.) From 1793 to 1816 the Union Jack, in both its pre- and post-1801 forms, served as an unofficial national flag for the Kingdom of Hawaii.

In 1816 King Kamehameha I designed the flag flown by the first Hawaiian ship to sail to a foreign country (China). That flag bore the British Union in the upper left and had nine stripes of white, red, and blue, signifying the nine islands under the king's dominion. The flag was altered in 1845 by reducing the stripes to eight, representing only the principal islands. Since then it has essentially been the sole flag to symbolize the Hawaiian Islands as a kingdom, republic, U.S. territory, and state.

In the 1990s some Native Hawaiians began an effort to preserve the remnants of their heritage. This has included demands for sovereignty similar to that enjoyed by indigenous peoples on the mainland, a call for "reservations" or lands set aside solely for the Native Hawaiian people and their culture, and even calls for independence from the United States.

Because the traditional flag of the Hawaiian people continues as the state's flag, it serves poorly as a symbol for those Hawaiians favoring sovereignty rights or independence. At least two groups use distinctive flags of their own design, while others use the state flag inverted, an international symbol of distress. Still other Hawaiians supporting sovereignty or independence movements continue to use the state flag—the symbol created for them by their greatest king, Kamehameha I.

The Independent and Sovereign Nation-State of Hawaii, a group that seeks to separate from the United States, has  promulgated its own constitution for an independent Hawaii and held demonstrations protesting continued "occupation" of Hawaii by the United States. Its flag employs the traditional colors of the Hawaiian people and their costumes. It is a horizontal tricolor (proportioned 1-2-1) of white over yellow over black (source: World Wide Web site for Nation-State of Hawaii). A purple *kahili*, a feather-covered staff symbolizing royalty, is centered on the wide yellow stripe. The brown-handled *kahili* is surrounded by a green wreath as a symbol of sovereignty.

The Ka Lahui Hawai'i sovereignty movement employs a blue flag bearing  nine fifteen-pointed stars, recalling the nine-striped flag of King Kamehameha I. Five of the stars, which vary in size, appear to stand for the Southern Cross or Crux Australis, the constellation on the flags of Samoa, Australia, New Zealand, and Papua New Guinea. It serves as a unifying symbol for the peoples of the Pacific (*NAVA News* [January/February 1994]: 5).

Yet another Hawaiian flag began appearing in the latter half of the 1990s. This has been called "the original Hawaiian flag" by its promoters. It consists of nine stripes of green, red, and yellow and bears a green shield in the center with Native Hawaiian emblems in yellow. The promoters claim that this flag predated the contact between European explorers and the indigenous population and that they have evidence for this claim. Unfortunately, they never specifically cite their source material. One major design flaw in the "original Hawaiian" flag is the shield in the center. It is a standard form of shield based upon European heraldry. The possibility that the Native Hawaiian people, who have no record of employing shields of this shape, would use it on a flag prior to contact with Europeans is extremely unlikely. Despite the efforts of promoters, this flag is considered a historical fabrication. It still serves as a modern emblem for the struggle to maintain the distinct Hawaiian culture, and as such should be noted.

Jatibonicù Taino Tribal Band of New Jersey

While the histories of most tribes in the United States today involve forced migration, voluntary migration has added a new tribe to the colorful palette of indigenous peoples of the United States: the Taino people, descendants of the Arawak Indians of Central and South America.

Centuries before Columbus met the Taino people, their ancestors the Arawaks had colonized the islands of the Caribbean (*ENAT,* 20–22). The Tainos became the first to trade glass beads with the Europeans, who would use them as a trade item for hundreds of years.

The warlike Caribs, who gave their name to the Caribbean Sea, followed the Arawaks from South America and forced the peaceful Arawaks from what are now the Lesser Antilles northward to the Greater Antilles, the Bahamas, and southern Florida. These isolated Arawaks intermixed with indigenous populations in these locales and evolved on the islands of Puerto Rico, Cuba, Hispaniola, and coastal regions of Florida into a distinct culture of their own; they became the Tainos. The modern Tainos continue to speak a dialect of the Taino language. The islands of the Caribbean became a major source of immigration in the second half of the twentieth century, when part of the Taino population settled in south Florida and the mid-Atlantic states. With sufficient density, the Tainos have now started to coalesce and form "outposts" of their culture and heritage in their new homes. In November 1993 the first Taino Tribal Council came to order in New Jersey under the leadership of Chief Peter Guanikeyu Torres, some sixty years after the Tainos first came to the area.

The Tainos of New Jersey, officially the Jatibonicù Taino Tribal Band of New Jersey, are originally from the *yucayeke* (village) of Jatibonuco (its

Taino name), which in current Puerto Rican geography covers the cities of Orocovis, Barranquitas, and Aibonito ("Jatibonuco History," http://www.hartford-hwp.com/Taino/jatibonuco.html).

The New Jersey tribe united with its kin in southern Florida, the Timucua Tainos, to form the Inter-Tribal Council of the Taino Nation, based in southern New Jersey. Both the Jatibonicùs and the Inter-Tribal Council use the same flag.

The flag is buff or off-white, the color of natural, unbleached cotton that predominates in the traditional "Jíbaro" mountain dress of the tribe (and the background color of the New Jersey state flag). The flag bears the seal of the Tainos, which features a hummingbird in blue, black, white, and red seeking nectar from a red hibiscus-like flower known to the Tainos as the *maga*. Circling the hummingbird is the title "The Taino Indigenous Nation of the Caribbean" across the top and "La Nación Indígena Taino del Caribe" in Spanish across the bottom.

The hummingbird or *colibrí* is a sacred symbol for the Taino people (http://www.hartford-hwp.com/taino/docs/bird.html) because it pollinates plants, bringing new life into the world. It symbolizes the rebirth of the Taino people. The most sacred species of the *colibrí* is the *guani,* once found throughout the Caribbean islands but now only in Cuba. The bird is greenish-blue—ancient legends say it was once a fly, converted into a bird by the Sun Father. Whatever its origins, the *colibrí* serves the Taino people as a striking emblem, connecting them with their heritage and their Caribbean homeland.

The Jatibonicù Tainos have recently altered their name, their flag, and their self-view. They have requested that they simply be referred to as a people (Beverly Carey Torres, secretary of the Jatibonicù Taino People, e-mail dated 3 June 1997). The old tribal name on the flag is "THE NEW JERSEY TAINO JATIBONUCO TRIBE," appearing in a half-circle above the *colibrí* logo. The text remains in English on the outer edge, in Spanish (and smaller) on the inner portion. All text now is in royal blue. The *colibrí* and flower have now been enlarged to reach from nearly the bottom edge to the top. The entire new device occupies about 75 percent of the length of the new flag.

Thanks to Chief Torres for information on the Jatibonicùs and their symbols.

Metis Nation in New England (MNNE)

The people called the Metis have traditionally been associated with Canada, where they spoke for those whose ancestry is both Native American and non-Native American. In Canada they have long been recognized as a distinct ethnicity—a part of, yet different from, the traditional tribes and bands that dwell in the northern part of the continent.

Though less well known, Metis organizations have been formed in the United States to accommodate the needs and pride in their ethnic heritage of those people who combine Indian and non-Indian blood. In Canada the most common origin of the Metis was a mixing of tribes such as the Ojibwes and the Iroquois with either French *voyageurs* or the British traders of the Hudson's Bay Company. In the United States the Metis have a virtually unlimited variation of ethnic origins. The United States Metis see themselves as a uniting force for all those of mixed ancestry, as long as part of that ancestry is Native American.

One such Metis organization is the Metis Nation in New England (MNNE). According to the group's constitution of 2000, the MNNE is open to those of mixed ancestry who live in the six New England states as well as New York and New Jersey. Four bands of the MNNE have thus far been established, one each in Maine, New Hampshire, Massachusetts, and Connecticut.

The flag employed by all four bands of the MNNE (and, as far as is known, all Metis groups in the United States) is the blue version of the standard Metis flag. According to the Canadian-based Metis Resource Centre (MRC), the flag of the Metis bears a horizontal figure eight or infinity symbol:

The infinity symbol represents the coming together of two distinct and vibrant cultures, those of European and indigenous North America, to produce a distinctly new culture, the Metis. . . . [The flag] was first used by Metis resistance fighters prior to the Canadian Battle of Seven Oaks in 1816. It is considered the oldest Canadian patriotic flag indigenous to Canada. The flag symbolizes the creation of a new society with roots in both Aboriginal and European cultures and traditions. The sky-blue background of the flag emphasizes the infinity symbol and suggests that the Metis people will exist forever.

The Metis flag has two variants: the more common blue flag and the red flag. Both bear the infinity symbol in white. According to the flag's history as documented by the MRC:

Nobody knows why the early Metis chose these two color patterns for their flags. However, conjecture seems to indicate that the Metis created the blue and white infinity flag because these were the colors of the North West Company, the fur-trading firm which employed most of the French Michif-speaking Metis. The blue Metis infinity flag bears a striking resemblance to the blue and white flag of St. Andrew, the national flag of Scotland. The blue and white colors of the Metis flag are also the traditional colors of French Canada, as seen on the provincial [flag] of Quebec. That the creators of the infinity flag may have had some Scottish and French Canadian input when creating their flag is not surprising, because these two groups dominated the North West Company and had the most Metis descendants. However, the flag was uniquely Metis and was recognized as such. The red Metis flag may have been created by Metis employees of the British Hudson's Bay Company [red being the predominant British color].

Although the definition of the flag refers to "sky" blue, the shade most frequently used is a dark blue; even in modern Canada, the red variant has all but disappeared.

With the Metis forming organizations in the United States, their flag joins a growing series of flags that span the international boundary. For example, the Abenakis, the Micmacs, and the Iroquois use the same flag in Canada as in the United States. It is a subtle but effective way of reminding us all that the people represented by this modern device have lived in this land for centuries. They predate the artificial borders created by the modern nation-state and are still one people, with one heritage—and now one flag.

Miami Nation
of Indiana

Unlike its cousins in Oklahoma, the Miami Nation of Indiana has not received the cherished federal recognition that increasingly brings prosperity and status to many American tribes. The federal government claims that the Miamis of Indiana have so integrated into the society of that state that their culture has been totally obliterated. The Miamis of Indiana disagree (*How the West Was Lost,* Discovery Channel, 5 February 1995).

The Miamis continue to pursue designation and recognition by the federal government. Such battles, often as long and tedious as any that the federal bureaucracy can devise, are being fought by many tribes. The majority of these nations are to be found in the eastern United States. For Native Americans to have survived there, they had to blend into society or be shipped west. Now the U.S. government punishes them for doing what it forced them to do in the last century.

The Miamis of Indiana continue to build a tribal entity that brings them closer to their historic past. They cherish the traditions of the Miami Nation and practice the rituals and ceremonies of their culture. Possibly because of the ongoing fight with Washington, D.C., the Miamis of Indiana have eschewed a more modern common flag like those adopted by so many federally recognized tribes.

The flag of the Miamis of Indiana emphasizes their heritage by being a true Native American type of flag. On a spear are attached either twelve eagle feathers or twelve turkey feathers, depending upon the situation, celebration, or ceremony. This is the sole flaglike object of the Miamis, and they do refer to it as their flag. This usage may be similar to the old traditions of the Kiowas and those still employed by certain bands of California Miwoks.

As a flag in the early twenty-first century, the flag of the Miamis of Indiana seems unique, but many tribes use both the modern interpretation of the flag—a rectangular piece of cloth—and a device similar to the flag of the Miamis of Indiana. At almost any powwow, one can see in the Grand March (the opening parade) not only the flags of the United States but also several others. Most frequently these include the flag of the host tribe and the "Prisoner of War–Missing in Action [POW-MIA]" flag as a way of honoring the tribal veterans of United States military service. Also included in this parade is a tribal "traditional flag"; this is a device similar to that of the Miamis of Indiana. Some tribes, such as the Comanches, utilize a coup stick; others, like the Miamis, a spear. For the Miamis, their flag flies in the face of the bureaucrats in Washington, D.C., who insist that the Miamis of Indiana have lost their heritage and tradition, as no other flag could.

While the Miamis of Indiana have not adopted a modern flag, they have a tribal seal. The circular seal is red, edged by a cord of red and white, and bears the head of a Miami chief in the center in white outline. It is possible that the chief represents Little Turtle, the greatest of the Miami chiefs. This bust is ringed by the tribe's name, "Miami Nation of Indians of Indiana," and the date "Sept. 30, 1827" (the date when the federal government aided the Miamis of Indiana in a dispute with the Delawares).

Micmac Nation— Maine

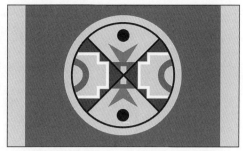

The Micmacs live in the northeastern United States and in the Maritime Provinces of Canada. They may have been the first Native Americans to have encountered white travelers, since their ancient lands included those areas of the American continent visited by intrepid Norse explorers nearly a thousand years ago (*ANAI*, 79–80).

This international nature of the Micmac family influences their use of symbols. Perhaps as a result, many Micmacs within the United States use an official flag of the Canadian Micmacs. This flag usage proclaims the unity of the tribe despite its division by an international boundary. (Other eastern Native American flags have a similar international usage—the Mohawk, Abenaki, and Iroquois flags fly in both the United States and Canada.)

The Micmac flag measures three by five feet and has a broad red central stripe bordered by vertical yellow stripes (one-tenth of the width of the red stripe) at each end. In the center of the red stripe is a yellow disk (whose diameter equals two-thirds of the height of the flag), which denotes the continuum, the cycle and fullness of life as viewed by Native American tradition. The central disk—representing for the Micmac unity amid their far-flung diversity—is edged by a wide yellow outer band and a narrower black outline that defines a circle divided into quarters by diagonal black lines. This apparent division into quarters is superficial, however, because the red, green, yellow, black, and blue elements inside the circle are part of a tightly knit and carefully thought-out symbolic structure, as outlined by Bernard Jerome, cultural director and member of Elders of the Micmac Tribe.

According to Mr. Jerome, the flag dates back to the late 1930s, and its

colors symbolize life and fire (red); Mother Earth, vegetable life, and medicinal protection (green); the growing season and the sun's heat (yellow); late season or winter (black); the sky and water (blue); and the supernatural (white). Viewed in the holistic, integrated light that informs most American Indian symbolism, the colors point to the fullness and cycle of creation, from its beginnings (red) to its midday (yellow) and finally to its dormant, wintery stage (black).

The design elements within the center integrate into a stylized view of a wigwam—the traditional domed dwelling of eastern and central Native Americans—both in its past form (diagonal black lines with black disks representing the entrance) and in its modern form (red semicircles within white-contoured yellow structures). Like the balance and continuity of life represented by the colors, the stylized allusions to traditional and modern dwellings bridge the old and the new, the past and present—symbolic of Micmac determination to honor and remember the past without living in it.

Beyond the mere physical access to the wigwam indicated by the black disks, the entrance is also a reminder of the need to journey inside oneself in the search for spirituality and to isolate oneself from the world for periods of introspection and meditation.

The flag description is taken from the most recent production run of polyester Micmac flags by TME Co., Inc., in May 2000, under the guidance of Bernard Jerome. Flag courtesy of TME Co. Thanks to Mr. Jerome for providing information on the flag's symbolism to Peter Orenski.

Oklavueha Band of the Seminole (Yamasee) Tribe— Florida

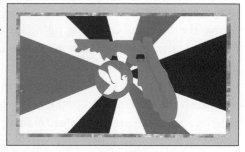

Although not federally recognized, the Oklavueha (sometimes spelled Okla-waha) Band of Yamasee Seminoles is centered at the Cox-Osceola Reservation in Orange Springs, Florida, about one mile from the Oklawaha River. That is roughly halfway between the cities of St. Augustine and Ocala.

The members of the Oklavueha Band of Yamasee Seminoles are the descendants of Seminoles who avoided deportation to the Indian Territory in the 1830s and hid out in the forests and swamps of a Florida dramatically different from today's crowded state. In the U.S. war against the Seminoles, the United States never achieved complete victory due to the harsh swampy conditions that the Seminoles had adapted to.

The lack of federal recognition keeps the Yamasee Seminoles far more economically deprived than their kin the Seminole Tribe of Florida, which maintains five separate parcels of land and operates several casinos. The Yamasee Seminoles, with recognition by the State of Florida, are able to offer a discount cigarette shop on their reserve to provide a source of income.

The flag of the Oklavueha Band is one of the most striking designs among the hundreds of tribal flags found within the United States. The basis of the design is what is called in heraldry a gyronny—a fan of rays of color emanating from a center point. The gyronny used by the Oklavueha Band has twelve segments. Starting with the wide ray that touches the left side of the flag, the segments alternate red, white, black, and white.

At the center of the gyronny (skewed slightly toward the left) is a light-blue disk with a white dove bearing an olive branch. This stands for the peace that now exists between the Seminole people and the United States. Above the disk and down its right side is a green map of the state of Florida. At the lowest point of the map is Lake Okeechobee, the northern edge of the Everglades. Coming out from the north end of the lake is a long river or waterway, representing the importance of Florida waters for the transit of the Seminoles in their canoes and their modern boats. Both the river and lake are light blue. A small black chickee, the traditional building of the Seminole people, marks the location of the Cox-Osceola Reservation.

This entire elaborate design is bordered by two stripes along all four edges of the flag. The outer stripe (about twice as wide as the inner one) is golden yellow, recalling the sun of Florida and hinting at the unproven legend that the Seminoles were sun worshipers before the arrival of the Spanish in the 1500s. Inside of this stripe is a narrow orange stripe, which may denote the importance of agriculture to both Florida and the Seminoles. The entire flag, employing some eight different colors, hints at the colorful traditional dress of the Seminole people. It also incorporates the four sacred colors of Native Americans throughout the United States— black, white, red, and yellow. These four colors are the main design elements in the flags of Florida's two federally recognized tribes—the Seminoles and Miccosukees.

Piqua Sept of the Ohio Shawnee Tribe—Ohio and Alabama

Like almost all tribes that originated in what is now the eastern United States, the Shawnees were repeatedly forced farther and farther west. Today the federally recognized Shawnee tribes (the Absentee Shawnees, Eastern Shawnees, and Loyal Shawnees) are all found in Oklahoma. While the homelands of the Shawnees—now the states of Kentucky, Ohio, Tennessee, and West Virginia—were filled by settlers, not all the Shawnees were evicted from these lands. Two hundred years ago these states were the wilderness, which provides a great place to hide if one does not want to be found.

The Shawnees who avoided the forced movement as well as those who had already integrated into the Eurocentric society that was quickly filling the western slopes of the Appalachians and Cumberlands are the ancestors of the Piqua Sept Shawnees.

The Shawnees were composed of five distinct subgroups, clans, or "septs": the Chillicothes, Hathawekelas, Kispokos, Mequachakes, and Piquas. Thus the Piqua Sept Shawnees means the Piqua Clan of Shawnees.

The Piqua Sept Shawnees, like cousins from many other tribes whose members were willing to accept assimilation rather than death or forced relocation, fight for the recognition denied them by the federal government. Based in Springfield, Ohio, they are also only one of two Shawnee tribes (the other is the equally nonrecognized United Remnant Band) still in the original homeland of the Shawnees. The Piqua Sept is not recognized by Ohio, but it is recognized by Alabama, where some of its members reside.

The flag of the Piqua Sept, while known, is not fully documented. The flag is light blue, with a variant of the tribal seal in the center. The seal displayed on the flag is also light blue. When it appears on letterheads, documents, or other representations, it is normally red. The seal is round and edged in black, with the shapes of a bird and a bear in the center. On the flag both images appear in white; in other media they are usually yellow or gold. Ringing these two images are thirteen yellow flames, forming a circle. Between the ring of flames and the black edge are the words "PIQUA SEPT OF OHIO" around the top, "SHAWNEE TRIBE" at the bottom, and the years "1780" to the left and "1990" to the right. All lettering is in black.

Because the Piqua Sept Shawnees are not federally recognized, information is scarce. A definitive interpretation for the animals could not be found, though most likely they are clan totems. It is not known what specific bird the image is supposed to represent, although it looks like either a hawk or game fowl of some sort.

The two dates are equally undefined. No treaty or land grant dated 1780 was found during the research for this book. The significance of 1990 is also unknown, although it may represent the year when Ohio is supposed to have granted recognition or when the tribe reorganized.

Powhatan Renape Nation— New Jersey

The Powhatan people are a branch of the Algonquin-speaking Indians who lived in the Northeast at the time of the colonization of North America. "Powhatan" is an Algonquin word meaning "At the Falls," describing the homeland of these people (*ENAT,* 198–200). "Renape" means "Human Beings." At their peak, the Powhatan people were part of the Powhatan Confederacy based in today's Virginia. In 1646 they became signatories of the first treaty written in America by England. Those Powhatan Renape Indians who remain today are a small part of the bands that once formed the great confederation.

The Powhatan Renape Nation adopted a flag in 1982, after receiving recognition from the State of New Jersey. The flag was white with the tribal seal in the center. The seal was divided in quarters: the upper left and lower right black, the other two white. Over the horizontal axis was a Powhatan longhouse. In front of it and covering the vertical axis was the great Sacred Tree borne on the back of a turtle, a reference to the legend that the earth itself was a turtle with people living upon its back. In the upper-left quarter was a crescent moon; in the other quarters (clockwise) were a blazing sun, a display of native fruits and vegetables, and an overhead view of a turtle's back. Circling the four quarters was a bright blue ring with a ghost eagle, a bird sacred to most Indians, at the top. A running bear straddled the right side; a Powhatan warrior stretched along the left side; and at the base lay a turtle.

About 1990 the nation modified its seal and its flag. The flag's background remains white; the new seal retains several elements of the original seal while eliminating much of the ancillary design. The main element is a rainbow, forming a nearly complete circle (see Navajo Nation). Its seven colors run from red at the center to violet at the outer edge; narrow white lines separate the colors. Centered on this rainbow is the Sacred Tree atop the shell of the turtle, with the white ghost eagle rising from the tree. The eagle's wings arch upward to encircle a yellow-and-orange sun against a red background.

The symbols have deep and multiple meanings for the Powhatan Renape people ("Symbols of the Powhatan Renape Nation," *NAVA News* [January/February 1989]: 1, 6). Chief Roy Crazy Horse explains its symbolism:

> The Powhatan Renape flag is based upon the circle and the number four. The circle symbolizes life, the cycle of life, and the shapes of living things. It is wholeness, completion, the all embracing, the people, the Great Hoop of the Nation, and the universe, all in one. The circle appears in this painting as a rainbow, the sun, the eye of the eagle, and the eyes, nostrils, scales, and entire body of the turtle. The number four symbolizes the four seasons, four times of the day, and the four ages of humankind. It manifests here as the four entities which we see—the turtle, the sacred tree, the white eagle, and the sun.
>
> The turtle represents Turtle Island, the ancient Native name for the continent now called North America. It also represents the entire earth, for many traditional cultures here and elsewhere in the world refer to the earth as a giant turtle . . . like riding on the back of a great turtle.
>
> The sacred tree symbolizes all life, and it grows at the center of the universe. Its condition is a reflection of the health and happiness of all living things in general. The left and right side of the sacred tree mirror each other, yet they are also opposite, but they are one in the oneness of the tree. This principle, which appears throughout this drawing, and everywhere in the outer world, is represented by the number, being both the duality of the one and the unity of the two. Thus multiplying three by itself, this sacred tree has nine tiers, or levels of leaves.
>
> The white eagle is a spirit eagle, a traditional American Indian symbol of sacredness, transformation, and watchfulness for the well-being of the coming generations. Some traditional elders say that there was once a great

Native American leader and spiritual leader named White Eagle, who traveled across this turtle island bringing a message of peace and unity to the people. As with the turtle and the sacred tree, the white eagle is a universal symbol, representing physical life taking spirit form and soaring skyward. Here we see the scales of the turtle, which represent the physical world, evaporating through the trunk of the sacred tree, which is rooted on this turtle island, to become the spirit being of the white eagle, whose head is turned sunwise as it looks towards rebirth.

The fourth entity is the sun, perhaps the most universally prominent of all symbols, which in unity with the earth is a giver of life. Its twelve rays represent the principles of three times four, which has many applications. Unity is expressed through the children as the third element. Also, there are legends among the Native people here and elsewhere that tell of twelve clans, twelve Nations, etc., that make up the whole of their kind, and great leaders are often spoken of as having twelve disciples. The sun is a great leader symbol. Twelve also plays a role in the turtle's make-up, with its twelve main scales, and the one in the center, which like the ball of the sun, symbolizes their oneness.

Thus we have four entities with their opposing, yet mirroring qualities—earth (turtle), sun, plant (tree), and animal (eagle). Turtle and tree of the land, eagle and sun of the sky. These four entities also represent the four elements; turtle—as water, tree—as earth, eagle—as air, and sun—as fire.

But there is also a fifth entity here, the rainbow, whose seven spectrum colors represent the principles of three and four together. As the fifth entity, it serves to unify the four, the duality of dualities, as the rainbow unifies the duality of earth and sky. Five also manifests in this painting as the five fingers of the turtle's hand and the eagle's wings. The circle of the rainbow connects all these beings into one ever-flowing life stream. Universally, the rainbow is a symbol of hope, the future, the beauty of the world, and the realization of our highest dreams.

Powhatan Chief Wahunsonakeh once said: "One must learn how to live. Not just how to make a living, but how to find a path of beauty in this life. We begin by knowing who we are." By understanding the symbols of the Powhatan Renape, we can begin to understand who they are.

Thanks to Chief Roy Crazy Horse and the Powhatan Renape Nation of the Rankokas Reservation for information on the seal and flag.

St. Francis Sokoki Band of Abenakis— Vermont

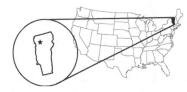

Once spread across what is now upper New England and Québec, the Abenaki Confederacy included the Passamaquoddy and Penobscot Indians of Maine, the Micmacs and Malecites of Maine and New Brunswick, and the Pennacooks of Vermont (*ENAT*, 3–4). Today the Abenakis are concentrated in Québec; one band is in Vermont.

The St. Francis Sokoki Band of the Abenaki Nation (sometimes referred to as the Western Abenakis) lives in the town of Swanton in northern Vermont. "Sokoki" is the Abenaki word for the Western Abenakis. Their original name, "Wabanakis," meant "Those Who Live at the Sunrise" or "Easterners."

On 24 July 1991 the Abenaki Nation adopted a tribal flag. The flag has a dark-green field recalling the Green Mountains and Vermont's green image, with the tribal seal in the center. The brown "shield" of the seal represents deer or beaver hide. It features three symbols. At the top is a red sun. Below it two blue waves denote the rivers and Lake Champlain. On a green grassy patch at the bottom of the seal are two deciduous and three conifer trees, which stand for the lush woodlands of western Vermont. White edging surrounds the symbols and the seal itself.

The tribe has been recognized by other Abenaki bands in Quebec as true Abenakis, and the State of Vermont extended recognition in 1976. That recognition was rescinded in 1977, however, because hunters and anglers protested the tribe's special hunting and fishing rights. The tribe is currently pursuing federal recognition, adopting its flag as part of that process. A large painting of the tribal flag appears over the main entrance of the Tribal Office in Swanton.

Thanks to Sokoki Band member Peter Flood for information on the tribe and its flag.

Southern Band of the Tuscarora Indian Tribe— North Carolina

When the average person hears the name "Tuscarora," he or she thinks of one of the Six Nations belonging to the Iroquois Confederacy, the Haudenosones of New York State and Canada. The Tuscaroras became the newest member of the Five Nations 280 years ago when they migrated north from their traditional homeland in what is today North Carolina. When the Tuscaroras ventured north, not everyone joined the journey. Those who clung to their traditional home now exist as the Southern Band of Tuscaroras based in Windsor, Bertie County, North Carolina. Other band members are descendants of those who returned from the North to their original homeland.

The Southern Tuscaroras have established their own tribal government, following by-laws based on those of the clans that make up the tribe. The tribal leader is the head sachem, Mud Turtle Clan Chief Edward Koona Haagw Livingston; the Grand Council is made up of six clan representatives—three clan mothers and three clan chiefs. Among the nearly 300 members of the Southern Band of the Tuscarora Tribe, representatives can be found from the Bear, Mud Turtle, Wolf, Snipe, Deer, Sand Turtle, and Eel Clans.

Since the Southern Band of the Tuscarora Tribe predates the merger of the northern Tuscaroras into the Six Nations Iroquois Confederacy, they do not employ the Iroquois flag or follow the Digahnahweda, Great Peace Law of the Six Nations. The Southern Band of the Tuscaroras uses a flag divided diagonally, white over red (the red starts at the upper left and terminates at the lower right). In the center of this field is the seal of the Southern Band of the Tuscaroras in black.

The seal is circular and features a longhouse in the center. Above it is a traditional Tuscaroran chief's headdress, called the Gustoweh, while below it is a grove of five pine trees. To the left of the longhouse is a clump of hemp bushes; to the right, entering through the eastern door of the longhouse, is a Tuscaroran man paddling a canoe. In the center of the longhouse is a fire surrounded by a ring of rocks. The central emblem is encircled by an inner ring bearing the words "SOUTHERN BAND" above and "TUSCARORA INDIAN TRIBE" below, featuring a sun, moon, and star. An outer ring is marked with an Iroquois pottery design with six slashes.

According to the Bear Clan Mother Marilyn Dreamwalker Mejorado-Livingston, the seal can be interpreted as follows:

> On our seal the skuarureaka, pronounced sca-ru-re-ah-ga, the hemp gatherers, are in the West, the katenuaka, pronounced ga-te-no-wah-ga, the people of the submerged pine, are in the South, the akawenteaka, pronounced ag-wan-te-ga, the people of the water, are in the East, and the Gustoweh, the chief's headdress, is in the North—the place where the elders gather, and of wisdom.
>
> The longhouse is in the center where we lived. The fire of our Great Nation burns in the center of the longhouse; we come in the eastern door. We are traditionalist and follow the longhouse customs. [We] are guided by the sun, moon, and stars as reflected in the inner circle, the circle of life. The outer circle is the Iroquoian pottery design, which is 6 slashes, one for each direction, North, South, East, West, one for the Creator above, and one for our Mother Earth or Turtle Island. Our tribe's traditional medicine colors are red/black/white.

The seal has been reproduced in many forms. It is black on the flag but has also been recreated in full color with black lettering and has been constructed out of wampum shells, which are closely associated with the Iroquois but were used by most of the Native American tribes along the Atlantic coast.

Thanks to Bear Clan Mother Marilyn Dreamwalker Mejorado-Livingston and the Wolf Clan Mother and secretary to the Grand Council, Pamela Miller Thomas, for their assistance in gathering the information about the symbols of the Southern Band of Tuscaroras.

Southern Cherokee Nation—Florida, Georgia, Illinois, Tennessee, Texas, and Other States

In 1834 the Ridge Band of Cherokees was established in Running Waters, Georgia, by Chief Major Ridge, John Ridge, Elias Boudinot, and Stand Watie. This new Cherokee entity was recognized by President Andrew Jackson, the U.S. Congress, and Governor Wilson Lumpkin of Georgia. This made the Ridge Band of the Cherokee Nation the oldest subset of the Cherokees to be officially accepted by Washington. It is the Ridge Band of Cherokees that forms the core of the modern Southern Cherokee Nation.

To date there has been no formal act by Congress to terminate that recognition or alter the tribe's status. U.S. Indian law and the U.S. Supreme Court hold that the federal status continues unless formally terminated by an act of Congress. Unfortunately, the Bureau of Indian Affairs disagrees with the Ridge Band, which thus is not considered to be a federally recognized tribe.

The Ridge Band, some 2,000 strong, negotiated a treaty of emigration with the United States in December 1835 and voluntarily moved to the Indian Territory (now Oklahoma) in 1837. When the remainder of the Cherokees arrived after the "Trail of Tears," the factions could not agree upon a reunion of the tribe; three distinct groups existed—the newly arrived Cherokees under Chief John Ross, the Ridge Band, and the pre-1830s resident Cherokees, sometimes called the "Old Settlers."

The leaders of the Ridge Band were assassinated in 1839, and Chief John Ross of the newly arrived Cherokees declared himself chief of all the Western Cherokees. Civil war broke out among the Cherokees, which lasted until 1846; during this time, the Ridge Band and the Old Settler Band fought as allies. A treaty between the three groups was signed at Washington, D.C., in 1846.

During the U.S. Civil War, the entire Cherokee Nation declared its independence from the United States and fought for the Confederacy at the beginning of the war, mostly because Chief Ross did not want the nation split. This lasted until the first battle, when Chief Ross and other Cherokees loyal to him switched over to the Union side.

In 1862 Brigadier General Stand Watie was elected principal chief of the Cherokee Nation government loyal to the Confederate States, since Chief Ross had sought refuge in Philadelphia and Washington, D.C., after changing allegiances. Under Chief Watie, the Cherokees never lost another battle during the Civil War. Watie became the highest decorated Cherokee general of the Confederacy and the last to surrender.

After the South collapsed, Chief Ross claimed the position of chief of the entire Cherokee Nation, because he was the leader of the Cherokees' loyalist side. Chief Watie objected, since he had served continuously in the role of chief; Chief Ross had switched sides while the Cherokees were fighting for their independence and that of the South. Yet another civil war continued within the Cherokee Nation between the Ross party and the Watie faction, now considered the Southern Cherokees.

In 1865 the Cherokees under Chief John Ross's control signed an agreement with the United States that renounced independence and came under the protection of the United States. Also in 1865 Chief Stand Watie signed a Cease-Hostilities Treaty with the United States (not a surrender agreement) until a favorable treaty could be ratified by all parties involved. This separate document pointed out the distinct Southern Cherokee independence. Watie thus became the final confederate general to give up the war.

In 1866 a second treaty was concluded with the Western Cherokees of John Ross. The treaty limited the sovereignty of the Western Cherokee Nation but also required the Cherokee Nation to grant concessions to the Southern Cherokees, including amnesty and 160 acres of land per head of household. Their district would not be subject to the laws of the Cherokee Nation of Oklahoma, having elected and appointed officials of its own and separate laws. It would have representation on the National Council of the Cherokee Nation of Oklahoma.

The Southern Cherokees, however, refused to sign this pact out of fear that they would dilute their sovereign status. All attempts to obtain a ratified treaty with the Southern Cherokees failed. In 1868 the Southern Cherokees and the Cherokee Nation signed a treaty to merge. The U.S. Senate again refused to ratify this treaty, because it would give the unified Cherokee Nation too much power. The merger failed. Over time government officials forgot that the Southern Cherokees existed as a distinct entity, but the Southern Cherokee people did not.

The Southern Cherokee Nation combines Cherokee people from across the former Confederacy in several bands scattered from Florida to Texas, including the Elk River Band of the Southern Cherokee Nation, Upper Mississippi River Band, Tennessee River Band, Ossahahatchee Creek Band, Buffalo Bayou Band, Brushy Creek Band, and Wolf Creek Band. All constituent parts of the Southern Cherokee Nation employ the same flag: the flag of the Cherokee Braves from the Civil War era.

That original flag—which essentially follows the pattern of the first flag of the Confederate States of America (CSA), the Stars and Bars—is still in existence in Oklahoma. It has three horizontal stripes: red, white, and red. In the upper-left corner of the flag is a dark-blue square canton equal in width to the first two stripes. The canton contains a ring of eleven five-pointed white stars, just like the first Confederate national flag. These symbolize the eleven states of the old CSA. Within that ring, however, is a large red star representing the Cherokee Nation. Between the large star and the ring are four small red stars recalling the four other "Civilized Tribes"—the Chickasaws, Creeks, Choctaws, and Seminoles—that also resided in the Indian Territory and were allied with the CSA during the war. Upon the white stripe appear the words "CHEROKEE BRAVES" in red. This was the local name of the unit of Cherokee warriors that fought for the CSA.

The use of the old flag of the Cherokee Braves reminds all Southern Cherokees that they remained loyal to the CSA and are separate from the current Cherokee Nation of Oklahoma. It also acts as a symbol of the continued belief in the independence of the Southern Cherokee Nation.

Taino Turabo Aymaco Tribe of Borikén— Puerto Rico

According to tribal spokesperson José A. Tureycu López, "The Taino Native American Indian Tribe of Turabo Aymaco, Borikén (Puerto Rico) is the modern-day rebirth of the ancient Taino Native American Indian Tribe of the regions of Turabo and Aymaco." The tribe "represents those Taino Native Americans who died, and fled their homelands during the massacre that came with the arrival of Christopher Columbus to the Americas in 1492." It is made up of descendants of the Taino Turabo and Aymaco Tribes as well as "other various Taino Tribes from the entire Caribbean and non Taino friends, families, and supporters of the Taino People."

In February 2002, under the leadership of hereditary tribal chief Carmen Baguanamey Delgado from the Manatee Clan, the Taino Turabo Aymaco Tribe adopted its first flag. The flag is called "Guamikini Bi Ara," which translates into "The Spirit Creator of the People."

That flag is light blue, with the tribal seal in the center and an object in each corner. In the upper left is a map of Puerto Rico in green, and in the upper right the outlines of a lounge chair in black. In the lower left is a photograph of a shark, and in the lower right a photograph of a manatee.

The green disk of the seal bears a red triangle containing the image of a special rock in black-and-white contours. Along the outer edge of the disk are twelve petroglyphs or rock markings. Enclosing the seal is a yellow ring with the tribal name in a black Matisse font. The name may appear in English, Spanish, or the native language of the Taino people, thus creating three separate flags. In Spanish the legend reads "TRIBU TAINO TURABO AYMACO DE BORIKÉN," in English "TAINO TURABO

AYMACO TRIBE OF BORIKÉN," and in the Taino language "YUKAYEKE TAINO TURABO AYMACO BORIKÉN."

According to Mr. López: "Blue represents the waters that our ancestors crossed to reach the Caribbean from South America and also represents the sky [Turey,] the realm of Father Sun.... Green represents our oneness with the land. Yellow represents the Father Sun who provides sustenance to the universe, Mother Earth, and our people and Red represents Mother Earth."

The central triangle "represents a pyramid since it has been declared by a Mayan shaman that our chief, Cacike Baguanamey, is recognized by the Mayans to be the Lady of Chichen Itza (The Princess Tukol Tuk)." Each of the four points of the pyramid that touch the ground represents "a stake which comes from the sky and touches the ground, the union of the divine with the earthly of Yucahu with his people; this is called 'Kaj Che' in classical Mayan." The top of the pyramid "represents the place of the top of the sky called 'Kaj Zuk' in classical Mayan. The ancients believed this to be Kaj Ajau or the residence of the creator. At the bottom of the pyramid, departing from its sides and meeting in the middle, a cross forms, each end being the four directions proper, and the middle, which sits inside the pyramid and, at the center of it, is called 'shaloat' in classical Mayan, meaning intersection."

The glyph to the left of the pyramid represents the sunrise or east; opposite it on the right is the glyph representing "the place of darkness called 'Shibal'ba,' the sunset." "When people die, they go into the sunset. This is why our ancestors [Tainos] would *never* venture at this hour if they could help it in fear of the 'Hupia' [spirit of the dead]." The petroglyphs represent "the different villages of our Taino people and the realm of the batey, the Sacred Ceremonial Plaza of our ancestors."

Mr. López also explained the significance of the elements in the corners of the flag. The island in the upper left-hand corner represents "the homeland of the Taino Boricuas called Borikén." The shark and the manatee are the animal totems of Aymaco village and Turabo village. The Duho chair in the upper right-hand corner stands for "the Chief of our village."

The Cemi (depicted as a rock) in the center of the pyramid symbolizes "the spirit messenger who takes messages to the Creator from the people." During the winter solstice, "the Cemis come to the Yunke [sacred mountain] to make an account to Yucahu of all our actions during the previous year; whether they be bad or good. Yucahu in his infinite wisdom measures these on his scale and decides whether we should live another year or not, whether to send the sun back in the morning or not."

The flag was designed through the combined efforts of Taino Turabo Aymaco tribal members Carlos Iuaonbo White Wolf Rivera, the tribal Fire Keeper, tribal spokesperson José Tureycu López, and Cacike (Chief) Carmen Baguanamey Delgado. Final drafts of the flag were completed on 25 February 2002.

Thanks to José Tureycu López for information on the flag.

Texas Cherokee Nation

The Texas Cherokees, based in Troup, Texas, are not federally recognized but are in the process of seeking recognition. They are not separate from the Cherokees of Oklahoma and the Eastern Band of Cherokees of North Carolina but are related by blood kinship to all other Cherokee people. The Tsalagiyi Nvdagi, as they are known in their native language, under the name of Texas Cherokees signed a treaty with the Republic of Texas on 23 February 1836. Texas violated that treaty when it drove the Texas Cherokees and their related bands from the area by force of arms on July 16, 1839. The head of the Texas Cherokees, Chief Diwali (principal chief at that time and known to the Texicans as Bowles), was killed. Those Cherokees who survived the massacre either fled to other locations or hid in the deep forest of East Texas so they would not suffer a similar fate.

It is the descendants of those refugees who make up the modern Texas Cherokees. On 14 August 1993 four men, D. L. Utsidihi Hicks, A. J. Bucktail Jessie, Douglas Wasini Watson, and David Adastiyali Hicks, Jr., met to reinstate the Tsalagiyi Nvdagi, "Cherokees in Texas." The tribe had been inactive in public since the events of 1839. Utsidihi Hicks was elected Ugu or head chief. The tribal national seal is to be kept within the old treaty area of the tribe received from the Republic of Texas no matter who becomes Ugu.

The flag of the Texas Cherokees is white, with the tribal seal in the center flanked by a set of three feathers on either side.

The white center of the tribal seal bears a single black-tipped eagle feather pointing to the top. Crossed in front of this feather (forming an "X") are the twin symbols of war and peace, a common thread running through Cherokee culture. Peace is represented by a pipe (with its bowl facing down). A stone war club (with its stone end facing down) symbolizes war. On a wide red band edged in black surrounding the central device is the tribal name "TSALAGIYI NVDAGI" in black at the top and the date "1819" at the bottom. That is the year of the treaty between the Cherokee Nation and the United States that recognized the Cherokees' claim to vast stretches of land in the area that is now Tennessee, western Georgia, western North Carolina, and surrounding states. The breaking of that treaty by Andrew Jackson led to the infamous "Trail of Tears."

When the two matching bundles of three feathers are combined with the single feather within the seal, they total seven. The Cherokees are known as the "Nation of Seven Clans," and the number seven recurs frequently in their history and culture.

Thunder Mountain Lenapé Nation— Pennsylvania

One of the requirements for federal recognition of an Indian tribe is geographical—the tribe must be resident either in its traditional homeland or in a place assigned to it by the federal government, as in the case of the more than three dozen tribes forcibly relocated to what is now Oklahoma. This requirement does not take into account those tribal members or their descendants who escaped forced relocation or "dropped out along the way." The Lenni Lenapé or Delaware people have two federally recognized components—the Delaware Tribe based in eastern Oklahoma and the Delaware Nation of western Oklahoma. Their traditional homeland includes the current states of Delaware, New Jersey, and parts of New York and Pennsylvania. In their move westward, the Lenni Lenapé people spent time in the area that is now western Pennsylvania, Ohio, Indiana, Missouri, and Kansas before finally settling in Oklahoma.

The Thunder Mountain Lenapé Nation is a descendant community of Delawares who never went beyond the Ohio border or voluntarily moved into the southwestern corner of Pennsylvania. The people of this independent Delaware nation do not have federal recognition as Native Americans, because their ancestors never made it to Oklahoma and therefore do not appear on the rolls of the Delaware Nations in Oklahoma.

Thunder Mountain Lenapé Nation members live throughout Pennsylvania and continue the traditions, religion, and ceremonies of the Lenapé people. They participate in many folk festivals and lecture on Lenapé culture and history. In recognition of their ancestry, the Thunder Mountain Lenapé Nation was asked by the federal government to act as caretaker of a sixteenth-century Eastern Woodland village site, checking on signs of land erosion and discouraging vandalism and graffiti.

Serving as a symbol of the Thunder Mountain Lenapé Nation is a flag of three horizontal stripes, red over white over black. These are essential colors in the art of the Lenapé people and can be seen in the flag of the Oklahoma-based Delaware groups. The three colors recall the three main dialect groups of the Delaware people (Munsee, Unami, and Unalactigo) and the three traditional clans (Wolf, Turtle, and Turkey).

Centered on the flag and overlapping the three stripes is the circular seal of Thunder Mountain Lenapé Nation. The seal is purple with a black zigzag pattern around the outer edge, suggesting a Native American shield. Within this is a ring bearing the words "Thunder Mountain" above and "Lenapé Nation" below in black. According to Pat Selinger, Turtle Clan Mother of the Thunder Mountain Lenapé Nation, this is a recent alteration: originally the wording read "Thunder Mountain Band." Centered on the seal is the black outline of a mountain, crossed by a yellow lightning bolt (running from the upper left to just past the center) ending in a black arrow point. The lightning acts as a graphic symbol for thunder; thus the image represents Thunder Mountain. Downward-pointing arrows are generally considered to be a symbol of peace in Native American iconography.

Tolowa Tribe— California

The Tolowas are located in northern California and share many of the customs, traits, and beliefs of the Miwoks and other tribes. Religious ceremonies are significant tribal events and in some instances take place only among members of the tribe.

For this reason, the Tolowas based in Fort Dick have a flag that is considered a religious relic and is thus used only in Tolowa ceremonies (unsigned letter dated 29 December 1994). It is not available for public view or dissemination, so it is not depicted here (see Kickapoo Tribe of Oklahoma).

Andrea Bowen designed the flag. Its "deerskin" field bears black elements pertaining to the Tolowa people. The background color of the flag is probably buff, tan, or brown, since the local mule deer is a light brown.

Wyandot Nation of Kansas

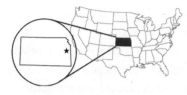

The Wyandot (or Wyandotte) people, descendants of the Hurons of the Great Lakes and upper New York regions, by 1842 had sold their lands east of the Mississippi River and settled in what is today Wyandotte County, Kansas. Most were later relocated to northeastern Oklahoma (see Wyandotte Tribe of Oklahoma), but some remained. These "absentee" Wyandots accepted citizenship under the Citizenship Act of 1924 and organized a tribe that was incorporated in 1959 (http://www.sfo.com/~denglish/wynaks/). The Wyandot Nation of Kansas has received state recognition as an authentic Indian nation. The Wyandots hold their ancestry dear and are currently seeking federal recognition as a branch of the great Wyandot Nation.

The flag of the Wyandot Nation of Kansas is probably blue, with the tribal seal edged in white in the center. Above the seal in bowed letters are the words "WYANDOT NATION" in white and "OF KANSAS" below. The seal depicts a Wyandot man sitting before a campfire (in natural colors) beneath a stylized green and brown willow tree. The fire recalls how the Hurons of old kept fires constantly burning in their camps (*ENAT*, 100).

Thumbnail Sketches

More extensive information was not available for the following flags.

BARONA BAND OF MISSION INDIANS—CALIFORNIA

This small tribe located east of San Diego has a single flag kept in the tribal head-quarters building. The flag is white and depicts elements from the tribal seal, including drums and rattles. All items on the flag are shown in reds and blues.

CHINOOK TRIBE—OREGON

This Oregon tribe began to consider the adoption of a tribal flag in the autumn of 2002. It was officially adopted in January 2003. The simple white flag (which has no legend) bears the image of a Chinook salmon in red, white, and black in traditional Northwest artistic style. The salmon has the contorted appearance it would have when it returned to an Oregon river to spawn. Centered on its stomach is a moonlike face (mask?) in red and white.

IOWA TRIBE OF KANSAS AND NEBRASKA

The Iowa Tribe adopted a white flag edged with green and bearing the tribal seal in black in the center in 1993. The seal features Chief White Cloud, founder of the tribe and its head from 1860 until his death in 1920. Chief White Cloud, like half the men of his tribe, served as a scout for the Union in the Civil War. Only about half of them returned from the war to establish the present tribe.

KETCHIKAN INDIAN COMMUNITY—ALASKA

This community adopted a striking red, black, and yellow flag in December 2002. In the center of a red field is a depiction of a Ketchican longhouse and totem pole in black. Arcing over the central image is the community's name, and below the longhouse is "Ketchican, Alaska" in yellow. Forty-six black palm prints (with the thumbs to the right) form the border of the flag: rows of fifteen each across the top and bottom, and ten each (including those in the top and bottom rows) on the left and right edges.

LOWER SIOUX INDIAN COMMUNITY OF MINNESOTA

This community has a single flag brought out only during powwows.

POKANOKET WAMPANOAG FEDERATION— MASSACHUSETTS AND RHODE ISLAND

The federation began to consider adoption of a red flag bearing the tribal seal in November 2002. The seal has a white line drawing of a Wampanoag with an elaborate headdress holding a turtle, upon whose back sits a howling wolf. The seal also contains a large dark-blue star and has three feathers dangling from it. The background of the seal is in light greens and yellows, with the official name in yellow.

PRAIRIE BAND OF POTAWATOMI INDIANS—KANSAS

The Prairie Band adopted a sky-blue flag bearing its name and seal in 1994.

SAC AND FOX NATION OF MISSOURI IN KANSAS AND NEBRASKA

The Sac and Fox Nation uses a blue flag bearing the tribal seal and its name in white.

SHOSHONE-BANNOCK TRIBES—IDAHO

The Shoshone-Bannock Tribes use a brown flag bearing the tribal seal in gold.

WESTERN SHOSHONES—CALIFORNIA, IDAHO, AND NEVADA

The Western Shoshones are an amalgam of small Shoshone bands scattered in the northern half of Nevada and neighboring states. All the bands employ one general flag: it is white with ornate red and green striping across the top and bottom. In the center of the flag is a full-color depiction of the seal of the Western Shoshones.

Index

Klamaths, 137
Klickitats, 53
Kootenais, Confederated Salish and
Kootenai Tribes of the Flathead
Reservation (Mont.), 44-45

Lac du Flambeau Band of Lake Superior
Chippewa Indians (Wis.), 118-19
Lake Band, Confederated Tribes of the
Colville Reservation (Wash.), 48, 49
Lakotas. *See* Sioux
Latgawa Band. *See* Takelmas, Confederated Tribes of the Siletz Reservation
(Ore.)
Leech Lake Band of Chippewas (Minn.),
120-21, 134
Lenni Lenapés. *See* Delawares
Little Osages. *See* Osages
Lower Brulé Sioux Tribe (S.Dak.), 122,
272
Lower Chinooks. *See* Chinooks
Lower Elwha Klallam Tribal Community (Wash.), 123-24
Lower Pimas, 85
Lower Sioux Indian Community of
Minnesota, 313
Lower Umpquas. *See* Umpquas
Loyal Shawnee Tribe (Okla.), 125-26
Lummi Tribe (Wash.), 127

Makahs, 123; Makah Indian Tribe
(Wash.), 128
Malacites, 296
Mandans, Three Affiliated Tribes of the
Fort Berthold Reservation (N.Dak.),
230-31
Maricopas, 37; Gila River Indian Community (Ariz.), 85-86; Salt River
Indian Community (Ariz.), 202
Mashantucket Pequot Tribe of Connecticut, 129
Menominees, 153; Menominee Indian
Tribe of Wisconsin, 130

Methow Band, Confederated Tribes of
the Colville Reservation (Wash.),
48, 49
Metis Nation of New England, 283-84
Miamis, 169; Miami Nation of Indiana,
285-86; Miami Tribe of Oklahoma,
131
Miccosoukees, 213, 290; Miccosoukee
Tribe of Indians of Florida, 132, 273
Micmacs, 164, 284, 296; Aroostook Band
of Micmac Indians of Maine, 10-11;
Micmac Nation (Maine), 287-88
Mikonotunnes. *See* Tututunnes, Confederated Tribes of the Siletz Reservation (Ore.)
Mille Lacs Band of Chippewas (Minn.),
133, 134
Miluks: Confederated Tribes of the
Siletz Reservation (Ore.), 52-54;
Coquille Tribe of Oregon, 59-60
Minnesota Chippewas, 134
Mission Indians: Barona Band of Mission Indians (Calif.), 312; Cabazon
Band of Cahuilla Mission Indians
(Calif.), 18-19; Torres-Martinez Band
of Cahuilla Mission Indians of California, 238-39
Mississippi Band of Choctaw Indians,
135, 273
Missourias. *See* Otoe-Missourias
(Otoes)
Miwoks, 286, 309. *See also* Yosemite
Miwoks (Calif.)
Modoc Tribe of Oklahoma, 136-37
Mohaves. *See* Mojaves
Mohawks, 100-101, 152, 287; St. Regis
Band of Mohawk Indians of New
York, 200-201
Mohegan Indian Tribe of Connecticut,
138-39
Mohicans, Stockbridge-Munsee Community of Mohican Indians of Wisconsin, 223-24

Mojaves, 236, 256, 261; Colorado River Indian Tribes (Ariz., Calif.), 40-41; Fort Mojave Indian Tribe (Ariz., Calif., Nev.), 82

Molalas: Confederated Tribes of the Grand Ronde Community of Oregon, 50-51; Confederated Tribes of the Siletz Reservation (Ore.), 52-54

Moses-Columbias: Confederated Tribes of the Colville Reservation (Wash.), 48, 49

Muckleshoot Indian Tribe (Wash.), 140

Muskogees. *See* Creeks

Nakotas. *See* Sioux

Narragansets, 129

Navajos, 115, 120, 256, 264; Colorado River Indian Tribes (Ariz., Calif.), 40-41; Navajo Nation (Ariz., N.Mex., Utah) 143-45

Nespelems, Confederated Tribes of the Colville Reservation (Wash.), 48, 49

Nestuccas. *See* Tillamooks, Confederated Tribes of the Siletz Reservation (Ore.)

Nett Lake Band of Chippewas. *See* Bois Forte Band of Chippewas (Minn.)

Nez Percés, 46, 268; Confederated Tribes of the Colville Reservation (Wash.), 48, 49; Confederated Tribes of the Umatilla Reservation (Ore.), 55-57; Nez Percé Tribe of Idaho, 141-42

Niantics, 129

Nimipus. *See* Nez Percés

Nooksacks, 127

Northern Cheyenne Tribe (Mont.), 148

Northern Utes, 246

Ogahpahs. *See* Quapaws

Oglala Sioux Tribe (S.Dak.), 149, 272

Ojibwes, 35, 156, 283; Bay Mills Indian Community of the Sault Ste. Marie Band of Chippewa Indians (Mich.), 13; Bois Forte (Nett Lake) Band of Chippewas (Minn.), 16-17, 134; Lac du Flambeau Band of Lake Superior Chippewa Indians (Wis.), 118-19; Leech Lake Band of Chippewas (Minn.), 120-21, 134; Mille Lacs Band of Chippewas (Minn.), 133, 134; Minnesota Chippewas, 134; Red Lake Band of Chippewas (Minn.), 134, 190; Saginaw Chippewa Indian Tribe of Michigan, 197-98; St. Croix Chippewa Indians of Wisconsin, 199; Sault Ste. Marie Tribe of Chippewa Indian of Michigan, 206-209; White Earth Band of Chippewas (Minn.), 134, 249

Okanogans, Confederated Tribes of the Colville Reservation (Wash.), 48, 49

Oklavueha (Oklawaha) Band of the Seminole Tribe (Fla.), 289-90

Omahas, 154; Omaha Tribe of Nebraska and Iowa, 150-51

Oneidas, 100-101; Oneida Nation of New York, 152; Oneida Tribe of Wisconsin, 153

Onondagas, 100-101, 152

Osages, 111, 155; Osage Tribe (Okla.), 154

Otoe-Missourias (Otoes), 98; Otoe-Missouria Tribe of Indians (Okla.), 155

Ottawas, 35; Ottawa Tribe of Oklahoma, 156-57

Pais: Hualapai Indian Tribe (Ariz.), 95-97; Yavapai-Apache Nation (Ariz.), 256-57; Yavapai-Prescott Tribe (Ariz.), 258-60; Yavapai Tribe of the Fort McDowell Indian Community (Ariz.), 261-62

Paiutes, 40, 46, 67, 270; Big Pine Band of Owens Valley Paiute Shoshone Indians (Calif.), 14; Cedar (Band of Utah Paiute), 158; Confederated Tribes of the Warm Springs Reserva-

Rogue River, Confederated Tribes of the Grand Ronde Community of Oregon, 50-51

Rosebud Sioux Tribe (S.Dak.), 193-94, 272

Sac and Fox Indians, 88, 114; Sac and Fox Nation (Okla.), 195; Sac and Fox Nation of Missouri in Kansas and Nebraska, 313; Sac and Fox Tribe of the Mississippi in Iowa, 196

Saginaw Chippewa Indian Tribe of Michigan, 197-98

St. Croix Chippewa Indians of Wisconsin, 199

St. Frances Sokoki Band of Abenakis (Vt.), 29

St. Regis Band of Mohawk Indians of New York, 200-201

Salish Indians, 117, 128; Coeur d'Alene Tribe (Idaho), 38-39; Confederated Salish and Kootenai Tribes of the Flathead Reservation (Mont.), 44-45; Coquille Tribe of Oregon, 59-60; Lummi Tribe (Wash.), 127; Muckleshoot Indian Tribe (Wash.), 140; Puyallup Tribe (Wash.), 183-84; Quileute Tribe (Wash.), 187-88; Quinault Tribe (Wash.), 189; Snohomish, 240; Spokane Tribe (Wash.), 133, 220; Squaxin Island Tribe (Wash.), 221; Suquamish Indian Tribe (Wash.), 225; Swinomish (Kikiallus, Lower Skagit, Samish) Indians (Wash.), 226-27; Tulalip Tribes (Wash.), 240-41; Upper Skagit Indian Tribe of Washington, 245

Salmon River. See Tillamooks, Confederated Tribes of the Siletz Reservation (Ore.)

Salt River Indian Community (Ariz.), 202

San Carlos Apache Tribe of the San Carlos Reservation (Ariz.), 83, 203-204

San Poil, Confederated Tribes of the Colville Reservation (Wash.), 48, 49

Santee Sioux Tribe (Nebr.), 205, 272

Santiams. See Kalapuya

Sault Ste. Marie Tribe of Chippewa Indian of Michigan, 206-209

Seminoles, 132, 141, 301; Oklavueha Band of the Seminole Tribe (Fla.), 289-90; Seminole Nation of Oklahoma, 210-11; Seminole Tribe of Florida, 212-13, 273

Senecas, 100-101; Seneca-Cayuga Tribe of Oklahoma, 214; Seneca Nation of New York, 215

Shastas: Confederated Tribes of the Grand Ronde Community of Oregon, 50-51; Confederated Tribes of the Siletz Reservation (Ore.), 52-54

Shawnees: Absentee-Shawnee Tribe of Indians of Oklahoma, 2; Eastern Shawnee Tribe of Oklahoma, 73-74; Loyal Shawnee Tribe (Okla.), 125-26; Piqua Sept of the Ohio Shawnee Tribe (Ohio, Ala.), 291-92; United Remnant Band, 291

Shingle Springs Miwuks. See Yosemite Miwoks (Calif.)

Shoshones, 270; Big Pine Band of Owens Valley Paiute Shoshone Indians (Calif.), 14; Eastern Shoshone Tribe (Wyo.), 75-76; Paiute Shoshone Indians of the Bishop Community of the Bishop Colony (Calif.), 159-60; Shoshone-Bannock Tribes (Idaho), 75, 313; Western Shosones (Calif., Idaho, Nev.), 59, 313

Siletz Indians, Confederated Tribes of the Siletz Reservation (Ore.), 52-54

Sioux, 148, 150, 231; Assiniboine and Sioux Tribes of Fort Peck Indian Reservation (Mont.), 12; Brulé, 29; Cheyenne River Sioux Tribe